MEDIA
LAW

*To Barbara Kay Martin
with love and thanks*

ESSENTIALS OF
CANADIAN LAW

MEDIA
LAW

ROBERT MARTIN

Faculty of Law
The University of Western Ontario

IRWIN
LAW

MEDIA LAW
© Publications for Professionals, 1997

Published in 1997 by
Irwin Law
1800 Steeles Avenue West
Concord, Ontario
L4K 2P3

ISBN: 1-55221-004-9

Canadian Cataloguing in Publication Data

Martin, Robert, 1939–
  Media law

(Essentials of Canadian law)
Includes bibliographical references and index.
ISBN 1-55221-004-9

1. Freedom of information – Canada.   2. Freedom of speech – Canada.
3. Freedom of the press – Canada.   4. Mass media – Law and legislation –
Canada.   I. Title.   II. Series.

KE4422.M36 1996   342.71'0853   C96-931598-8
KF4483.C524M36 1996

Printed and bound in Canada.

1 2 3 4 5   99 98 97 96

SUMMARY
TABLE OF CONTENTS

DETAILED
TABLE OF CONTENTS

FOREWORD

Robert Martin has written a delightful, valuable book. I recommend to every lawyer and journalist that they read the entire book as quickly as they can. He has created a seamless logical view of all the issues which confront a reporter or a lawyer. The book is cohesive and persuasive. If one follows the book one will have a lexicon of conduct, a touchstone. He is opinionated but he stresses the responsibility of the journalist to get it right before publishing.

I was excited when I finished the book. I have been a courtroom lawyer dealing with libel for more than 30 years and this text created a whole new vista on several important areas of the law. Professor Martin is a persuasive teacher and I found myself to be a beguiled student. I trust the reader will also.

Julian Porter, Q.C.

ACKNOWLEDGMENTS

It is a pleasure to thank the many people who have contributed to this book.

My friend and colleague Stuart Adam deserves a great deal of credit for the structure of the book. It is based on one we developed over several years of collaboration and is found in our joint work, *A Sourcebook of Canadian Media Law*, 2d ed. (Ottawa: Carleton University Press, 1994).

I also want to thank the law students who have been my research assistants over the years. Prominent among them are Shelley Appleby-Ostroff, Elaine Crossland, Maureen Dennison, Eve Donner, Karen Douglas, Nathan Golas, Kathryn Hazel, James Newland, Lynda Rogers, Michael Rumball, Federico Soda, and Helen Song. Particular thanks, although there are far too many of them to name, go to the working journalists to whom I have tried to teach Media Law and from whom I have learned so much about the way the media actually work.

Special gratitude goes to my colleague Margaret Ann Wilkinson, who read the entire manuscript and saved me from many errors, and to Rosemary Shipton, for her fine editing of the book. Barbara Martin and Alan Swann prepared the figures, which are entirely the product of their skill and creativity. Barbara Martin also helped prepare the index.

Finally, I have had the pleasure of working with Kathleen Adair for twenty-one years. Once again I thank her for her ability, hard work, kindness, and good cheer.

INTRODUCTION

The title of this book is designed to indicate both its subject-matter and its purpose. The focus is on *Canadian* media law. There is some reference to cases or approaches from other countries, but the bulk of the case-law and the legislation discussed is Canadian.

"Media law" is a term that requires some explanation. It is not a term of art, which is simply to say that it does not refer to a recognized, discrete area of the law such as contracts, torts, or constitutional law. In fact, media law brings together elements from a number of different areas — most prominently criminal law, constitutional law, and the law of torts. What unites these elements is that, taken together, they represent the law which directly affects the mass media and the people working in the mass media.

I have made certain, possibly arbitrary, decisions about what is to be included, or not included, under the rubric "media law." In particular, I have not discussed questions relating to copyright or, more generally, to the law of intellectual property. These matters deserve a separate treatment of their own. I have also not directly addressed the vexed issues of hate propaganda and obscenity. These two matters should not be of practical concern to persons working in the mass media.

Media law should, and does, apply equally to all media of communication. Most of the material in this book deals with newspapers, radio, and television — the media where legal issues have arisen. I do not address issues relating to the use of computers or online computer services, because these areas have not yet been addressed by our legal system. Nonetheless, there is no reason of principle or of logic to treat online computer services differently from any other medium of communication. I can only assume, for example, that a libel published through the Internet would be dealt with in exactly the same way that a libel published in a newspaper is dealt with.

The central concept around which this book is organized is freedom of expression. First, however, we need to clarify a number of definitions. The most important addresses distinctions among four different, though related, notions: freedom of speech, freedom of the press, freedom of expression, and freedom of information. It is essential to keep the four separate, even though they are often used interchangeably. Although they relate to similar things, they are not identical.

Freedom of speech is probably the phrase with the longest tradition. It is found in the first amendment to the US Constitution: "Congress shall make no law . . . abridging the freedom of speech." Freedom of speech addresses the ability of individuals to communicate ideas and information without interference from the state. When we talk about interference by the state, as a legal notion, we are referring to the imposition of prior restraint. Freedom of speech has typically meant the freedom to publish — publish being used here in its widest possible meaning as writing, speaking, printing, or broadcasting ideas and information — without prior restraint imposed by the state. A prior restraint is any state-created limit whereby individuals must seek some form of official permission before they may lawfully publish material. Two examples, one from an old Supreme Court of Canada decision and one from my university, will illustrate what is meant.

The Supreme Court decision is from the 1953 case *Saumur* v. *Quebec (City)*.[1] *Saumur* was one of a series of cases where notions of civil liberties developed in a long struggle between, primarily, the Jehovah's Witnesses and the Quebec government of Maurice Duplessis. It dealt with a municipal by-law in Quebec City which said that anyone who wished to distribute any kind of printed material on the streets had first to take the material to the chief of police. The chief would look the material over and decide if it was acceptable. If the chief decided positively, the material could be lawfully distributed; if he decided negatively, it could not. Such power is a classic example of a prior restraint. Whenever you have to have the permission of a state official before you can publish — before you can print, write, or speak — you have a prior restraint. The Court struck the law down.

---

1   [1953] 2 S.C.R. 299.

At my university we have a system called Poster Pollution. If anyone wants to put a flyer, poster, or handbill on a bulletin board anywhere on the campus, the person must submit the material to the Students' Council. The Council decides whether it is acceptable and, if it is, puts a dated Poster Pollution stamp on it. Students acting for the Students' Council patrol the bulletin boards and, if they discover anything that does not have the required stamp or that has an expired stamp, they pull it down.

Traditionally, then, freedom of speech meant the ability to publish, write, speak, or print without prior restraint. Censorship, strictly defined, is any form of prior restraint. Thus, when we speak of censorship as a legal concept, we mean prior restraint.

Freedom of the press is a related notion, but it is not identical. Freedom of the press includes the absence of prior restraint, but there can be circumstances where distinctions, even contradictions, arise between freedom of speech and freedom of the press. An example is found in a 1979 decision of the Supreme Court of Canada, *Gay Alliance Toward Equality* v. *Vancouver Sun*.[2] The title of the Vancouver group, Gay Alliance Toward Equality, expressed its politics and its objectives. It sought to take out a classified advertisement in the Vancouver *Sun* that read: "Subs.[cribe] to GAY TIDE, gay lib[eration] paper," followed by the cost of a subscription and a street address in Vancouver. That was all. There were no extravagant graphics or exuberant political statements. The Vancouver *Sun*, however, declined to print the ad. The Alliance took a complaint to the BC Human Rights Commission on the basis that the classified advertising pages of a newspaper were a service or a facility customarily available to the public and, as a result, the Commission had jurisdiction to deal with the matter under the BC Human Rights legislation. The Commission ordered the *Sun* to print the advertisement. The *Sun* took the Commission to court and the case ended up before the Supreme Court. In the event, the Court decided that the Commission did not have the necessary legal authority to make such an order.

For our purposes, the case points up a contradiction between the freedom of speech of the Gay Alliance Toward Equality and the freedom of the press of the Vancouver *Sun*. Many people have argued that if freedom of speech is to be meaningful in the kind of society in which we live, it must include some notion of access to the mass media. If freedom of speech simply means that I can set up my soapbox in the corner of a field and rave at the blue sky, it may not be a practical or useful freedom.

---

2   *Sub nom. British Columbia (Human Rights Commission)* v. *Vancouver Sun*, [1979] 2 S.C.R. 435.

Given the role that the mass media play in our society, access to them is crucial if one is going to communicate one's ideas or information effectively. Thus, freedom of speech for the Gay Alliance Toward Equality, in the circumstances of this case, meant having its classified advertisement appear in the Vancouver *Sun*. But while freedom of the press contains elements of free speech, it also ensures that the managers or proprietors of a newspaper, journal, radio station, or television network are free to have the last word about what they will or will not print or broadcast. Freedom of the press must mean that no one outside a newspaper, for example, can set editorial policy for that newspaper. In the circumstances of this case, freedom of the press for the Vancouver *Sun* meant that it should be free to choose whether to run this ad or not. The simple point is that, while freedom of speech and freedom of the press may often be synonymous, there can be instances where there is tension or even direct contradiction between the two.

Freedom of expression is the general term used in the *Canadian Charter of Rights and Freedom*.[3] Freedom of expression contains many of the basic elements of freedom of speech, but it is a consciously broader and more expansive notion. It clearly embraces the freedom to speak, write, print, and publish, but it also means that pure physical acts can attract the same kind of protection. While freedom of speech, then, protects the communication of information and ideas through speaking, writing, printing, or publishing, freedom of expression may also protect the communication of ideas or opinions through purely physical acts. For example, the Supreme Court of Canada has decided that picketing during a labour dispute is a form of expression.[4] Thus, freedom of expression may include more than would traditionally be regarded as falling within freedom of speech. The obvious question is whether we dilute the significance of free speech by adding to it protection for purely physical acts.

The fourth phrase has little to do with the three previous ones. Freedom of information is a very different notion from freedom of speech, freedom of the press, or freedom of expression. Freedom of information is a phrase which was invented in the United States and which is misleading. It has to do with the ability of individuals to gain access to information in the possession of the state. Freedom of information legislation in the United States gives people a legal right of access to such information. The federal legislation in Canada is more accurately titled

---

3   Part I of the *Constitution Act, 1982*, being Schedule B to the *Canada Act 1982* (U.K.), 1982, c. 11, s. 2(b) [hereinafter *Charter*].

4   *R.W.D.S.U. v. Dolphin Delivery Ltd.*, [1986] 2 S.C.R. 573.

as the *Access to Information Act*.[5] This title describes what the statute is about. Many people who do not understand what freedom of information means have, in recent years, confused freedom of information and freedom of speech and expression. The confusion is compounded by the fact that freedom of information is a phrase with little inherent meaning. Provincial access to information statutes tend to be called Freedom of Information Acts.

In this book we will consider only those limits on freedom of expression that are imposed by the state. We will not look at limits that arise from the structure of ownership of the mass media. By and large, the law does not deal with these matters. We will briefly address why this should be the case, but in order to do so, we have to note distinctions between the structures of the broadcasting media and the print media, and the proprietary rights of the owners of each.

The history of broadcasting regulation in Canada began, for practical purposes, in 1928, when the government of William Lyon Mackenzie King set up a Commission under the chairmanship of Sir John Aird, a prominent banker. The mandate of the Aird Commission was to consider what kind of system should be set up to regulate radio broadcasting in Canada. In the 1920s, broadcasting meant radio broadcasting, and commercial radio broadcasting was limited to what we would now describe as the AM frequency band. Because there was a limited range of broadcasting frequencies that could be used commercially, the response in all countries was for the state to take over the regulation and, more important, the allocation of broadcasting frequencies. If the state had not done so, the result would have been chaos. Given recent fundamental changes in the technology of broadcasting, however, this scarcity is either no longer with us or is about to disappear. In an era when everyone who has a telephone and a computer is, arguably, engaged in broadcasting, scarcity has little significance. One reason that newspaper publishing has not for many years been subjected to state regulation is that there has never been a situation of scarcity in relation to newspapers. Anyone with a piece of paper and a pen can produce a newspaper. No one may read it, but that is a different question. There is no technological barrier, comparable with the one that existed in the early days of radio broadcasting, to anyone producing a newspaper. Thus, the most basic justification for state regulation of broadcasting may well have disappeared, or be in the course of doing so.

---

5   R.S.C. 1985, c. A-1.

A major concern of the Aird Commission *Report* in 1929 was the growing domination of commercial radio broadcasting in Canada by American broadcasters.[6] What should the Canadian response be? The Commission made a number of fundamental recommendations, many of which are still with us. First, it urged that the state should regulate broadcasting, not simply to allocate frequencies, but to ensure that there was a broadcasting system in Canada which reflected and promoted Canadian identity, Canadian values, and Canadian culture. The Commission's report said it had discovered "unanimity on one fundamental question — Canadian radio listeners want Canadian broadcasting." Further, the Aird Commission recommended not only that the state should regulate broadcasting but that it should itself provide broadcasting services. Indeed, the Commission recommended that the state have a monopoly on providing broadcasting services, as was the position of the British Broadcasting Corporation in the United Kingdom at the time. This crucial recommendation was not adopted by the government of Canada and, from the outset, limited private radio broadcasting was permitted. Most important for present purposes, the Aird Commission recommended that the airwaves be regarded as public property, to be regulated by the state in the public interest. This principle, although it has been much watered down, continues in the current *Broadcasting Act*.[7]

There have been many *Broadcasting Acts*. The first was enacted under the R.B. Bennett government in 1932.[8] One interesting fact in the history of broadcasting in Canada is that every time there has been a change in the party in power, there has been fresh broadcasting legislation. The only exception was the short-lived Clark government of 1979.

How has the principle that broadcasting frequencies are public property worked in practice? First, no one may legally operate a broadcasting undertaking without a licence issued by the state through the agency of the Canadian Radio-Television and Telecommunications Commission. Second, the CRTC administers regulations that apply to all broadcasters. There are three sets of regulations: the *Radio Regulations*; the *Television Regulations*; and the *Cable Regulations*.[9]

---

6   Royal Commission on Radio Broadcasting, *Report* (Ottawa: King's Printer, 1929) (Chair: J. Aird).

7   S.C. 1991, c. 11.

8   *The Canadian Radio Broad-casting Act, 1932*, S.C. 1932, c. 51.

9   The *Radio Regulations* are SOR/86-982; the *Television Broadcasting Regulations* are SOR/87-49; and the *Cable Television Regulations* are SOR/86-831. All three have been much amended.

Although the proprietary rights of the owners of the broadcasting media are limited through being subject to control and regulation by the state, the state or public role in Canadian broadcasting in recent years has become far more apparent than real. There has been continued growth and expansion in private broadcasting. For many years private broadcasting was formally regarded as subordinate to the Canadian Broadcasting Corporation, the state-run broadcasting operation, but during the Diefenbaker era private broadcasting was given legal recognition as having the same status as the CBC. More recently, the CRTC has largely taken itself out of the business of directly regulating Canadian broadcasting. It no longer aggressively enforces the broadcasting regulations. Indeed, it has formally embraced the principle of "self-regulation" on the part of private broadcasters,[10] largely through encouraging the development of voluntary codes.

The CRTC has three levels of authority over licensees. First, it can cancel a licence. Yet every broadcaster in Canada knows the CRTC has never cancelled a licence because of a breach of the applicable broadcasting regulations. Second, the CRTC can suspend licences. It has suspended licences, not for any breach of the general broadcasting regulations, but usually for a breach of the specific terms of a particular licence. When an application is made for a licence, especially a radio licence, it is necessary to fill out a promise of performance form. The CRTC has established various program categories and, in the promise of performance, the applicant sets out the number of hours per week it intends to broadcast in different performance categories. What has happened many times in the history of radio licensing is that someone, especially in one of the larger urban markets, applies for a licence and promises to provide, say, X hours a week of innovative, Canadian-written and -produced radio drama, Y hours a week of uplifting talks, and Z hours a week of Canadian public affairs programming. The submission sounds ideal and the applicant gets a licence. Immediately, the station begins to broadcast twenty-four hours a day of Top 40 music. The CRTC has suspended licences for flagrant violations of the promise of performance.

Third, the CRTC can also refuse to renew a licence. Licences are granted for specific terms, usually five years. Even the CBC has to apply every five years for a new licence. Where there have been refusals to renew, they have usually arisen because of problems with the financial or technical elements of the regulations. The simple fact is that the

---

10   See generally M. Raboy, *Missed Opportunities: The Story of Canada's Broadcasting Policy* (Montreal: McGill-Queen's University Press, 1990).

CRTC plays a muted role in regulating the content of what is broadcast in Canada. As a result, the proprietors of the broadcasting media, rather than the state, determine what is broadcast in Canada.

There would appear to be substantial distinctions between the authority of the owners of the broadcasting media and the owners of the print media. While there is a seemingly elaborate system of broadcasting regulation, the print media are unregulated. The significance of this ostensible distinction has diminished in recent years. In practice, there is little difference between owning a radio station or a television network and owning a newspaper.

From the standpoint of the law, owning a newspaper is much the same as owning any other form of private property. The proprietor of a newspaper stands in the same relation to his newspaper as the proprietor of a soap factory or a used car lot does to his property. Owners have, within provincial employment laws, absolute authority over hiring and firing. This authority includes the right to dismiss journalists who express uncongenial opinions in the pages of the newspaper or outside the workplace.[11] Owners have authority over all financial matters affecting their newspapers. They decide how much or how little money will be spent on hiring and keeping editorial staff and how newspaper profits will be disposed of. Will profits be reinvested in improving the newspaper or, as often happens where newspapers are part of conglomerate corporate empires, will they be used to finance other corporate ventures? Finally, owners have complete freedom to dispose of newspapers. They can sell them to whomsoever they choose or they can simply fold them.

Disputes over the authority wielded by owners arise periodically, because there are people who believe there are significant social differences between newspapers and detergent or used cars. Such beliefs are widely expressed only when something especially outrageous occurs.

Something outrageous happened in the summer of 1980. The Southam corporation closed the Winnipeg *Tribune*, and the Thomson chain closed the Ottawa *Journal*.[12] Both Winnipeg and Ottawa were left as one-newspaper towns. A degree of public concern was expressed and

---

11   General questions relating to the extent of employer authority over journalist employees are discussed in *Cashin v. Canadian Broadcasting Corp.*, [1988] 3 F.C. 494 (C.A.), and *Canadian Broadcasting Corp. v. Canada (Labour Relations Board)*, [1995] 1 S.C.R. 157.

12   These acts were made legally possible because of a Supreme Court of Canada decision which, in effect, told newspaper owners that the existing federal competition legislation did not apply to them. *R. v. K.C. Irving Ltd.*, [1978] 1 S.C.R. 408.

the federal government responded by setting up a royal commission to look into newspapers. The commission was chaired by Tom Kent. Kent began his career as a journalist in the United Kingdom, then moved to Canada where, among other things, he headed Prime Minister Lester Pearson's war on poverty in the mid-1960s and later became dean of management studies at Dalhousie University. He had, despite the often critical views of some newspaper owners about him, an abiding faith in capitalism.

The Kent Commission produced its report in 1981 and recommended certain limitations on the proprietary rights of newspaper owners.[13] In response, Kent was roundly vilified on editorial pages from sea to sea. The Commission's recommendations were portrayed as a monstrous scheme to destroy freedom of expression and freedom of the press in Canada. Yet the reality was different. Kent proposed the enactment of a *Canada Newspapers Act* to inhibit further concentration of newspaper ownership and to reverse it in severe cases. The Act would have guaranteed a degree of independence for newspaper editors and journalists. Advisory committees would be set up across the country to permit members of the local community to express their views about local newspapers. Draft legislation was prepared, but as the hysteria of denunciations of Kent and all his works mounted, the government lost its nerve. The draft bill went nowhere and the report was quickly forgotten.

The only lasting significance of the Kent Commission lies in the impetus it gave to press councils. Newspaper owners apparently decided that, having torpedoed the Commission, they should make some symbolic concession to one of its recommendations. Perhaps they wished to give the appearance of limiting their ownership rights and of recognizing the legitimacy of a public interest in the content of newspapers. So they decided to join press councils. To what degree, if any, do these councils limit the proprietary authority of newspaper owners?

The Ontario Press Council, Canada's first, was formed in 1972, with eight newspapers as members: the *Toronto Star*, the *London Free Press*, and a number of Southam papers. Membership grew slowly, with only one daily and a few weeklies joining before 1981. But 1981 was, as the Council put it, a "record year for growth." One daily and nine weeklies joined. The *10th Annual Report* for 1982 stated, "Council membership booms." The number of dailies belonging to the Press Council increased from ten to thirty-two, and included the *Globe and Mail* and some other Thomson papers. Membership among weeklies jumped from fourteen

---

13   Royal Commission on Newspapers, *Report* (Ottawa: Minister of Supply & Services, 1981) (Chair: T. Kent).

to forty-nine. Eighteen more dailies joined the Council in 1983 and, by the beginning of 1985, all forty-two English-language daily newspapers in Ontario were members.[14]

The activity was not confined to Ontario. The Ontario Council stated in its 1982 *Report*: "The press council movement got into high gear across Canada in late 1982." In 1996 there are press councils in Quebec, Manitoba, Alberta, and British Columbia, in addition to the Atlantic Press Council.

The Ontario Press Council was based on the model provided by the UK Press Council. Its structure is bipartite, in that there are two parties — the newspapers and the public. The parties receive equal representation in all the committees and organs of the Council. The Atlantic Press Council and the press councils in Western Canada all follow the Ontario model. The Quebec Press Council is different, having a tripartite structure: the newspapers, the public, and the journalists. This tripartite structure would seem to reflect more accurately the nature of newspaper organizations. The problem with the Ontario Press Council structure is that it defines the interests of proprietors and reporters as being identical, something which, in the experience of anyone who has ever been a reporter, is questionable. The tripartite structure in Quebec not only allows members of the public to complain about newspapers but also allows journalists to complain about newspapers.

The essential function of press councils is to hear complaints. Normally, persons must have exhausted all available legal remedies before a press council will entertain a complaint. Where a council determines that a complaint has some substance, it will set up a committee to conduct a formal hearing into it. This committee will reach a decision as to whether the newspaper's coverage of particular stories was proper or adequate, whether the photograph on page 1 was tasteless, and so on. In Ontario, the committee hearing a complaint reflects the bipartite structure of the Council. An equal number of representatives of the newspapers and of the public will be on the committee. The rules provide that where the decision is adverse to the newspaper, the offending newspaper is obliged to print the text of the decision. The problem with the Ontario Press Council is that there is no mechanism in its constitution for enforcing decisions. The normal mechanism that all private or voluntary associations use for enforcing their rules is expulsion: if a member does not obey the rules, the member is thrown out. The

---

14   Copies of Ontario Press Council *Annual Reports* and other documents can be obtained from the Council's Office at Ryerson Polytechnic University, 350 Victoria Street, Toronto, Ontario, M5B 2K3.

Ontario Press Council's constitution contains no power to expel a member. So a newspaper can consistently refuse to print the text of adjudications that are critical of it. Press councils, in effect, do little to limit the proprietary authority of newspaper owners.

The proprietary authority of owners of newspapers and radio and television undertakings can be used to shape and define freedom of expression. The law simply does not address this matter. The law speaks only to limitations on freedom of expression that are imposed by the state. To take a leading illustration of this fact, the *Canadian Charter of Rights and Freedoms* creates rights only as against the state. The *Charter's* guarantee of freedom of expression cannot be enforced against media owners or managers.

The bulk of this book looks at freedom of expression in Canada. First, it addresses the issue in relation to the Constitution of Canada, and then focuses attention on the various and substantial limitations on freedom of expression that are found in our law. Because it is often difficult to dissociate general or abstract questions about freedom of expression from concrete issues that confront working journalists, a recurring theme throughout the book is whether the law should recognize any special rights or special status for journalists.

FURTHER READINGS

A useful, if somewhat dated, survey of Canadian newspapers is found in the report of the Kent Commission: Royal Commission on Newspapers, *Report*, (Ottawa: Minister of Supply & Services, 1981) (Chair: T. Kent). The fullest current survey of the regulation of broadcasting is M. Raboy, *Missed Opportunities: The Story of Canada's Broadcasting Policy* (Montreal: McGill-Queen's University Press, 1990).

For a detailed collection of primary materials on media law, see R. Martin and G.S. Adam, *A Sourcebook of Canadian Media Law*, 2d ed. (Ottawa: Carleton University Press, 1994). A very useful practical guide is R.S. Bruser and B.M. Rogers, *Journalists and the Law: How to Get the Story without Getting Sued or Put in Jail* (Ottawa: Canadian Bar Foundation, 1985). An excellent source for keeping up with developments is "The Press and the Courts" service of the Canadian Daily Newspaper Association, Suite 1100, 890 Yonge Street, Toronto, Ontario, M4W 3P4, telephone (416) 923-3567.

CHAPTER 1

FREEDOM OF EXPRESSION AND THE CONSTITUTION

What effect has Canada's federal structure had on freedom of expression? To answer this question it is necessary to examine the division of powers and responsibilities between the two levels of government and to see how this division has been interpreted to provide a limited degree of constitutional protection for freedom of expression. Similarly, the *Canadian Charter of Rights and Freedoms* has created a substantive guarantee of freedom of expression.[1]

One of the basic principles of constitutional government is that the state is subject to the law. The state and all its organs must act within the rules set out in the constitution. Section 52(1) of the *Constitution Act, 1982*,[2] expresses this principle clearly by stating that "[t]he Constitution of Canada is the supreme law of Canada." Consequently, any act of the state which is not in accordance with the requirements of the Constitution is invalid. Thus, to the extent that the Constitution protects freedom of expression, state acts that interfere with free expression may be open to challenge before the courts and, if the challenge is successful, may be declared invalid by the courts.

---

1   Part I of the *Constitution Act, 1982*, being Schedule B to the *Canada Act 1982* (U.K.), 1982, c. 11, s. 2(b) [hereinafter *Charter*].
2   Being Schedule B to the *Canada Act 1982* (U.K.), 1982, c. 11, s. 52(1).

A. FEDERALISM

1) General Considerations

For 115 years after Confederation, Canada's written Constitution consisted largely of the *British North America Act*[3] of 1867. Nowhere in the text of that Act is there reference to freedom of speech, freedom of expression, freedom of the press, or anything similar. The central purpose of the *B.N.A. Act* was to create Canada's institutions of government. More specifically, it set out the basic elements of the federal system, dividing the authority to make laws between the Parliament of Canada and the provincial legislatures. The *B.N.A. Act* did not contain any formal protection for rights. The limits it established on law-making authority were functional rather than substantive.

The task of interpreting the *B.N.A. Act* and, more particularly, the way it apportioned law-making powers between Ottawa and the provinces was left to the courts. It is worth spending some time describing the federal structure set out in the Act and the way that structure was elaborated by the courts. The *B.N.A. Act*, like all federal constitutions, is organized around lists of legislative subject-matters. Section 91 lists the areas in which Parliament, the federal legislature, has the authority to make laws. These areas tend to be national in scope and significance. Sections 92, 92A, and 93 list the areas in which the provincial legislatures may make laws, areas that are more local in scope. Section 95 is the joint list, setting out those areas — agriculture and immigration — where both levels of government may make laws.

The judicial approach to dispute resolution, despite substantial oscillation over the years between preferences for either a centralized or a decentralized approach to Canadian federalism, is quite simple. When someone challenges the validity of a statute, for example, a provincial statute, the court must determine whether that statute is within the powers of the provincial legislature to enact (*intra vires*, and, therefore, constitutional) or whether it is beyond the powers of the provincial legislature to enact (*ultra vires*, and, therefore, unconstitutional). The court will follow a two-stage approach. In the first stage, it will examine the impugned law to determine its subject-matter and to discover what that law is really all about. This stage is described as "characterizing" the law. Having determined the subject-matter of the law, the court will then go to the lists in the Constitution to see where this subject-matter

---

3   (U.K.), 30 & 31 Vict., c. 3.

is to be found. Since we are hypothetically dealing with a provincial law, if the court finds its subject-matter in the provincial list, the law is valid. But if the court finds the subject-matter of the law under scrutiny in the federal list, it is invalid. It is a provincial enactment dealing with a subject-matter about which only Parliament can make laws.

2) The "Implied Bill of Rights"

The Supreme Court of Canada was able to create a limited degree of constitutional protection for freedom of expression out of the division of powers. This protection originated in a decision called *Reference Re Alberta Legislation*[4] — the first major discussion of the significance of freedom of expression by the Court. It is noteworthy that such a crucial concern did not receive extensive judicial consideration until 1938.

The background to the decision is of interest.[5] In the 1930s Canada experienced a major economic depression, and the areas most hard hit were the three prairie provinces of Manitoba, Saskatchewan, and Alberta. Not only were these provinces devastated economically but the effects of the depression were exacerbated by prolonged drought. The economies of the prairie provinces were, at the time, based on agriculture. Oil of a commercially exploitable quality and quantity was not discovered in Alberta until 1947.

These extreme economic conditions in western Canada, as in other places undergoing similar stresses at other times, led to extreme political responses. The response in Manitoba and Saskatchewan was the Cooperative Commonwealth Federation (CCF), founded in Regina in 1933; in contrast, the response in Alberta was Social Credit. In the 1935 Alberta election the world's first Social Credit government was voted into office. The new government was determined to bring about the Social Credit millennium in Alberta.

One of the many difficulties Social Credit experienced in Alberta was a lack of enthusiasm among the province's newspapers. The newspapers, and in particular the Edmonton *Journal*, were highly critical of Social Credit. The *Journal*, in fact, became the only Canadian newspaper ever to win a Pulitzer Prize, when it received an honorary award for some of its writing about Alberta politics. This criticism became increasingly annoying to Social Credit, and as part of its legislative package, it introduced a statute called *An Act to Ensure the Publication of Accurate News*

---

4   [1938] S.C.R. 100.

5   The classic account is C.B. Macpherson, *Democracy in Alberta: Social Credit and the Party System*, 2d ed. (Toronto: University of Toronto Press, 1962).

and Information. When governments enact statutes with titles like this, their objectives are likely to be opposite to what the words indicate.

For our purposes, the *Act to Ensure the Publication of Accurate News and Information* said three things. The first had to do with any story about a Social Credit policy or program which the authorities believed to be inaccurate or misleading. Social Credit did not believe in the institution of government, so it was in an embarrassing position when it found itself the government of Alberta. It announced that it was not really the provincial government and passed legislation setting up the Social Credit Board, which was in fact the government of Alberta. The leader of Social Credit, William Aberhart, likewise did not want to call himself the premier of Alberta, so he took the title of chairman of the Social Credit Board. The legislation stipulated that the chairman of the Social Credit Board had the power, when he believed that a newspaper story was inaccurate or misleading, to order the offending newspaper to print a story setting out the official Social Credit position on the matter.

Is that censorship? The newspaper was free to print its inaccurate, biased, or distorted story. It did not have to take its story to the chairman of the board to receive permission before being allowed to publish it. If censorship necessarily involves prior restraint, there does not appear to be any restraint here. The power given to the chairman of the Social Credit Board could be said to be a prior restraint only to the extent that, by being required to use space to carry the official Social Credit story, the freedom of the proprietors of the newspapers to choose what to put in their pages was limited. The implication in the Act was that the official Social Credit position should receive the same prominence as the inaccurate or misleading story. If the inaccurate and misleading story was on page 1, then presumably the official Social Credit story had to go on page 1.

It could be argued that the Social Credit Board demanded a kind of free advertising. The government had conferred on itself a power to secure free advertising. Formerly, in American broadcasting law, there was a doctrine known as the "fairness doctrine."[6] This doctrine was invented by the courts ostensibly to promote freedom of speech. The fairness doctrine said that if a broadcaster presented one side of a controversial issue, that broadcaster had to afford time to those on the other side of the issue to present their point of view. This first provision in the *Act to Ensure the Publication of Accurate News and Information* was a sort of state-based fairness doctrine.

---

6   *Red Lion Broadcasting Co. v. Federal Communications Commission*, 395 U.S. 367 at 368 (1969).

The second provision in the Alberta legislation was more ominous: it was a kind of anti-leak provision. If the chairman of the Social Credit Board was not happy with a story dealing with one of his party's policies, programs, or initiatives, he could require the proprietors of the offending newspaper to disclose their sources for the story.

The third element in the legislation was the most ominous: where the chairman of the Social Credit Board had either directed a newspaper to print a story giving the Social Credit version, or had required the newspaper to disclose its sources for a particular story and the newspaper had refused to do so, he could order the newspaper to be closed. That clearly would be a prior restraint.

The government of Canada, which was not sympathetic to Social Credit, took the extraordinary step of referring the entire package of legislation enacted under Social Credit directly to the Supreme Court of Canada for a determination of its constitutionality. What did the Court say about the *Act to Ensure the Publication of Accurate News and Information*, or, more colloquially, the Press Bill?

The problem with the Alberta Press Bill was that it seemed to place limits on freedom of expression. But since the phrase freedom of expression was not to be found in the text of the *B.N.A. Act*, how could it be argued that there was a constitutional problem with this statute? The answer lies in the realm of judicial creativity. Chief Justice Lyman Duff, who gave the most important judgment, concluded that freedom of expression, which he defined as the "free public discussion of public affairs," was the essential precondition to the operation of democratic government. As he put it, "[F]ree public discussion of public affairs . . . is the breath of life for parliamentary institutions." Parliamentary institutions, and, therefore, democratic government, could not function without freedom of expression. Indeed, freedom of expression was fundamental to the Canadian constitutional system, transcended any provincial interest, and underlay the "peace, order and good government of Canada." The significance of this conclusion was that, under the *B.N.A. Act*, only Parliament was given the authority to make laws that address the peace, order, and good government of Canada.

Put another way, Chief Justice Duff saw in the Press Bill a law that restricted the free public discussion of public affairs. What was the subject-matter of such a law? Chief Justice Duff concluded that the true subject-matter of a law that limited the free public discussion of public affairs was the peace, order, and good government of Canada. Only Parliament had the constitutional authority to make such a law; a province could not make a law about the peace, order, and good government of Canada. The Chief Justice decided that the Press Bill was an attempt on the part of a provincial legislature to enact a law dealing with a subject-matter that did not belong to it. Thus, the law was invalid.

Duff was able to create a degree of constitutional protection for freedom of expression out of a Constitution that nowhere referred to freedom of expression. When he talked about freedom of expression, it is clear that he was referring to political expression. He meant political expression when he talked about the free public discussion of public affairs. It would seem that in 1938, Duff had a hierarchy of forms of expression in mind. Some forms were clearly more important than others, and most important of all was political expression.

There was, further, no discussion of individual rights in Duff's judgment. Freedom of expression was deserving of protection, in his opinion, not because it was a right claimed by individuals, but because it was an essential precondition to democratic government. The basis for freedom of expression was not individual but social.

There was also a concurring judgment by Mr. Justice Cannon. He added two further arguments in support of the conclusion that the statute was beyond the competence of a province. He looked historically and comparatively at legislation that sought to restrict or control political expression. He looked at the United Kingdom and concluded that laws which placed limits on political expression were historically part of that country's criminal law. He also looked at the existing *Criminal Code* of Canada and noted that there already was a provision, the offence of sedition, which sought to define the limits of acceptable political expression. He concluded that to attempt to set limits on political discourse was to make criminal law. But in the division of powers between Ottawa and the provinces under the *B.N.A. Act*, it was only Parliament that had the constitutional authority to make criminal law. Once again the legislature of a province had tried to enact legislation dealing with a subject-matter — criminal law — that belonged exclusively to Ottawa. Therefore, once again, the Press Bill was *ultra vires*.

Mr. Justice Cannon's second argument had to do with something he called "the status of Canadian citizen," odd terminology, given that the first citizenship legislation in Canada was not enacted until 1946. He said that both the incidents that flowed from the status of Canadian citizens and the status itself were matters relating to the peace, order, and good government of Canada. Only Parliament could place limits or conditions on the status of Canadian citizens. More particularly, he said that one of the incidents of possessing the status of a Canadian citizen was that a person was free to take part in political debate. To limit the ability of Canadians to take part in political debate, Cannon decided, was to place limits on the status of Canadian citizen; it made a law about the peace, order, and good government of Canada — an area beyond the competence of a province. Again, the provincial legislation was invalid.

A number of general observations may be made about these decisions. First, Chief Justice Duff did not say that there was a discrete constitutional subject-matter called "newspapers" or that the press, as a legislative subject-matter, belonged entirely to Ottawa. As he said in his judgment, "Some degree of regulation of newspapers everyone would concede to the provinces." What aspects of newspapers could provinces regulate? Their jurisdiction extended to the business aspects of newspapers, one obvious example being the employment relations affecting newspapers. Also, as the Supreme Court decided in a number of cases over the following years, questions of newspaper advertising should be dealt with under provincial law.[7] The Court said that it was open to the provinces to regulate newspaper advertising, because to do so was to regulate a contractual relationship, an element of property and civil rights, a matter listed in section 92 as within provincial jurisdiction. In saying this, the Court was reinforcing the notion of a hierarchy of forms of expression. There was political expression and there was commercial expression, and they clearly stood on different footings.

Second, although the result of the Alberta Press Bill decision was the creation of a degree of constitutional protection for freedom of expression, it was only protection against limits imposed by a province. Canadian federalism has been viewed as an either/or system. Every conceivable subject is to be found somewhere in the division of powers between Ottawa and the provinces. If a particular matter is not something that can be regulated by the provinces, then, by definition, it is something that can be regulated by Ottawa. The clear implication of the Press Bill decision is that, had this legislation been enacted by Parliament, it would have been held to be valid. There was no absolute protection for freedom of expression arising out of this decision.

This decision is often referred to as the beginning of the "Implied Bill of Rights" theory. It is a Bill of Rights because it gave a degree of constitutional protection to certain rights, but these rights are implied because they were not set out explicitly in the text of the Constitution.

The Implied Bill of Rights theory stayed around for a number of years. An important Supreme Court decision of the 1950s — *Switzman v. Elbling*[8] — addressed the constitutionality of a Quebec statute called

---

7   The last such decision was *Canada A. G. v. Law Society (British Columbia)*, [1982] 2 S.C.R. 307.

8   [1957] S.C.R. 285.

An Act to Protect the Province Against Communistic Propaganda. The title of the Act made its purpose clear, but the operative section said:

> It shall be illegal for any person, who possesses or occupies a house within the Province, to use it or allow any person to make use of it to propagate communism or bolshevism by any means whatsoever.

This wording raises an obvious question. If Quebec wanted to protect itself against communist propaganda, why did it not just say: "It shall be illegal for any person to propagate communism or bolshevism by any means whatsoever." Why tie the prohibition to the use of a house? Why draft a statute in such an odd fashion? The answer is that the people who wrote this statute had obviously addressed the same concerns that underlay the Supreme Court's decision in the Press Bill case. They could see that if a statute said directly that it was unlawful to propagate communism or bolshevism in Quebec, such legislation would amount to a province attempting to place limits on the free public discussion of public affairs, something it seemed a province could not do. The drafters attached the statute to the use of houses because land use was clearly an element of property and civil rights in the province. There is no doubt that a province can say that a house may not be used as a brothel or a bar or a glue factory or a law office. That is land-use legislation. The argument advanced by Quebec was that a law saying you cannot use a house to propagate communism or bolshevism was also a law about land use, which is to say about property and civil rights and, thus, valid.

The teeth in this Act provided that if the attorney general of the province was satisfied that a house was being used to propagate communism or bolshevism, he could order that the house be locked up. The house could be closed without any requirement of a charge or a hearing. That is why this statute came to be known popularly as the Padlock Act.

A dispute arose between a landlord and a tenant in Montreal. The landlord sought to end the lease on the ground that the leased premises had been used unlawfully for the purpose of propagating communism. The tenant conceded this fact, but argued that the Padlock Act was unconstitutional and, therefore, of no relevance. The dispute ended up before the Supreme Court.

A majority of the judges in the Court, and this was especially true in the judgment of Mr. Justice Ivan Rand, reiterated the principles of the Press Bill decision. Mr. Justice Rand suggested that freedom of expression was as important to human beings as the ability to draw breath. More to the point, he held that free expression was an essential element in a democratic society. Thus, legislation which limited that freedom, as the Padlock Act clearly did despite its transparent attempt to appear to address land use, was beyond the competence of a province. It was beyond the competence of a province because it dealt with the peace, order, and good government of Canada and because it dealt with matters properly belonging to the criminal law.

The judgment of Mr. Justice Douglas Abbott is interesting. His judgment is unique, even though most commentators agree that it is wrong. Mr. Justice Abbott concluded that not only was legislation of this kind beyond the competence of a province to enact but it was also beyond the competence of Parliament. What was his basis for saying so? He relied on the preamble to the *B.N.A. Act*, which said that Canada was to have a constitution "similar in Principle" to that of the United Kingdom. Abbott focused on those words and said that one of the principles of the UK Constitution was the protection of free expression. He then said that the effect of the preamble to the *B.N.A. Act* was to place freedom of expression on a constitutional basis, making it impossible for either a province or Parliament to enact legislation to limit it. This point is wrong for a very simple reason. There is, or has traditionally seemed to be, only one principle in the Constitution of the United Kingdom: the absolute, unlimited, unqualified supremacy of Parliament. There are no legal limits on the law-making authority of the UK Parliament, so, if it had at any time wanted to enact legislation restricting or denying freedom of expression, it was constitutionally free to do so.

In the 1970s the Implied Bill of Rights theory began to fall into disfavour in the Supreme Court. This is exemplified in a decision called *McNeil v. Nova Scotia (Board of Censors).*[9] Gerry McNeil was a journalist who was living at the time in Dartmouth and wanted to see the movie *Last Tango in Paris*. He went to the Court twice in his attempt to do so. Nova Scotia had a statute called the *Theatres and Amusements Act*. The Act created an Amusements Regulation Board, which was the province's movie censorship agency. There is a long-standing tradition in Canada of provinces censoring movies, although in recent years they have moved from censoring to classifying. McNeil questioned whether there was any constitutional basis for this censorship.

Why do governments censor movies? What are they trying to accomplish? Nobody has ever censored movies because they are badly acted, poorly written, boring, abysmally directed, or totally lacking in originality. They are censored in order to remove the "naughty" bits and, more recently, violence. The problem that arises is that the underlying goal in creating such a system of censorship is the preservation of

---

9   [1978] 2 S.C.R. 662.

public morality. But when the state acts to uphold public morality, it is, arguably, making criminal law. This was the basis of McNeil's argument before the Supreme Court.

As with most of the division of powers cases, this one came down to a matter of characterization, to a determination of the true subject-matter of the legislation that was being challenged. What was the subject-matter of the censorship provisions in the Nova Scotia *Theatres and Amusements Act*? Was it the regulation of public morality, which would mean they were about criminal law, or was it the regulation of a particular business in the province, which would make them about property and civil rights in the province? McNeil's argument seemed to be strengthened by the fact that the *Criminal Code* already contained express prohibitions against obscenity and against offering an immoral or indecent performance in public — and, by the fact that when the state censors movies, it is placing limits on free expression. In the end the Court split five to four. The majority decided the subject-matter of the legislation was the regulation of a business in the province. Clearly, a provincial legislature can enact legislation regulating businesses. The mere fact that the statute might have incidental effects on matters such as criminal law that were within federal jurisdiction would not affect its validity.

3) Broadcasting

For obvious reasons, the original text of the *B.N.A. Act*, which dates from 1867, made no reference to broadcasting. When commercial broadcasting began to develop in Canada in the 1920s, this lack immediately became an issue. Did Ottawa or the provinces have the necessary constitutional authority to regulate broadcasting? When the Aird Commission was set up in 1928, the assumption around Ottawa was that Ottawa had the authority. The matter was forced before the courts in 1929 when the Quebec legislature enacted a statute called the *Radio Act*, which purported to establish a mechanism for regulating broadcasting. The case ended up before the Judicial Committee of the Privy Council, then the final court of appeal for Canada, in 1932.[10]

The Judicial Committee decided that broadcasting was a matter exclusively within federal jurisdiction. The judges reached this conclusion for three reasons. First, they saw broadcasting as a matter of such significance to the country as a whole that it went to the peace, order,

---

10   *Reference Re Radio Communications in Canada (Regulation and Control of)*, [1932] A.C. 304 (P.C.).

and good government of Canada. Broadcasting transcended purely local or provincial interests and was of importance to the entire nation. Second, the court upheld federal jurisdiction over broadcasting under section 132 of the *B.N.A. Act.* This section gave Parliament the jurisdiction to legislate so as to implement treaty obligations. By this time Canada was a party to treaties with the United States and Mexico allocating broadcasting frequencies among the three countries. The Judicial Committee said Parliament must have the law-making authority to implement these obligations. Finally, section 92(10) of the *B.N.A. Act* deals with "Works and Undertakings." It talks about steamships, railways, canals, and telegraphs. The Judicial Committee thought that this provision had some application because it saw an analogy between broadcasting and telegraphs. "Work" here is meant in a nineteenth-century engineering sense — a bridge, a canal, a line of rail. An "undertaking" is a commercial enterprise that uses a "work." So a railway company is an undertaking and the work it uses is the railway track. Section 92(10) says that *local* works or undertakings are within provincial jurisdiction. That meant, for example, that a railway which operated entirely within one province would be under provincial jurisdiction. On the other hand, section 92(10) went on to say that where a work or an undertaking extended beyond the boundaries of a province or connected one province with another, it would be within federal jurisdiction. This is why national railways are within federal jurisdiction.

A similar issue was argued in litigation for many years concerning jurisdiction over provincial or local telephone systems. The Supreme Court resolved it in 1989 by noting that although local telephone systems continue to exist, they are all connected together through the Telecom Canada system. This interconnected system extends beyond the boundaries of any province and is, thus, within federal jurisdiction.[11]

In understanding the Judicial Committee's decision on broadcasting, it is important to be clear on its definition of broadcasting. The Committee saw broadcasting as the transmission and reception through the air of Hertzian waves. If we think about broadcasting today, it clearly means a lot more. But for the Judicial Committee the deciding factor about broadcasting was that Hertzian waves, by their nature, did not respect provincial boundaries. Thus, broadcasting was a work or undertaking which extended beyond the boundaries of the province or which connected one province with another. It was, therefore, a matter within federal jurisdiction.

---

11 *Alberta Government Telephones v. Canada (Radio-Television & Telecommunications Commission),* [1989] 2 S.C.R. 225.

Subsequent decisions have gone further. In 1973 the Ontario Court of Appeal, in *C.F.R.B.* v. *Canada (A.G.) (No. 2)*, said broadcasting should now be regarded as if it were *de facto* one of the enumerated heads of section 91 of the *B.N.A. Act* — that is, as if the section which gives jurisdiction to Parliament to make laws actually said "broadcasting."[12] Other decisions have held that federal jurisdiction over broadcasting includes not only the technical aspects of broadcasting, but the financial aspects and all matters related to content.[13] The general view taken by the courts has been that everything involved in broadcasting is subject to federal jurisdiction.

Certain difficulties have arisen over the years. Cable television is one. Cable television works by taking signals from a large antenna that receives them off-air — called the head end — and then feeding them out to subscribers along copper wires or, increasingly, fibre optics. From the head end to the subscriber there is no transmission or reception of Hertzian waves through the air. The argument was made in the 1960s that cable television systems were, as a result, not broadcasting, or at least not broadcasting as understood by the Judicial Committee of the Privy Council in 1932. The argument was further made that it was technically feasible to create a cable television system wholly situated within one province — that is, a local work or undertaking and, as such, within provincial jurisdiction. This issue was a matter of ongoing negotiation between Ottawa and several of the provinces for many years. The *Broadcasting Act* was amended by Parliament to say that broadcasting included the operation of a cable television system. The basis for the dispute, of course, was the enormous amounts of money involved.

Parliament, through the *Broadcasting Act*, had said that anyone who wanted to operate a cable television system anywhere in Canada had to have a federal licence. The province of Quebec then amended its *Public Service Board Act* to state that anyone who wanted to operate a cable television system anywhere in Quebec had to have a provincial licence. Both regulatory bodies, the CRTC and the Public Service Board of Quebec, operated in the same fashion. They issued licences that were geographically exclusive. There is no competition in the cable business in Canada. Anyone who receives a cable licence receives an exclusive licence to provide cable services within a defined geographical area.

Both Ottawa and the province of Quebec were demanding that cable operators be licensed by them. For many years all cable operators in the

---

12   [1973] 3 O.R. 819 (C.A.).
13   *Capital Cities Communication Inc.* v. *Canada (Radio-Television & Telecommunications Commission)*, [1978] 2 S.C.R. 141.

province of Quebec simply got two licences — one federal and one provincial. Unfortunately, something went wrong in the town of Rimouski. At its most basic, the CRTC gave one cable operator an exclusive federal licence to operate a cable system in the town, and the Public Service Board gave a different operator an exclusive provincial licence. The matter ended up being litigated. The provincial argument looked at cable systems from the head end to the subscriber and said these systems were undertakings wholly situate in the province and, therefore, within provincial jurisdiction. The majority in the Supreme Court said that although the signal which cable systems sent to the subscriber was carried over copper wire, these systems nonetheless relied on the reception of Hertzian waves off-air. The wire-based delivery system did not alter the fact that cable systems were part of the general broadcasting system. As a result, cable systems were broadcasting and within federal jurisdiction.[14]

4) Advertising

Until the late 1970s, broadcasting was treated by the courts as if it were a monolith. Anything involved in what could be characterized as broadcasting was within federal jurisdiction. Then a problem was created by a regulation made under the Quebec *Consumer Protection Act*.

Quebec had in the 1970s, and still has, probably the most active system of consumer protection legislation in Canada. A regulation dealing with advertising directed at children said, "No one shall prepare, use, publish or cause to be published in Quebec advertising intended for children which . . . employs cartoons." This regulation raised a number of questions. First, the Supreme Court of Canada had earlier decided that the provinces could regulate print advertising. But clearly, and this has never been open to doubt, Ottawa can regulate broadcasting advertising as part of its general jurisdiction over broadcasting. The drafting in the Quebec regulation was very careful. It did not purport to prohibit the broadcasting of advertising intended for children which employed cartoons. Such a regulation would have been invalid, as its subject-matter would clearly have been broadcasting. The wording, that no one should "prepare, use, publish or cause to be published," was consciously aimed at advertisers, not broadcasters. Another feature was concealed here, one that fooled the Court. When "cartoons" was used in the regulation, it did not mean newspaper cartoons, but moving cartoons. There is only one medium that can employ such cartoons in advertising directed at chil-

---

14   *Dionne v. Quebec (Public Service Board)*, [1978] 2 S.C.R. 191.

dren, and that is television. The point about this regulation was that it could only have meaning in relation to television.

The majority in the Court held that the regulation was directed towards advertising — that is, towards a contractual relationship. This meant that its subject-matter was property and civil rights in the province and, as a result, the regulation was valid provincial legislation. Thus, by means of some careful drafting, the province of Quebec was able to control part of the content of what was broadcast on television.[15]

The next logical step is found in a more recent Supreme Court decision about freedom of expression and the division of powers: *Irwin Toy Ltd. v. Quebec (A.G.)*.[16] There had been a further amendment to the Quebec *Consumer Protection Act*, and this amendment, in sections 248 and 249, absolutely prohibited all commercial advertising directed at persons under the age of thirteen. Now, if you live in the real world and you want to advertise to persons under the age of thirteen, you put your advertising on television, which, of course, is why the challenge to the legislation came from the Irwin Toy Company. But the majority of the judges was baffled by the form of the legislation. It did not expressly address broadcasting — the word "television" was not used. The statute spoke only of advertising. Once again the Court held that to deal with advertising was to deal with a contractual relation; as a result, the subject-matter of the legislation was property and civil rights in the province — and, thus, it was valid.

The issue of advertising and its regulation continues to be important in relation to the division of powers. In 1994 the Supreme Court released its decision as to the validity of a federal statute called the *Tobacco Products Control Act*.[17] This Act prohibited the advertising in any medium in Canada of any tobacco product. There should be no division of powers problem with Parliament enacting legislation that prohibits the advertising of tobacco products over radio or television, because such legislation would clearly be characterized as being in relation to broadcasting. The more difficult question is whether Parliament has the authority to prohibit tobacco advertising in newspapers and magazines, because print advertising has been held, as we have seen, to involve matters of property and civil rights in the province. Where did Parliament get the authority to do this? The Supreme Court decided that the prohibition on advertising could be upheld as an exercise of Parliament's exclusive authority to make criminal law, a majority being

---

15   *Quebec (A.G.) v. Kellogg's Co.*, [1978] 2 S.C.R. 211.

16   [1989] 1 S.C.R. 927 [hereinafter *Irwin Toy*].

17   *RJR-MacDonald Inc. v. Canada (A.G.)*, [1994] 1 S.C.R. 311.

convinced that the protection of public health was a valid objective to be achieved in making criminal law.

A brief digression to discuss certain other legal issues relating to advertising is in order. The central policy issue with respect to advertising has been the regulation of false and misleading advertising. What should the state do about it? Many people might say that all advertising is, by its nature, false and misleading. In the early days of mass consumer advertising the possibility was briefly created that false and misleading advertising could be regulated through the law of contract. An ad says, Use our toothpaste and you will become enchanting, alluring, exciting. You faithfully use the toothpaste for several months, but remain the same dull, boring person you always were. Can you sue the advertiser for breach of contract, arguing that it promised that if you used its toothpaste all sorts of wonderful things would occur, but you did and nothing happened?

There was an interesting case along these lines before the English courts in the latter part of the nineteenth century. The Carbolic Smoke Ball Company marketed something called the Carbolic Smoke Ball. The user held the ball in his hand, removed the top, and fumes came out. These fumes were supposed to cure a range of ailments. A newspaper advertisement had said: "[A hundred pound] . . . reward will be paid by the Carbolic Smoke Ball Company to any person who contracts the increasing epidemic of influenza, colds, or any disease caused by taking cold, after having used the ball three times daily for two weeks according to the printed directions supplied with each ball." The company deposited £100 with a bank to show its sincerity. A Mrs. Carlill bought a Smoke Ball and followed the directions, inhaling the fumes three times a day for two weeks. Despite this routine, she got sick. She sued the company and won, the court holding that the advertising claims were a term of her contract with the company.[18] Quickly, however, the courts reversed their direction and, since then, have consistently said that advertising claims are "mere puffs." They are not contractual terms and cannot be treated as contractual terms. As a result, the law of contract has been rendered useless as a legal mechanism for regulating advertising. The approach employed in Canada has been to use direct state intervention. A host of both federal and provincial statutes purports to regulate false and misleading advertising directly.

Comparative advertising involves an attempt to demonstrate the ways in which one's product is superior to those of one's competitors. Engaging

---

18   *Carlill v. Carbolic Smoke Ball Co.*, [1893] 1 Q.B. 256 (C.A.).

in this sort of advertising carries the risk that one may get involved in an obscure civil proceeding known variously as the tort of slander of goods, injurious falsehood, or malicious falsehood. To succeed in this action a plaintiff must establish that a statement about his product was false, that it was intended to disparage his product, and that it actually resulted in his suffering a loss of business. There are very few recent Canadian cases.[19]

5) Conclusion

The division of powers in the Constitution has been at the heart of major litigation. This has raised questions concerning both the protection of freedom of expression and the regulation of the mass media.

In 1982 major changes were made to the Constitution of Canada. The *British North America Act* was renamed the *Constitution Act, 1867.* Although the Act's name was changed, its content remained essentially as it had been. At the same time, a major new element, the *Constitution Act, 1982,* was added to our Constitution. The most important part of the *Constitution Act, 1982,* was the *Canadian Charter of Rights and Freedoms,* to which we now turn.

B. THE *CHARTER* GUARANTEE OF FREEDOM OF EXPRESSION

1) General Considerations

The adoption of the *Charter* in no way ended or transformed the federal division of powers. As a result, there could be two distinct challenges to any state act that appears to limit freedom of expression: the traditional challenge arising from the division of powers; and the direct substantive challenge based on the guarantee of freedom of expression in the *Charter.* This dual challenge is precisely what happened in the *Tobacco Products Control Act* litigation before the Supreme Court. The statute was argued to be both *ultra vires* Parliament and an unjustifiable limit on freedom of expression.

With the adoption of the *Charter,* the Canadian Constitution for the first time expressly recognized the existence and protection of certain rights. It would, however, be wrong to imagine that none of these rights had existed in Canada prior to April 1982. Although the *Charter* gave formal constitutional recognition to freedom of expression, it would be

---

19 See *Rust Check Canada Inc. v. Young* (1988), 47 C.C.L.T. 279 (Ont. H.C.J.). Actual loss need not be proved in Ontario.

incorrect and a serious misreading of Canadian legal and political history to think that freedom of expression was unknown before 1982. Since 1982 the belief has tended to grow that unless something is formally recognized in a constitution it simply does not exist.

The guarantee of freedom of expression is found in section 2 of the *Charter* which purports to guarantee "fundamental freedoms." Four fundamental freedoms are set out in this section. The one with which we are concerned is found in section 2(b), which guarantees freedom of "thought, belief, opinion and expression." At our current level of technological development, a guarantee of freedom of "thought, belief and opinion" does not mean much. No one else has any way of knowing what I think or believe or what my opinions are until such time as I actually *express* them.

Section 2(b) goes on to talk of "freedom of . . . expression, including freedom of the press and other media of communication." This subsection appears to be saying that freedom of the press is part of freedom of expression, but that may be misleading. As we noted in the discussion of the *Gay Alliance* case, circumstances can arise where there appears to be conflict between freedom of expression and freedom of the press.

The structure of the *Canadian Charter of Rights and Freedoms* is such that all litigation involving it has two separate and distinct stages. In the first stage, the court must determine whether there has been a denial or an infringement of a right or a freedom guaranteed in the *Charter*. At this stage, it is up to the party relying on the *Charter* to prove that one of his rights or freedoms has been infringed. In technical terms, the burden of proof rests initially with the party relying on the *Charter*. Logically, in order to determine whether there has been an infringement of a *Charter* right, the court must first determine the boundaries or the definition of the *Charter* guarantee in question. This has been one of the major tasks confronting the courts in applying the *Charter*. For example, section 2 also guarantees freedom of association. Freedom of association is most directly relevant to political parties and trade unions. Clearly, freedom of association guarantees some sorts of rights with respect to trade unions, but what are they? Does freedom of association guarantee a constitutional right to strike? Does it guarantee a constitutional right to bargain collectively? Is there a right *not* to belong to a union? The point is that the wording of the *Charter* itself does not provide answers to these questions. The *Charter* simply says that freedom of association is guaranteed, but does not define its specifics. That task was left to the courts.[20]

---

20   See *Reference Re Public Service Employee Relations Act (Alberta)*, [1987] 1 S.C.R. 313 and *Lavigne v. O.P.S.E.U.*, [1991] 2 S.C.R. 211.

Similarly, the task of defining the limits and the precise content of freedom of expression was left to the courts. A host of issues was litigated. The courts were asked, for example: Does freedom of expression include pure commercial advertising? Does freedom of expression include hate propaganda? Does it include obscenity or pornography? What about communications on the street between prostitutes and potential clients? Advertising by dentists? Sticking posters or handbills on telephone poles?[21]

These are some of the issues that had to be addressed to give shape and dimension to the guarantee of freedom of expression. Again, the point is that in order to determine whether freedom of expression has been limited, one must first set out a definition of freedom of expression itself.

The second stage in *Charter* litigation involves the application of section 1 of the *Charter*. Section 1 says:

> The *Canadian Charter of Rights and Freedoms* guarantees the rights and freedoms set out in it subject only to such reasonable limits prescribed by law as can be demonstrably justified in a free and democratic society.

As a general principle, section 1 makes clear that the state may impose limits on *Charter* rights. The various guarantees set out are not absolute. Indeed, a substantial motivation underlying the adoption of section 1 was to give considerable leeway to legislatures to enact limits on rights.

The courts have determined that if the party relying on the *Charter* is successful in proving that one of his rights has been limited, the burden shifts to the other party — usually the state — to satisfy the court that the particular limit can be justified in a free and democratic society. If the limit on the *Charter* guarantee is found to be justified, the particular state act that created it is constitutional; if the limit cannot be justified, the state act creating it is unconstitutional and will be declared invalid by a court.

In *R. v. Oakes* the Supreme Court of Canada created a detailed methodology for applying section 1.[22] This methodology seeks to assess both the end that the state is seeking and the means it has chosen to achieve that end.

Rather than looking in detail at the general methodology to be followed in *Charter* litigation, we will now investigate the specific approach that is used in cases involving freedom of expression. This approach was set out by the Supreme Court of Canada in *Irwin Toy Ltd.*

---

21   In each instance the Supreme Court of Canada decided the activity was expression.
22   [1986] 1 S.C.R. 103.

v. *Quebec (A.G.)*, a decision we have already looked at in relation to division of powers issues.[23] The *Irwin Toy Ltd.* methodology seeks to define an approach to freedom of expression which all courts are supposed to follow. It is very complicated. The essential steps in this methodology are summarized in figure 1.

Figure 1   How to Apply the Guarantee of Freedom of Expression in Section 2(b) of the Charter

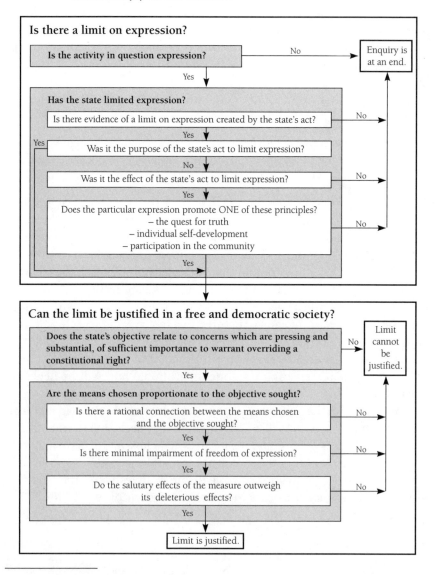

---

23   *Supra* note 16.

2) The Meaning of Expression

The first phase in the *Irwin Toy* analysis involves determining whether the freedom of expression of the party relying on the *Charter* has been limited. This simple question is broken down into a series of subquestions. The first subquestion addresses the activity in question — that is, it seeks to discover whether what the party relying on the *Charter* was engaged in amounted to expression. The traditional Canadian approach was set out in the Press Bill case. The Supreme Court in that decision saw the essence of expression as the free public discussion of public affairs. It accepted that there was a hierarchy of forms of expression, with political expression at its summit. In *Irwin Toy* the Supreme Court consciously rejected any notion of a hierarchy of forms of expression. The Court said that if the activity in question had expressive content, if it sought to convey a meaning, then it qualified as expression and was constitutionally protected.

This is a broad definition. It excludes little from expression and, to reinforce the point, the Court accepted that even pure physical acts could qualify as expression. The Court chose the example of someone knowingly and intentionally parking a car in a restricted parking zone as a form of political protest. The Court said that such an act would qualify as constitutionally protected expression. Thus, everything from the free public discussion of public affairs to the way you park your car can be subsumed within expression. The only exception the Court was prepared to recognize in *Irwin Toy* was for pure physical acts of violence. These acts would not qualify as expression.

The implications of this approach were made clear in subsequent cases. The *R. v. Keegstra* decision is a good illustration.[24] James Keegstra, the accused, was a school teacher in the small town of Eckville, Alberta. In the course of his historical research he apparently discovered a Jewish plot to take over the world, and he believed that he was under an obligation to inform his students about it. He was eventually charged under what is now section 319(2) of the *Criminal Code* with wilfully promoting hatred against any group of people identifiable on the basis of their race, religion, or national origin. Keegstra claimed, among other things, that the existence of this offence amounted to a limit on his constitutionally guaranteed freedom of expression. The first question the courts had to answer was whether promoting hatred qualified as constitutionally protected expression. One argument advanced by the Crown was that to promote hatred was to encourage violence, so that the pro-

24   [1990] 3 S.C.R. 697.

motion of hatred could be regarded as analogous to physical acts of violence and thus not be constitutionally protected. The Supreme Court
said no. It said there was a difference between threats of violence and
acts of violence. Hate propaganda was expression. A year later the
Supreme Court heard the *R. v. Butler* case.[25] This case dealt with the
constitutionality of section 163(8) of the *Criminal Code*, the section that
proscribes obscenity, or, in more common usage, pornography. Butler
ran a video shop in Winnipeg. The typical contemporary obscenity
prosecution involves a video shop; there has not been a prosecution of
a book for more than two decades. Butler was charged with possessing
and selling obscene material. Like Keegstra, he argued that the section
of the *Criminal Code* under which he was charged was a limit on his constitutionally guaranteed expression. Was obscenity expression? In the
Irwin Toy case the Supreme Court had said that anything that attempted
to convey a meaning qualified as expression. But in *Butler* the Manitoba
Court of Appeal concluded that pornographic videotapes were not an
attempt to convey meaning because they contained nothing but a series
of physical acts devoid of intellectual content. The Supreme Court disagreed. It said pornographic videotapes do attempt to convey some sort
of meaning. The meaning might be odious or distasteful to many, but
nonetheless there was an attempt to convey meaning. Therefore, said
the Court, obscenity, like hate propaganda, qualified as expression.

There is still a problem here. At some stage in applying a constitutional document like the *Charter* the courts, whether they like it or not,
are going to have to discriminate, to make choices. They are going to
have to uphold some limits on constitutionally guaranteed rights and to
strike others down. Some sort of ranking of different forms of expression
is inescapable. The approach taken to date has led, as we will see, to some
serious inconsistencies in the judicial decisions on these matters.

If a court determines that the activity in which the party relying on
the *Charter* is engaged is, indeed, expression, it must move to the second part of the first phase of the analysis. This part involves determining
whether the state has acted in such a way as to limit expression.

Ordinarily, the *Charter* can only be invoked against the state. Unless
the act complained of emanates from the legislative, executive, or
administrative branches of the state, there is no basis for claiming any
of the rights guaranteed in the *Charter*. Thus, a newspaper reporter
could not raise a *Charter* claim against an editor who refused to print
one of his stories.

---

25   [1992] 1 S.C.R. 452.

This principle has been somewhat qualified by the Supreme Court of Canada in two recent decisions — *Dagenais* v. *Canadian Broadcasting Corp.*[26] and *Hill* v. *Church of Scientology of Toronto.*[27] In these decisions it was suggested that the *Charter* might be relied on as a basis for shaping or altering rules of the common law even where there was no direct state act involved. Although *Charter* rights may still be invoked only against the state, the Court held that judges have the authority to alter the common law so as to make it consistent with what it described as *Charter* "values." The difficulty with this interpretation is that since the word "value" does not appear anywhere in the text of the *Charter*, it is impossible to state with any degree of certainty what constitutes, or does not constitute, a *Charter* value.

The party relying on the *Charter* is obliged to prove, through evidence, that his expression is being limited. The courts have said that it is not enough simply to assert that one's expression is limited. Real proof is required.[28]

At this point, two possibilities arise. The first applies if the *purpose* underlying the state's act was to limit expression. The cases of *Keegstra* and *Butler* illustrate this situation. If the wilful promotion of hatred amounts to expression and the state makes it a crime to promote hatred, then clearly the state's purpose in so acting was to limit expression. Likewise, if the state says that no one may distribute obscene material and obscenity is a constitutionally recognized form of expression, then, once more, the clear purpose of the state's act was to limit expression. In such a case there has been an infringement of freedom of expression and it becomes incumbent on the state to show that the particular infringement can be justified in a free and democratic society.

The other possibility is that the state may have acted to achieve some quite different purpose, but the *effect* of its act, perhaps an unintended effect, has been to create a limit on expression. This is what happened in *Committee for the Commonwealth of Canada* v. *Canada.*[29] The respondents wished to engage in political discourse with travellers in an airport owned by the government of Canada. Such activity was prohibited under the *Government Airport Concession Operations Regulations*, the clear purpose of which was to provide for the orderly operation of airports. The Court held that the public areas of airports could be analogized to traditional "public arenas" in which individuals were entitled to express themselves freely. It concluded that, whatever the state's pur-

---

26 [1994] 3 S.C.R. 835.
27 [1995] 2 S.C.R. 1130 [hereinafter *Hill*].
28 *MacKay* v. *Manitoba*, [1989] 2 S.C.R. 357.
29 [1991] 1 S.C.R. 139.

pose might have been, since the effect of its action was to limit free expression, there was an infringement of a *Charter* guarantee which would have to be justified under section 1. There is a qualification on this point, however. In *Irwin Toy* the Court said that where it is only the effect of the state's act, rather than its purpose, to limit expression, the party relying on the *Charter* would also be required to show that the expression in question promoted one of the following principles or "values":

(1) seeking and attaining the truth is an inherently good activity;

(2) participation in social and political decision-making is to be fostered and encouraged; and

(3) the diversity in forms of individual self-fulfilment and human flourishing ought to be cultivated in an essentially tolerant, indeed welcoming, environment not only for the sake of those who convey a meaning, but also for the sake of those to whom it is conveyed.[30]

Why is such a distinction warranted? If the state's purpose in acting is to restrict expression, then all forms of expression are protected; if it is merely the effect of the state's having acted that restricts expression, then only those types of expression that promote one of the three principles set out above are protected. There does not appear to be any basis for this distinction in the *Charter* text.

If a court decides that expression has indeed been limited by the state, it must move on to determine whether that limit can be justified under section 1.

3) Applying Section 1

There are two parts to the second phase of the *Irwin Toy* analysis. The first involves an assessment of ends; the second of means.

In the first part, the state must persuade the court that the objective sought through the creation of the limitation on freedom of expression relates to concerns that are pressing and substantial in a free and democratic society, or which are, to use the phraseology of other cases, of sufficient importance to warrant overriding a constitutional freedom. In *Irwin Toy* the Court believed that the objective behind a prohibition against all commercial advertising directed at persons under thirteen was the protection of a group that was vulnerable to manipulation. This objective was held to meet the required standard. In *R. v. Keegstra*,

---

30   *Irwin Toy, supra* note 16 at 976.

which dealt with the *Criminal Code*'s ban on the wilful promotion of hatred, the state's objective was seen as two-fold — to prevent the pain suffered by persons who were the objects of hate propaganda and to reduce racial, ethnic, and religious tension and "perhaps even" violence in Canada. *R. v. Butler* dealt with the constitutionality of the *Criminal Code* offences directed against obscenity. The Supreme Court concluded that the state's objective was "the avoidance of harm to society." The harm was seen to lie in an enhanced propensity towards violence, degradation of women, and the reinforcement of "male-female stereotypes" on the part of men who were exposed to obscene material.

There is considerable subjectivity in the judicial approach to these matters. If protecting children from commercial manipulation is "pressing and substantial," why should not the protection of adults, many of whom are also credulous and gullible, be pressing and substantial? Although it would seem that preventing racial, religious, or ethnic violence is of sufficient importance to justify overriding a constitutional right, it is not self-evident that making sure people's feelings do not get hurt, which is what the first objective identified in *Keegstra* appears to amount to, is similarly important. In *Butler* the Court conceded that there was no solid evidence that obscenity caused any anti-social behaviour.

If the state's objective does not meet the required standard, the limit cannot be justified and the particular state act creating it will be struck down by the court. If, however, the objective sought by the state is acceptable, then the court must turn to an assessment of the means selected by the state for the achievement of its objective. The purpose of this assessment is to determine whether the means selected by the state are "proportionate" to the end it is seeking. Three separate inquiries are required here.

First, the court must ask whether there is a "rational connection" between the end sought and the means chosen. In practice this comes down to a test of efficacy, with judges attempting to divine whether the means chosen will actually work and lead to the achievement of the end. In *Keegstra*, for example, three judges of the Supreme Court were not convinced there was a rational connection between criminalizing hate propaganda and successfully suppressing it. They were not persuaded that the offence in the *Criminal Code* was an "effective way of curbing hate-mongers." The stringency of this part of the assessment was much diluted in the *Butler* decision. There it was suggested that all that was necessary was a "sufficiently rational link between the criminal sanction [against obscenity] . . . and the objective." This assertion avoided a serious logical difficulty. If there was, indeed, no evidence that exposure to obscenity led to anti-social behaviour, it would have been impossible to accept that criminalizing obscenity would suppress or control such behaviour.

The state must next show that the means it has chosen result in the "minimal impairment" of the right in question. Logically, of course, this is not possible, since it involves proving a negative. It cannot be proved that no conceivable means exist which might have resulted in a less serious infringement of the right than those actually selected. A court is, at this stage, really being asked to determine whether the measure in question goes too far. Limitations on rights that are "overbroad" or excessively vague will likely be seen as going too far. In *Osborne* v. *Canada (Treasury Board)*[31] the Supreme Court struck down a prohibition against all federal civil servants "engag[ing] in work" for or against a political party on the ground that it was not "carefully designed to inpair freedom of expression as little as reasonably possible" and went "beyond what is necessary to achieve the objective of an impartial and loyal civil service." Likewise, in *R.* v. *Zundel*,[32] a section of the *Criminal Code* which made it an offence to publish false news that "causes or is likely to cause injury or mischief to a public interest" failed the minimal impairment requirement because the words "injury or mischief to a public interest" were "undefined and virtually unlimited."

The third and final question with respect to the means adopted involves an analysis of any "deleterious effects" that may result from them. According to Chief Justice Antonio Lamer in *Dagenais* v. *Canadian Broadcasting Corp.*,[33] "it is necessary to measure the actual salutary effects of impugned legislation against its deleterious effects." This statement appears to suggest that the judge, at the end of the day, must somehow balance the good likely to be achieved through the state act in question against the bad that may occur as a necessary by-product of it. It is difficult to see how judges can do this in a way which is consistent and which produces objective principles that can be generalized to other cases.

If the means chosen fail to meet any of these three standards, they are not proportionate to the objective and the limit on the *Charter* guarantee cannot be justified. The court will then declare the state act that has been challenged to be of "no force or effect" — that is to say, invalid. If the means chosen are proportionate to the objective, the limit is justified in a free and democratic society and the challenged state act is constitutionally valid.

---

31   [1991] 2 S.C.R. 69.

32   [1992] 2 S.C.R. 731.

33   *Supra* note 26 at 888.

4) Conclusion

Charter analysis has generally been seen to involve two stages, but, particularly in relation to cases involving freedom of expression, this process is open to doubt. Since, as the Supreme Court decided in *Irwin Toy*, "if the activity conveys or attempts to convey a meaning," it qualifies as constitutionally protected expression, this stage of the analysis is largely without substance. It is a hurdle that is so low as to be virtually non-existent. The serious analysis, on which the validity of the state act stands or falls, inevitably takes place in the second stage.

The problem is that, having accorded equal constitutional protection to all forms of expression, by refusing to make any distinctions among them, the Supreme Court, in order to avoid striking down every existing limit on any form of expression, has had to make the process of justification under section 1 an easy one. In fact, having said at stage one that it will not discriminate among forms of expression, the judges found it necessary to introduce precisely that sort of discrimination at stage two. So we have the Supreme Court saying in *Butler* that obscenity "does not stand on equal footing with other kinds of expression which directly engage the 'core' of the freedom of expression values." This assertion appears to directly contradict the *Irwin Toy* approach of not discriminating among forms of expression.

It is difficult to suggest any theory about the meaning of freedom of expression as guaranteed in the *Charter*. The main reason is that each of the Supreme Court's decisions on free expression and the *Charter* tends to stand alone. It is difficult to generalize about them. It could be argued that what we have in these cases is little more than a random collection of ad hoc policy analyses. This is where the Court's methodology has led it. When we read *Butler*, we discover what the Court thought about the virtue or desirability of a particular criminal prohibition against obscenity. When we read *Keegstra*, we discover what it thought of a similar prohibition against hate propaganda. The decisions do not tell us very much about freedom of expression, about what it means and why it matters, and, most important, why it should have received constitutional protection.

Chief Justice Duff, in his judgment in the Alberta Press Bill case, clearly understood the essential significance of freedom of expression in a democracy. And, in some of their judgments, judges of the contemporary Supreme Court have tried to adopt a principled approach to freedom of expression. In *Edmonton Journal* v. *Alberta (A.G.)*,[34] Mr. Justice Peter Cory observed, "It is difficult to imagine a guaranteed right more impor-

---

34   [1989] 2 S.C.R. 1326 at 1336.

tant to a democratic society than freedom of expression." This approach has not been the norm. Madam Justice Bertha Wilson took a "contextual" approach to expression, deciding that it would mean one thing in one context and other things in other contexts.[35] The contextual approach makes a general theory of freedom of expression impossible.

The *Irwin Toy* methodology is fundamentally flawed. It has frustrated the development of a useful jurisprudence. Legal decision making, particularly by the highest court of appeal, should lead to the creation of general principles. The purpose of these general principles is to provide a framework that will give direction to judges in resolving each new case that arises. The Supreme Court's decisions about freedom of expression do not provide such direction. As Professor Peter Hogg has concluded, the Court's approach to expression is "unprincipled and unpredictable."[36]

The courts have given some guidance in one area. They have seen freedom of expression as involving a process. That process begins with the gathering of information. If freedom of expression is, in concrete terms, about the publication of information and opinions and we recognize that that information and those opinions have to come from somewhere, then the protection afforded by freedom of expression should also extend to the collection of the information. A Federal Court decision, *International Fund for Animal Welfare Inc.* v. *Canada (Minister of Fisheries & Oceans)*,[37] addressed the *Seal Hunting Regulations*. These regulations set up a permit system that was designed to limit the access of reporters to the Atlantic coast seal hunt. The court decided that the guarantee of freedom of expression would extend to protecting the ability of reporters to gather information. Going further, while freedom of expression clearly includes the publication of information, it must, in addition, as the Ontario Court of Appeal determined in *Information Retailers Assn. of Metropolitan Toronto* v. *Metropolitan Toronto (Municipality)*,[38] extend to the sale and distribution of information and opinions. Freedom of expression protected the ability of booksellers to operate bookshops and to sell and distribute books and periodicals. Finally, as the Federal Court held in *Luscher* v. *Deputy Minister of National Revenue (Customs & Excise)*,[39] freedom of expression includes the right to receive information. Luscher was a Canadian whose hobby was importing pornography from the United States. He challenged cer-

---

35   *Ibid.* at 1354–1356.
36   P.W. Hogg, *Constitutional Law of Canada*, 3d ed. (Toronto: Carswell, 1992) at 965.
37   [1987] 1 F.C. 244 (T.D.).
38   (1985), 52 O.R. (2d) 449 (C.A.).
39   [1985] 1 F.C. 85 (C.A.).

tain provisions of the *Customs Tariff* which limited his ability to do this. The court accepted that the receipt of information was a necessary part of expression. The Supreme Court has recognized the same principle, stating in one decision that freedom of expression "protects listeners as well as speakers."[40] Expression is a process, then, that extends from gathering information to publishing information, to selling and distributing information, and finally to receiving information. All the stages in the process are protected under the guarantee of freedom of expression.

As a final point, the courts have not interpreted section 2(b) as creating any special rights or special status in the mass media or in reporters.[41] Freedom of expression can be exercised by everyone — high school teachers, video shop owners, dentists, and cigarette manufacturers.

FURTHER READINGS

The leading and the most comprehensive work on Canada's Constitution is P.W. Hogg, *Constitutional Law of Canada*, 4th ed. (Toronto: Carswell, 1996).

---

40   *Ford* v. *Quebec (A.G.)*, [1988] 2 S.C.R. 712 at 767.
41   See *Hill, supra* note 27, and *Moysa* v. *Alberta (Labour Relations Board)*, [1989] 1 S.C.R. 1572.

CHAPTER 2

STATE SECURITY
AND PUBLIC ORDER

Limitations on freedom of expression are imposed by the state to achieve some purpose peculiar to the state. These limitations include emergency powers and the control of confidential information.

A. EMERGENCY POWERS

Emergency powers are an anomalous phenomenon in any constitutional democracy. As we have seen, the basic tenet of constitutional democracy is that the state is bound by the constitution. That is the rule of law principle. Just as each individual has no choice but to obey the law, so the state is obliged to act within the constitution. We have long since abandoned the idea that the state can do whatever it likes simply because it is the state. The very notion of emergency powers is anomalous because it posits that in times of national crisis or national emergency the state may step outside the constitution. The state may do things in a time of national emergency which it would not be permitted to do in normal times. The justification is that in extreme circumstances the state can take extreme measures to ensure its own existence. There is a useful analogy between the notion of emergency powers as far as the state is concerned and the defence of self-defence in criminal law. The ordinary rule of the criminal law is "Thou shall not kill." However, self-defence has always recognized an important exception to the rule that one person may not take another's life. That exception arises when one individual is directly threatening to kill another. To preserve his own life, that individual could lawfully kill the person who was threatening his life. Under extreme circumstances, then, an individual may lawfully do something that is prohibited under normal circumstances. The justification is, once again, found in the extreme circumstances.

What do states most commonly seek to do during states of emergency? First, they give themselves the power to arbitrarily arrest and detain people — to arrest people without charges and hold them without trial. Second, they impose censorship.

1) The *War Measures Act*

In Canada, emergency powers were found for a long time in a federal statute called the *War Measures Act*.[1] The statute was first enacted in August 1914 to give the national government the powers it believed to be necessary to prosecute the war. The *War Measures Act*, although substantially amended after the First World War, remained part of Canadian law from 1914 to 1988. The important thing to remember about it, however, was that, unlike most statutes, the *War Measures Act* was not normally in operation. It was law throughout those years, but remained dormant in ordinary times. It came into operation only when it was invoked by a proclamation issued by the Governor General. The Act was invoked on three separate occasions: immediately after its passage in 1914; in 1939 on the outbreak of the Second World War; and once in peacetime by the government of Pierre Trudeau in October 1970.

What actually happened with the *War Measures Act*? The mechanism was a simple one. Once the Act had been proclaimed, plenary law-making authority was transferred from Parliament to the Governor in Council — that is, to the federal cabinet. Under the Act Canada was transformed from a parliamentary democracy into an executive dictatorship. The Cabinet was given a power, which was practically limitless, to make regulations having the force of law. The operative part of the Act was section 3 which, when stripped of its extra words, said: "The Governor in Council may do . . . such . . . things . . . as he may . . . deem necessary." The legal authority to do such things as are deemed necessary is an authority pretty much without limit. During both world wars Canada was largely ruled by orders in council made under the *War Measures Act*. There were literally thousands of them, dealing with every aspect of Canadian life. Inevitably they included orders that provided for censorship.

---

1   S.C. 1915, c. 2.

Various publications were prohibited during the First World War. Many of these publications were, for obvious reasons, German language newspapers, but the list also included Irish nationalist publications and a number of left-wing publications. Many of the existing orders in council were brought together in the *Consolidated Orders Respecting Censorship* of 1918.[2] The chief censor was given broad authority to withhold from public consumption any material that commented unfavourably on the causes or operations of the war. Thus, criticism of the consistently abysmal leadership of the British Army on the Western Front, which was where most Canadians were killed, could lead one to run afoul of the censors.

In addition to the censorship regulations imposed under the *War Measures Act*, extensive use was made of the *Criminal Code* offence of sedition. In 1916, in a case called *R. v. Trainor*,[3] a man was chatting with some people in a drugstore in a town in Alberta and said that he approved of the sinking of the *Lusitania*. He was charged with sedition and convicted. His appeal was allowed, and one of the judges observed: "There have been more prosecutions for seditious words in Alberta in the past two years than in all the history of England for over a hundred years and England has had numerous and critical wars in that time."

A major change was made in the censorship regulations after the Russian Revolution of 1917. The timing seems unusual, given that Canada was at war with Germany, Austria, and their allies, not with Russia. The list of censored publications was extended to include a considerable number of pro-Bolshevik or communist-oriented publications.

Also subject to suppression during the First World War were publications that advocated temperance. Somehow, promoting temperance was seen as interfering with the war effort. In addition, many organizations were declared to be unlawful under the *War Measures Act*, so that membership in any of them was subject to sanctions.

The *War Measures Act*, once invoked, stayed in operation until its proclamation was revoked by the Governor in Council. Hostilities ended in November 1918, but the Act remained in operation until 1920. It was next invoked in 1939, and immediately regulations were adopted for the defence of Canada. These regulations imposed limitations on expression and created offences with respect to the expression of opinion and the communication of information. Regulation 39A(c) said:

> No person shall print, circulate or distribute any book . . . card, letter, writing, print, publication or document of any kind containing any

---

2   P.C. 1918-1241, C. Gaz. 1918. 4376.
3   (1917), 10 Alta. L.R. 164 (C.A.).

material, report or statement . . . which would or might be prejudicial to the safety of the State or the efficient prosecution of the war.[4]

That is about as broad a censorship regulation as you could find anywhere. In one case a high school teacher was prosecuted for breaching this regulation because, during a discussion in his classroom, he had encouraged the presentation of pacifist opinions. He was convicted. The court that convicted him said: "The whole intention [of the regulations] is to compel individuals to maintain silence or speak in the unconquerable spirit by which troops in action must be moved if they are to win."[5] Any other expression of opinion would presumably be an offence under the *Defence of Canada Regulations*. Various organizations were proscribed. In addition, a range of publications was prohibited, including for a period left-wing publications. Given that the war was being fought against Nazi Germany, this censorship seems strange.

There was little criticism of the aggressive suppression of opinion and basic rights under the *War Measures Act*, although the leader of the Cooperative Commonwealth Federation (CCF), M.J. Coldwell, did speak out about the *Defence of Canada Regulations*. In May 1940 he said in the House of Commons: "We are prepared to support the struggle against aggression and for the preservation of democratic institutions, but we insist that democratic institutions shall be respected and safeguarded in our own country. . . . Ever since the outbreak of war we have been governed by decree . . . largely in secrecy."[6]

Once again, while the fighting in Europe ended in May 1945 and in the Pacific in September 1945, the *War Measures Act* stayed in effect until 1947. There was no legal mechanism in the Act by which the government could have been compelled to revoke the proclamation.

2) The *Emergencies Act*

In 1988 Parliament repealed the *War Measures Act* and replaced it with a new statute called the *Emergencies Act*.[7] The *Emergencies Act* is in many respects an improvement on the *War Measures Act*. The first problem with the *War Measures Act* was its all or nothing nature. Taking the case of the invocation of the Act in October 1970, let us assume that on the island of Montreal, or even in the province of Quebec, there existed a serious and substantial threat to the security of the state. Once the *War*

---

4   P.C. 1939-2891, C. Gaz. 1939. 1126.
5   *R. v. Coffin*, [1940] 2 W.W.R. 592 at 602 (Alta. Prov. Ct.).
6   House of Commons, *Debates*, 20 May 1940, at 51.
7   S.C. 1988, c. 29.

Measures Act was proclaimed in October 1970, however, it applied throughout Canada, not just in Montreal or Quebec. In October 1970 Vancouver was not a hotbed of extreme Québécois nationalism. Nonetheless, the city authorities there were having considerable problems with what they regarded as undesirable elements on the streets — drug dealers, panhandlers, petty criminals, transients, prostitutes, and so on. Under the *Public Order Regulations*,[8] which had been made pursuant to the *War Measures Act*, there was a generally unlimited power to arrest people and detain them for ninety days. The streets of Vancouver were cleaned up for a while by arresting all the undesirables under the *War Measures Act*.[9] It was not possible to have a state of emergency in one province or in one defined locality. Second, the proclamation of the *War Measures Act* created a full-scale national emergency. There was no gradation or levels of emergency. Nor, third, was there any requirement that the government of Canada consult with provincial governments before invoking the Act. Finally, there was only limited opportunity for involvement by Parliament in determining whether a real state of emergency existed or how long the emergency should continue.

The *Emergencies Act* addressed a number of these concerns. It makes it possible for states of emergency to be declared either in a province or in a limited area; it provides for consultation with provincial governments; and it substantially increases the oversight role of Parliament in the emergency process. It provides for finite limits on the duration of states of emergency and also for different levels of emergency.

There are four levels of emergency in the Act: public welfare emergency, public order emergency, international emergency, and war emergency. Various levels of power are given to the authorities in each specific level of emergency. The one worth talking about for present purposes is a war emergency, because this is the only level of emergency under the Act during which the imposition of censorship is permitted. A war emergency is the big one, the all-out state of emergency. In fact, the powers available to the state during a war emergency are as broad as the powers that were available under the *War Measures Act*. Section 38 of the *Emergencies Act* says:

> When the Governor in Council believes, on reasonable grounds, that a war emergency exists and necessitates the taking of special temporary measures for dealing with the emergency, the Governor in Council ... may, by proclamation, so declare.

---

8   SOR/70-444.
9   R. Haggart and A.E. Golden, *Rumours of War*, 2d ed., (Toronto: New Press, 1979) at 111.

Section 40 goes on:

> While a declaration of war emergency is in effect, the Governor in Council may make such orders or regulations as the Governor in Council believes, on reasonable grounds, are necessary or advisable for dealing with the emergency.

The Governor in Council may do whatever it believes is necessary to deal with the war emergency. The authority created clearly would include the power to impose various forms of censorship.

An important question has to do with the status of the *Charter* guarantee of freedom of expression during a war emergency. There are two possibilities. One involves the use of section 33, the notwithstanding clause in the *Charter*. Section 33 allows either Parliament or a provincial legislature to declare that a particular statute is to operate notwithstanding many of the guarantees, including freedom of expression, set out in the *Charter*.[10] The federal *Emergencies Act* would be an obvious candidate for a section 33 clause. The *Canadian Bill of Rights*,[11] a statute introduced under the Diefenbaker government, gave to Parliament the power to declare that any federal statute was to operate notwithstanding the *Bill of Rights*. That power was used only once — in the *War Measures Act*. Parliament, however, has not exercised its authority under section 33 of the *Charter*, although two provincial legislatures have, but there is nothing to prevent it doing so in the future. The second possibility is that, since section 33 has not been relied on, it would be open to individuals who were subject to any regulations made under a war emergency declared pursuant to the *Emergencies Act* to challenge those regulations on the basis of the *Charter*. The courts would then have to decide whether those limitations — for example, a regime of censorship imposed on the mass media — could be justified in a free and democratic society.

B. STATE INFORMATION

1) Official Secrets

What about confidential information in the possession of the state? The *Official Secrets Act*,[12] a federal statute, is based on legislation first enacted

---

10   *Canadian Charter of Rights and Freedoms*, Part I of the *Constitution Act, 1982*, being Schedule B to the *Canada Act 1982* (U.K.), 1982, c. 11, s. 33 [hereinafter *Charter*].

11   S.C. 1960, c. 44, reprinted in R.S.C. 1985, App. III.

12   R.S.C. 1985, c. O-5.

in the United Kingdom in 1889. The original purpose of the UK *Official Secrets Act* was to address espionage. An embarrassing situation arose in the United Kingdom when a number of individuals were arrested on the ground that they had been spying on behalf of a foreign power and, to considerable official consternation, it was discovered that this activity was not against the law. Canada's *Official Secrets Act* also addresses espionage and creates offences in respect of it. It is difficult to question the legitimacy of any state making it an offence to spy against it on behalf of foreign states, so there is little that can usefully be said about the espionage provisions in the Act. However, other parts of the Act relate to the communication of certain kinds of information that are in the possession of the state. These parts are problematic and worth discussing. Indeed, on the face of it, the *Official Secrets Act* is unacceptably oppressive legislation.[13]

The first and most basic difficulty with the Act is that it is not at all clear to what it applies. For example, section 4(3) makes it an offence to receive any "secret official code word, password, sketch, plan, model, article, note, document or information." There is a simple, but fundamental, problem with that wording. The list set out begins with two adjectives, "secret official," and following them is a series of nouns, "code word, password, sketch, plan, model, article, note, document or information." Do the two adjectives "secret official" modify only the immediately following nouns "code word," or do they modify all the subsequent nouns in the series? That is to say, does this statute apply only to *secret official information* — presumably, the real state secret security information — or does it apply to *any* information? The distinction matters because if this section applies to *any* information, it is possible that offences could be committed under the *Official Secrets Act* by a journalist simply having in his possession some sort of information that the government of Canada did not want him to have.

The second difficulty has to do with this odd offence of receiving information. Section 4(3) makes it clear that one commits the offence by the very act of receiving any information to which the Act applies. Strictly speaking, then, as soon as a plain brown envelope filled with photocopied documents arrives at someone's desk in a newsroom, an offence has been committed.

Furthermore, as a third difficulty, section 4 contains a reverse onus provision. The state does not have to prove the guilt of the accused person; rather, the accused has to prove his innocence. An accused person

---

13   For background see W.S. Tarnopolsky, "Freedom of the Press" in *Newspapers and the Law* (Ottawa: Minister of Supply & Services, 1981) 1 at 19–21.

is deemed to be guilty of an offence by the very act of receiving information unless he can prove that the communication to him of the code word, password, sketch, plan, model, article, note, document, or information was "contrary to his desire." How would a reporter prove that it was contrary to his desire that an envelope had landed on his desk?

The fourth difficulty is that the Act creates a practically unlimited power of arrest. Under Canadian law there are two ways a person can lawfully be arrested: either with a warrant — that is, pursuant to a formal authorization issued by a judicial officer — or without a warrant. Our law says that police officers can arrest persons without a warrant only when they have reasonable and probable cause to believe that an offence has been committed. Without going in detail into a complicated area of law, it can be said that reasonable and probable cause is substantially more than suspicion. This provision is an important protection for basic liberties. Section 10 of the *Official Secrets Act*, however, says that an individual can be arrested without a warrant if he is found committing an offence, or if he is reasonably suspected of having committed or having attempted to commit or *being about to* commit an offence under the Act. Thus, if a police officer reasonably suspects that a plain brown envelope containing documents to which this Act applies is about to land on a reporter's desk, that reporter can be arrested.

Fifth, this statute is the only one in effect today which allows police officers to authorize searches. Under the *Criminal Code*, search warrants can be issued only by a judicial officer. If the police cannot get a judicial officer to issue a search warrant under the *Criminal Code*, they cannot legally conduct a non-consensual search. The *Official Secrets Act* is unique in that it gives to RCMP officers of the rank of superintendent or above the power to authorize searches.

Sixth, in section 14, the Act makes express provision for secret trials. Such trials, again, are contrary to fundamental principles of the Canadian legal system.

The final difficulty is found in section 15, which states that the maximum penalty that can be imposed in respect of an offence under the Act is fourteen years. The next most serious punishment available in our criminal justice system is life imprisonment.

The former Law Reform Commission of Canada described the *Official Secrets Act* in 1986 as "one of the poorest examples of legislative drafting in the statute books."[14] I agree.

---

14   Law Reform Commission of Canada, *Crimes against the State* (Working Paper 49) (Ottawa: The Commission, 1986) at 30 [hereinafter *Crimes against the State*].

How has the *Official Secrets Act* been applied in practice? Its most extensive use stemmed from the Gouzenko affair. In 1945 Igor Gouzenko, a cipher clerk at the Soviet Embassy in Ottawa, went to the RCMP and claimed that a spy ring was operating out of the embassy. The official response to Gouzenko's claims was extraordinary. The *War Measures Act* was pressed into service. As we have already noted, even though the Second World War was over, the Act was still in operation. A large number of people were rounded up under regulations made pursuant to the *War Measures Act*. They were arbitrarily arrested, not brought before a court, held incommunicado, and forced to appear without legal representation before a royal commission composed of two Supreme Court of Canada judges. It should be a matter of some concern that two Supreme Court judges were prepared to take part in this investigation. The detainees were required to give evidence against themselves before the royal commission. This evidence was then used as the basis for laying charges. Some persons were charged with actual breaches of the *Official Secrets Act*, but in fact more were charged with *conspiring* to breach the Act. Conspiracy is a strange criminal offence. Its essence is an agreement to commit an unlawful act, not necessarily a criminal act, but *any* unlawful act. The crime of conspiracy is perfected when the agreement is made to commit the unlawful act. The unlawful act itself does not have to be committed. By relying on the offence of conspiracy in the Gouzenko affair, the Crown did not have to prove that a particular accused person had actually breached the *Official Secrets Act*, just that he had agreed with someone else to do so. One of the many people eventually convicted was a member of Parliament, Fred Rose.[15]

In recent years there have been few prosecutions, and these few have mainly dealt with the espionage sections of the Act. One non-espionage prosecution was the *R. v. Treu* case. It involved a civil servant who took some files home which, he said, he forgot about. He later left the government, went into business, and just happened to use some of those files.[16]

The only recent prosecution involving a journalist or the media was that of Peter Worthington in 1979, when he was the publisher of the Toronto *Sun*. He and the *Sun* had become convinced there was a Soviet spy network operating in Canada and that the government was not doing anything about it. Worthington claimed to have top secret documents that outlined Soviet espionage activities. To seek to prove his point, he published one of these documents in the pages of the *Sun*. As

15   See *R. v. Mazerall*, [1946] O.R. 762 (C.A.) and *Rose v. R.*, [1947] 3 D.L.R. 618 (Que. C.A.).

16   (1979), 104 D.L.R. (3d) 524.

a result, he was charged under section 4 of the *Official Secrets Act*. He went to trial before an Ontario provincial court judge who acquitted him on the ground that the document in question, which the judge clearly accepted had once been subject to the *Official Secrets Act*, no longer was. The reason, according to the judge, was that disclosures had brought the document, "now 'shopworn' and no longer secret, into the public domain." Surely this reasoning is wrong. It suggests that the way to avoid conviction under the *Official Secrets Act* is simply to publish any secret documents one has in one's possession. The Crown did not appeal Worthington's acquittal because the matter had by this point become quite embarrassing to the government of Canada.[17]

Canadians can take a certain amount of comfort in the Doug Small prosecution. What happened to Small suggests that the *Official Secrets Act* does indeed apply only to actual security information, and not simply to any information in the possession of the government of Canada. In 1989 Small, a reporter for Global Television, was leaked a copy of a summary of the federal budget in advance of its announcement by the minister of finance. This leak annoyed the government. Small was prosecuted, but the important point is that he was *not* prosecuted under the *Official Secrets Act*. Presumably, the opinion of the government of Canada's lawyers must have been that the *Official Secrets Act* did not apply to budget documents. These documents were clearly "information," but one must assume the advice was that they were not "secret official information." To repeat, the fact that Small was not prosecuted under the *Official Secrets Act* strongly suggests that the official view of the Act is that it applies only to actual security information. Small was prosecuted for theft, but the difficulty faced by the prosecution was the principle that information as such cannot be stolen. You can misappropriate information that is presented in a particular form — which is what copyright law is all about — but there cannot be property in the information itself. Small was acquitted. He was acquitted because the document he had in his possession was in fact a photocopy of the budget document. He had nothing that was the property, or could be proven to be the property, of the government of Canada. The implication was that, if he had had an actual budget document, he probably could have been convicted of theft for stealing those specific pieces of paper. One simple lesson to be learned from this case is that when journalists receive leaked documents, they should make sure they are photocopies.

---

17   *R. v. Toronto Sun Publishing Ltd.* (1979), 24 O.R. (2d) 621 (Prov. Ct.).

2) Access to Information

The federal *Access to Information Act*[18] serves as a balance to legislation like the *Official Secrets Act*. The purpose of the *Access to Information Act* is not to maintain the tradition of governmental secrecy as exemplified in the *Official Secrets Act*, but to change it substantially, if not end it completely.

The Access to Information Act, passed in 1983, sets out its objective and its limitations in section 2(1):

> The purpose of this Act is to extend the present laws of Canada to provide a right of access to information in records under the control of a government institution in accordance with the principles that government information should be available to the public, that necessary exceptions to the right of access should be limited and specific and that decisions on the disclosure of government information should be reviewed independently of government.

We will analyse the Act according to the structure set out in this provision: the right of access; limits; and review.

a) The Right of Access

The general right of access created by the Act is not so broad as might appear. First, "government institution" does not, in fact, mean *any* government institution; it means only those institutions that are listed in the schedule to the Act. Any institution not mentioned in the appendix, such as, for example, the Canadian Judicial Council or the CBC, is not subject to the Act. Second, while the right of access is granted to "all individuals present in Canada,"[19] it does not appear to extend to corporations. Since, however, an application may be made by an agent acting for a corporation, this is not a substantial obstacle. Third, and perhaps most important, finding something, whether as a general matter or under the *Access to Information Act*, is very much a matter of knowing what you are looking for. The request for information must be sufficiently full and detailed for an experienced government employee familiar with the subject-matter to locate the record requested with a reasonable effort. If this condition is not met, there is no obligation to provide the information. To make the task easier, however, the Act requires the government to produce an annual *Access Register*. This publication describes in detail what each department or agency of the government of Canada does and the types of records it controls. Fur-

---

18   R.S.C. 1985, c. A-1.
19   *Privacy Act Extension Order*, No. 2, SOR/89-206.

thermore, each department or agency has an access coordinator, whose job is to assist persons applying for information. Any reporter whose responsibilities cover particular federal departments or agencies would do well to establish good working relations with the appropriate access coordinators. Fourth, there is provision in the Act for fees to be charged. There is a basic application fee of $5.00, as well as charges for photocopying and any time in excess of five hours spent searching for the records sought. Applicants may ask for a waiver of all fees and should do so as a matter of course. Finally, the Act makes no reference to the purpose behind an application. As a result, at no stage of the process is the applicant required to establish that he wishes the information for some useful or legitimate purpose, nor, indeed, should the applicant even be asked why he wants the information.

b) Limits

Various categories of information are exempt from disclosure under the Act. The Act provides for both mandatory exemptions and discretionary exemptions.

i) Mandatory Exemptions

Under the Act, the head of the government institution "*shall* refuse to disclose" [emphasis added] information that falls into any of the following categories:

- Any personal information as defined in the *Privacy Act*. The *Privacy Act* was enacted at the same time as the *Access to Information Act*. Its purpose is to protect the confidentiality of personal information about individuals which is in the possession of the government of Canada. This exemption prevents applicants having access to personal information about other people, but not about themselves.
- Any information being sought in a business context which contains trade secrets or other confidential commercial information. The Act is not intended to provide a competitive edge to any business enterprise. This is not to say that the Act cannot be used to further purely commercial ends. There are businesses, for example, which have used the Act to gain access to rulings and decisions made under the *Income Tax Act*. This material has then been published commercially.
- Any documents prepared for the work of the Cabinet, or Cabinet confidences. The traditional principle of Cabinet secrecy is maintained.
- Any information obtained by the government of Canada in confidence from a foreign government, an organization of states, a provincial government, or a municipal government.

- Information obtained or prepared by the RCMP while performing contractual policing services for a province or municipality, where there has been a prior agreement not to disclose such information.
- Any information that may not be disclosed pursuant to some other statute.

ii) Discretionary Exemptions

The head of a government institution *may* refuse to disclose any record from a long list of categories of information. These categories include:

- Information that could reasonably be expected to be injurious to the conduct of federal-provincial affairs, or the conduct of international affairs and the defence of Canada, or of any state allied with Canada, or the "detection, prevention or suppression of subversive or hostile activities."
- Information relating to law enforcement, including the detection, prevention, and suppression of crime.
- Information that could reasonably be expected to facilitate the commission of a crime. As examples, the Act includes in this category technical information relating to weapons or potential weapons or information on the "vulnerability" of particular buildings.
- Information that could reasonably be expected to threaten the safety of individuals.
- A great deal of information of an essentially economic nature. This includes information injurious to the "financial interests" of the government of Canada or the ability of the government to "manage" the country's economy, such as information about contemplated changes in the bank rate, or tariffs or taxes. It further includes government trade secrets and scientific or technical information obtained through government research.
- Any information subject to solicitor-client privilege.
- Information the government was already planning to release within ninety days of the request being made. Additional time may be allowed for the translation and publication of such information.

Even if a reporter is unable to gain access to certain information following the rules laid down in the Act, it may well be that he is still able to get the information through other means. Assuming that the information is not subject to the *Official Secrets Act*, no offence will be committed through the publication of such information. A denial of access does not amount to a prohibition against publication.

c) Review

The person applying for information is supposed to receive an answer within thirty days of making the request, although the government agency has the ability to extend this period for a further thirty days or, sometimes, even longer. The applicant should either get the information sought or, if disclosure is not to be granted, written reasons for the refusal. These reasons must either indicate the section of the Act under which access is being refused or state that the record being sought does not exist. If the record sought belongs to a class to which access is not permitted, there is no obligation to inform the applicant whether the particular record exists. A complaint against a refusal to grant access to the information sought can be taken within a year of the refusal to the information commissioner. The commissioner can also address issues concerning fees and delays. The procedure followed by the commissioner is closer to an investigation than to a hearing, but the applicant, the relevant government institution, and any third party opposing the release of information about itself are all allowed to present arguments to the commissioner.

Once the information commissioner has reached a decision, that decision is communicated to the government agency in question. The agency is not bound to follow the information commissioner's decision. If the agency still refuses to grant access, either the applicant or the information commissioner may have the agency's refusal reviewed by the Federal Court of Canada. It is the refusal of access that is to be reviewed, not the decision of the information commissioner.[20] The Federal Court has shown a general inclination in favour of disclosing information rather than withholding it. In a 1986 decision, *Canada (Information Commissioner)* v. *Canada (Minister of Employment & Immigration)*,[21] the court said: "[T]he purpose of the *Access to Information Act* is to codify the right of access to information held by the government. It is not to codify the government's right of refusal. Access should be the normal course. Exemptions should be exceptional and must be confined to those specifically set out in the statute."

All the provinces except Prince Edward Island have access legislation. The majority of these statutes use the misleading phrase "freedom of information." All the statutes follow the broad path of the federal legislation in setting out a general right of access to information, qualifying that with specific exemptions, and, at the same time, seeking to protect

---

20 *Dagg v. Canada (Minister of Finance)*, [1995] 3 F.C. 199 (C.A.).
21 [1986] 3 F.C. 63 at 69. (T.D.).

the privacy of individuals. In five provinces — Alberta, British Columbia, Ontario, Quebec, and Saskatchewan — the access legislation also applies to municipal governments.

C. CRIMINAL LIBEL

There are two broad categories of libel in Canada: civil libel and criminal libel. Civil libel is the mechanism whereby individuals may seek to protect their reputations (see chapter 4). The broad purpose of criminal libel is to preserve public order. Criminal libel punishes certain forms of expression largely because they are seen as creating potential threats to public order. There are three forms of criminal libel in the *Criminal Code*: seditious libel, defamatory libel, and blasphemous libel.

1) Seditious Libel

Seditious libel is the crime that has traditionally been used to prosecute unacceptable political speech. The *Criminal Code* deals with sedition in sections 59 to 62. These sections are exceedingly unsatisfactory. Section 59(1) says, "[s]editious words are words that express a seditious intention," and goes on in subsection 2 to note that a "seditious libel is a libel that expresses a seditious intention."[22] Unfortunately, the *Code* does not tell us exactly what is meant by a seditious intention. It does, however, set outer limits. It tells us that it is seditious to advocate the use of force as a means of accomplishing a governmental change within Canada. At the other extreme, section 60 provides that certain things are not seditious. For example, it is not seditious, to use the classic formulation, to say or argue in good faith that "Her Majesty has been misled or mistaken in her measures." It is not sedition to engage in reasonable criticism of the government of the day. Nor is it sedition to criticize in good faith the Constitution of Canada or of a province, or to criticize the Parliament of Canada or the legislature of a province, or the administration of justice. At the one extreme, then, advocating the overthrowing of the government of Canada by force is seditious, but, at the other, engaging in normal political discourse is not. What conduct falls in the middle?

There has not been a proscution for sedition since the 1940s. The last prosecution arose out of the ongoing struggle in Quebec between the Jehovah's Witnesses and the government of Maurice Duplessis. It

---

22   *Criminal Code of Canada*, R.S.C. 1985, c. C-46, s. 59 [hereinafter *Criminal Code*].

focused in particular on a tract circulated in Quebec by the Witnesses. The tract was in French, but its title translated into English was "Quebec's Burning Hate for God and Christ and Freedom Is the Shame of All Canada." In the kind of society that existed at the time in Quebec, and especially rural Quebec, those words were inflammatory. The persons who had been circulating this pamphlet were prosecuted for sedition. The case, *Boucher* v. *R.*,[23] went to the Supreme Court, where the judges divided five to four. The nature of their division is important, and has been important, in ensuring a substantial degree of freedom of political expression. All the judges agreed that in order for there to be a conviction, the Crown would have to prove that the words used by the accused, whether in a speech, a book, a pamphlet, or whatever, were seditious in and of themselves. What does that mean? The Court looked to older case-law, especially older English case-law, and suggested that words are seditious if they tend "to create discontent or disaffection among His Majesty's subjects or ill-will or hostility between groups of them." On that definition, a great many utterances could be regarded as seditious — and this is where the key distinction lay between the majority and the minority in the Court in *Boucher*. The minority judges were prepared to say that an accused person could be convicted on the basis of words alone. If the words that the accused published were seditious in and of themselves, then, said four of the nine judges, that is enough, he is guilty. Five of the nine judges, however, said that there must be another element. They decided that not only does the Crown have to show that the statements made were seditious in and of themselves, but it must show in addition that when the accused uttered the seditious words he did so with the intention of inciting riot, tumult, or disorder. The point is simple, but important, that five of the nine judges were saying the purpose of the offence of sedition is not to punish expression pure and simple. The purpose of the offence, rather, is to punish people who would seek to undermine public order. Sedition exists not to protect society against unpleasant words, but against real threats to social peace.

The result of this decision has been to make it extremely difficult to convict someone of sedition. How is the Crown to prove that the accused actually intended to incite riot, tumult, or disorder? This is undoubtedly the main reason there has not been a prosecution for sedition since *Boucher*.

The Law Reform Commission of Canada described the offence of sedition as an "outdated and unprincipled" law, and further took the

---

23   [1951] S.C.R. 265.

view that, as a result of the *Boucher* case, it was so narrowly circum-
scribed as no longer to have any practical utility. The Commission recommended that it be removed from the *Criminal Code*, but it is still there,
even though there have been no prosecutions for close to fifty years.[24]

2) Defamatory Libel

Defamatory libel is the most prolix offence in the *Criminal Code*, its definition occupying sections 297 to 316. In these sections, the offence
sounds very similar to civil libel, but there are some distinctions. Mere
insults exchanged between two people can amount to defamatory libel,
for example, whereas with civil libel publication to a third person is
required (see chapter 4(1)(C)).

What is defamatory libel all about, and what is the point of it? There
are few prosecutions, but as the Law Reform Commission of Canada
noted in a 1984 study, some prosecutions still take place.[25] An interesting one occurred in Vancouver in 1969 when the *Georgia Straight*, one
of the better known of the underground publications of the 1960s, was
prosecuted.[26] The *Georgia Straight* did not like a particular magistrate in
Vancouver, Lawrence Eckhardt, and was highly critical of him. It also
conferred a number of awards upon him. On one occasion it gave him
the Order of Abundant Flatulence, and on another awarded him the
Pontius Pilate Certificate of Justice. In the citation for this certificate the
paper said: "To Lawrence Eckhardt, who, by closing his mind to justice,
his eyes to fairness, and his ears to equality, has encouraged the belief
that the law is not only blind, but also deaf, dumb and stupid. Let history judge your actions — then appeal." The trial court was not at all
clear what the crime of defamatory libel was about. It did refer to perhaps the best-known Canadian prosecution, which occurred in Alberta
in the 1930s.[27] Unwin, the accused in this case, had circulated a pamphlet showing on one side the names of nine prominent citizens of
Edmonton, all under the heading "Bankers' Toadies." On the other side
were the words: "God Made Bankers' Toadies, just as He made snakes,
slugs, snails and other creepy-crawly, treacherous and poisonous
things. NEVER therefore, abuse them — just exterminate them!" He
was charged with defamatory libel and convicted. The court said that

---

24   *Crimes against The State, supra* note 14 at 35–36.
25   Law Reform Commission of Canada, *Defamatory Libel* (Working Paper 35)
     (Ottawa: Minister of Supply & Services, 1984).
26   *R. v. Georgia Straight Publishing Ltd.* (1969), 4 D.L.R. (3d) 383 (B.C. Co. Ct.).
27   *R. v. Unwin*, [1938] 1 D.L.R. 529 (Alta. C.A.).

the distinction between civil libel and criminal libel was that civil libel was a private matter between individuals. If you say insulting and untrue things about someone which tend to harm that person's reputation, then he can sue you civilly and be awarded compensation. By way of contrast, a defamatory libel prosecution is a public matter between the state and the accused. In *Unwin*, the court suggested that the purpose of such a prosecution was not so much for the redress of a private wrong as it was to punish the accused for the wrong done to the public. The theory appears to be that some statements can be so extreme that they cease to be a purely private matter between individuals and become a public matter engaging the attention of the state.

That is all very well until we look into the history of the offence of defamatory libel in England. The offence was created by the Court of Star Chamber in the seventeenth century as an anti-duelling measure. The theory was that if A made extreme and insulting statements to B, B might be so offended that he would feel obliged to challenge A to a duel. And A or B would probably end up dead. The point of the crime was to discourage A from making the outrageous statements about B which would lead B to challenge A to a duel. This may have made a great deal of sense in seventeenth-century England, but duelling is not a widespread phenomenon in late twentieth-century Canada. Despite that, we continue to have this anti-duelling measure in our *Criminal Code*. The Law Reform Commission of Canada said there was simply no justification whatsoever for having this offence and recommended that it be removed. That was twelve years ago, and the offence is still in the *Criminal Code* and people are still being prosecuted. Once again, it must be noted that the purpose of the offence, at least in the seventeenth century, was to maintain public order by punishing expression that would tend to undermine it.

3) Blasphemous Libel

Blasphemy is the third and final form of criminal libel. Once again, it would seem that the justification for the offence is that extreme statements made about the religious beliefs of individuals can lead to a breakdown in public order.[28] For this reason, the uttering of such statements may properly be limited by the state.

Section 296 of the *Criminal Code* deals with blasphemy. As is the case with sedition, the *Code* does not define blasphemy. It simply states that: "It is a question of fact whether or not any matter that is published

---

28   R. v. *Rahard* (1935), 65 C.C.C. 344 (Que. S.C.).

is a blasphemous libel." One qualification provides that it is not blasphemous to express "an opinion upon a religious subject" as long as such opinion is expressed in "good faith" and "decent language."

There are two significant problems with this offence. First, it has been held that in order for there to be a conviction, the Crown does not have to prove that the accused intended to blaspheme; it is enough to prove that the accused intentionally uttered statements that were found to be blasphemous.[29] Second, while the matter has not been the subject of a judicial decision in Canada, an English court has decided that the offence of blasphemy applies only to the Christian religion. Statements made about other religions, no matter how extreme, cannot, by definition, result in a prosecution for blasphemy.[30]

As with defamatory libel, although there are few prosecutions for blasphemous libel, they do occur from time to time.

4) The *Charter*

What about these three offences and the *Charter*? Since there have been no recent sedition prosecutions, there has been no opportunity to question the constitutionality of the offence.

In the case of defamatory libel, the Manitoba Court of Appeal dismissed a challenge based on the *Charter*'s guarantee of freedom of expression in 1995.[31] The court held that the state's objective in creating this offence was the protection of reputation, and that this objective was "pressing and substantial." There are two difficulties with this conclusion. First, this seems to suggest that the state's objective has somehow shifted since the crime was originally created. Second, and more problematic, if the purpose underlying this offence was indeed the protection of reputation, then its true subject-matter would seem to be "Property and Civil Rights in the Province." On this approach, the offence appears to address a matter not within the jurisdiction of Parliament. The Manitoba court's decision is under appeal to the Supreme Court of Canada.

All three offences seem to be questionable limits on freedom of expression. Furthermore, in the case of blasphemous libel, if the offence were to be held to apply in Canada only to statements made about Christianity, this would seem to conflict with the equality guarantee in section 15 of the *Charter* and the affirmation of "multicultural[ism]" in section 27.

---

29   *R. v. Gay News Ltd.*, [1979] 1 All E.R. 898 (H.L.).
30   *R. v. Chief Metropolitan Stipendiary Magistrate; ex parte Choudhury*, [1991] 1 Q.B. 429.
31   *R. v. Stevens*, [1995] 4 W.W.R. 153 (Man. C.A.).

FURTHER READINGS

No single work deals specifically and in detail with the matters addressed in this chapter. An essay by W.S. Tarnopolsky, "Freedom of the Press," in a volume prepared by the Royal Commission on Newspapers, *Newspapers and the Law* (Ottawa: Minister of Supply & Services, 1981) 1, is helpful. A compendious source on access to information and related issues, which is regularly updated, is C.H. McNairn and C.D. Woodbury, *Government Information: Access and Privacy* (Toronto: Carswell, 1992).

FREE EXPRESSION AND THE COURTS

What is the law on reporting about the legal system? Detailed rules govern what may and may not be reported concerning proceedings that are pending or actually before the courts. There are also difficulties that can arise for journalists who get caught up with the legal system.

A. THE OPENNESS PRINCIPLE

In our system the courts are public institutions. The courtroom is a public place, and what takes place there is public business. Thus, what happens in the courtroom should, as a matter of principle, be open to the public and, more to the point, to reporters and to the media. This principle of the openness and the public nature of the judicial system had been recognized even prior to the adoption of the *Charter*.

The clearest source is a 1981 decision of the Supreme Court of Canada, *Nova Scotia (A.G.)* v. *MacIntyre*.[1] Linden MacIntyre, a CBC reporter, went to a court-house in Halifax and asked both to inspect some search warrants and to be allowed to see whatever had been discovered as a result of the search. A justice of the peace was not sympathetic to the request and told MacIntyre it was impossible. MacIntyre disagreed and litigation ensued. The litigation was initially between

---

1   [1982] 1 S.C.R. 175.

MacIntyre and the attorney general of Nova Scotia, but that official was joined by the attorney general of Canada and the attorneys general of six other provinces, all of whom were opposed to allowing MacIntyre to see this material.

In his judgment, Mr. Justice Brian Dickson [as he then was] laid down some important principles, although perhaps it is more accurate to say affirmed them, because it was his view that they had always been part of the Canadian legal system. He said that the basic principle governing judicial proceedings was their openness. Openness was to be the rule; covertness the exception. He said further that what must be sought was maximum public accessibility: "At every stage the rule should be one of public accessibility and concomitant judicial accountability."

Any limit on openness, any limit on the access of the public to the courts, would have to be justified as an exception to this basic principle. Dickson formulated his approach in the following words: "[C]urtailment of public accessibility can only be justified where there is present the need to protect social values of superordinate importance." Although it is not clear what is meant by "social values of superordinate importance," Mr. Justice Dickson obviously had in mind something substantial.

By way of illustration, Dickson gave two examples of social values of superordinate importance which he believed would justify limiting the principle of openness. He put them in the context of access to search warrants and to the material discovered as a result of a search. Since a search warrant is a court document and since material discovered as a result of a search comes into the possession of the court, the openness principle would generally require that members of the public be entitled to see search warrants and any material that had been discovered during their execution. What social values could justify limiting access in such a situation? First, the administration of justice was a value of superordinate importance. This meant that members of the public could not see search warrants before they were executed. Clearly, a major part of the value of search warrants as tools in law enforcement is the element of surprise. Thus, the administration of justice would justify limiting the openness principle to this extent. The second social value of superordinate importance was the protection of the privacy of the innocent. What did that mean? Mr. Justice Dickson said that where a search warrant had been executed but nothing was found, it would be justifiable to limit access to that warrant. That does not seem as clear-cut and as self-evident as the first instance. If, for example, I claimed to a reporter that I was being harassed by police searches of my home or office, one of the things I would want to do to substantiate my claim would be to produce search warrants authorizing the searches I claimed to have taken place. Dickson's second social value might make this impossible.

Subsequent cases have held that section 2(b) of the *Charter*,[2] the guarantee of freedom of expression, has the effect of putting the openness principle on a constitutional basis. Here we want to look at some of the earliest litigation in which a media organization attempted to rely on the *Charter*: the decision of the Ontario Court of Appeal in *Reference Re S. 12(1) of Juvenile Delinquents Act (Canada)*.[3]

The Southam corporation has been aggressive in using the *Charter* as a means of expanding what it sees as the legal and constitutional rights of journalists. Is litigation a useful means of improving journalism? Has the litigation the Southam corporation has been involved in actually made a concrete contribution to enhancing the legal status of journalists? Furthermore, one can question whether paying the lawyers who conduct this litigation is a useful or desirable means of investing the funds of a media corporation.

A federal statute, the *Juvenile Delinquents Act*,[4] was replaced in 1983 by the *Young Offenders Act*.[5] Section 12 of the earlier Act said that the trials of juveniles were to take place "without publicity." Towards the end of 1981 the Supreme Court decided that the phrase meant that during the trial of a juvenile the courtroom was to be closed.[6] Nobody was to get in, except, of course, lawyers, social workers, psychologists, police, parents, and so on. But no reporters.

In the spring of 1982 the *Charter* became part of the Canadian Constitution and, shortly after that, the Ottawa *Citizen* decided to use it as the basis for challenging the constitutionality of section 12 of the *Juvenile Delinquents Act*. The *Citizen* sent a reporter to the court-house in Ottawa to attend the trial of a juvenile and, when she was turned away, the newspaper instituted its challenge.

A digression is necessary here to deal with the issue of standing. Standing addresses the important question of who is entitled to raise issues before the courts and, more particularly, who is entitled to challenge the constitutionality of legislation. By way of illustration, standing

---

2   Canadian *Charter of Right and Freedoms*, Part I of the *Constitution Act, 1982*, being Schedule B to the *Canada Act 1982* (U.K.), 1982, c. 11, s. 2(b) [hereinafter *Charter*].

3   (1983), 41 O.R. (2d) 113 (C.A.).

4   R.S.C. 1970, c. J-3.

5   R.S.C. 1985, c. Y-1 [hereinafter *YOA*].

6   *B.(C.) v. R.*, [1981] 2 S.C.R. 480.

was a central issue in the attempts of both Henry Morgentaler and Joe Borowski to change the law about abortion.[7]

Borowski was challenging section 251 of the *Criminal Code* because it permitted abortions under certain circumstances, and Morgentaler was challenging the same section because it did not give women complete freedom of choice. They were both relying on section 7 of the *Charter* for their challenges, but from different perspectives. Borowski said that by permitting abortions at all, the state was infringing the right to life of fetuses, a right he argued was guaranteed in that section. Morgentaler claimed that by placing restrictions on access to abortion, the state was infringing the liberty and security of the person of women, also guaranteed by section 7. The major procedural difference between the two cases was that Morgentaler, when he raised these challenges, was actually in court accused of violating section 251 of the *Criminal Code* by performing abortions other than in accordance with the procedure laid down in that section.[8] He had run concretely and directly up against the section. Since he was directly affected by the law, he thereby had the necessary standing to challenge its constitutionality. But Borowski's situation was different. He had not run up against section 251 in the course of actual litigation; he simply did not agree with it. As a result, there was controversy before the courts as to whether Borowski should be granted the necessary standing to challenge the law,[9] although in the end the Supreme Court concluded that he could be heard. It should be added that being granted standing simply means that a court has agreed to hear an individual's case. It in no way guarantees that the court will actually decide the case in that person's favour.

There is a deeper problem here. If we broaden the notion of standing, we come very close to the point of allowing people to raise constitutional challenges to laws solely on the basis that they do not like them. This has the obvious effect of politicizing the role of the courts. If I can challenge the constitutionality of a law for no reason other than my distaste for it, it would seem that I am attempting to use the courts as a political, rather than a legal, forum.

The issue of standing arose at once in the Ottawa *Citizen*'s challenge to section 12 of the *Juvenile Delinquents Act*. The *Citizen* reporter was seeking to raise an issue in the course of a proceeding to which she was

---

7   As general background, see F.L. Morton, *Morgentaler v. Borowski: Abortion, the Charter, and the Courts* (Toronto: McClelland & Stewart, 1992).

8   *R. v. Morgentaler*, [1988] 1 S.C.R. 30.

9   *Canada (Minister of Justice) v. Borowski*, [1981] 2 S.C.R. 575. See also *Borowski v. Canada (A.G.)*, [1989] 1 S.C.R. 342.

not a party. The proceeding was entirely a matter between the Crown and a particular juvenile. Now along comes someone who is an outsider to this proceeding, yet wants to raise legal arguments relevant to it. How can she do this? On what basis did the *Citizen* have the standing to challenge the constitutional validity of section 12 of the *Juvenile Delinquents Act*, when it was not a party to any proceeding involving that section?

Take another example, one that has happened from time to time. While conducting a trial a judge orders, "I do not want this witness identified by name by the mass media." A reporter might stand up and assert to the judge, politely, "I think that order is an infringement of rights guaranteed under section 2(b) of the *Charter* and I think you should reconsider it." Where does that reporter get the standing to raise this issue when, once again, he is not a party to the proceeding actually before the court?

For a long time the generally held view was that the necessary standing was provided by section 24(1) of the *Charter*. That section says,

> Anyone whose rights or freedoms, as guaranteed by this Charter, have been infringed or denied may apply to a court of competent jurisdiction . . . [for a] remedy. . . .

Now the section cannot mean what it says literally. No one can know for sure whether his rights or freedoms have been infringed or denied until a court decides they have been. What the section has to mean, and can only mean, is that anyone who *claims* that his rights or freedoms have been infringed or denied may apply to a court for a remedy. It had been assumed until December 1994 that this was the basis on which journalists claimed standing to challenge rulings made during proceedings to which they were not parties. But the Supreme Court of Canada in its *Dagenais* v. *Canadian Broadcasting Corp.*[10] decision complicated the issue as to how exactly journalists may bring these challenges before the courts.

The *Dagenais* decision casts doubt on the idea that section 24(1) gives journalists, or other third parties, the necessary standing. *Dagenais* says that when a judge makes an order that results in imposing an unjustifiable limitation on freedom of expression, that judge has made "an error of law." The process of challenging an error of law is more complex than simply getting up in court and suggesting that a particular ruling was incorrect. If the ruling was made by a judge of an inferior court, an application may be made to have it reviewed by a judge of a superior court. The decision of that superior court judge may then be

---

10   [1994] 3 S.C.R. 835.

appealed to the provincial court of appeal and, thence, where appropriate, to the Supreme Court of Canada. If, however, the original order was made by a superior court judge, it is, according to *Dagenais*, to be appealed directly to the Supreme Court of Canada.

To return to the *Reference Re S. 12(1) of Juvenile Delinquents Act (Canada)* case, the court accepted that the requirements of standing were met. The substantive question raised by the *Citizen* was whether the guarantee of freedom of expression in section 2(b) should be interpreted as including a constitutional guarantee of the openness of the courts. The Ontario Court of Appeal said it should.

The reasoning adopted by the court in reaching this conclusion is not clear. To begin with, it is not immediately apparent that the phrase "freedom of expression" necessarily includes a guarantee of the openness of the courts. The judges in the *Reference Re S. 12(1) of Juvenile Delinquents Act (Canada)* case talked about the Constitution as a "living tree." Whenever judges talk like this, they are really saying that the constitutional text does not actually authorize them to do what they want to do, but if they call the Constitution a living tree, they can feel free to put a broader interpretation on it. The court referred to a number of American decisions that had reached the same conclusion. The court further recognized that access to the courts was not specifically enumerated in the fundamental freedoms part of the *Charter*, but said that, having regard to the historic origin and necessary purpose of public access, it was reasonable to regard public access to the courts as an integral part of the fundamental freedom of expression. The argument is that freedom of expression includes both a right to gather information and a right to comment publicly about the operations of fundamental state institutions. Obviously, however, no one can either gather information or comment publicly about the way these institutions operate unless he can get into them. Since the courts are clearly key state institutions, the guarantee of freedom of expression is, thus, interpreted as including a right of access to them.

This approach to interpreting section 2(b) of the *Charter* has been affirmed by the Supreme Court of Canada. Giving judgment in *Edmonton Journal* v. *Alberta (A.G.)*,[11] Mr. Justice Cory asserted:

> There can be no doubt that the courts play an important role in any democratic society. They are the forum not only for the resolution of disputes between citizens, but for the resolution of disputes between the citizens and the state in all its manifestations. The more complex

---

11   [1989] 2 S.C.R. 1326.

society becomes, the more important becomes the function of the courts. As a result of their significance, the courts must be open to public scrutiny and to public criticism of their operation by the public.

In recognizing that the openness principle had a constitutional basis, Mr. Justice Cory also recognized an essential practical corollary to the principle. This is the special role of the mass media in making the principle concrete. He said:

> [A]s listeners and readers, members of the public have a right to information pertaining to public institutions and particularly the courts. Here the press plays a fundamentally important role. It is exceedingly difficult for many, if not most, people to attend a court trial. Neither working couples nor mothers or fathers house-bound with young children, would find it possible to attend court. Those who cannot attend rely in large measure upon the press to inform them about court proceedings — the nature of the evidence that was called, the arguments presented, the comments made by the trial judge — in order to know not only what rights they may have, but how their problems might be dealt with in court. It is only through the press that most individuals can really learn of what is transpiring in the courts. They as "listeners" or readers have a right to receive this information. Only then can they make an assessment of the institution. Discussion of court cases and constructive criticism of court proceedings is dependent upon the receipt by the public of information as to what transpired in court. Practically speaking, this information can only be obtained from the newspapers or other media.

Indeed, to take another illustration, Madam Justice Boland of the Ontario High Court advanced the matter a step further in R. v. Robinson.[12] She suggested that the mass media have a duty, not necessarily legal, but certainly moral or professional, to inform the public of what is happening in our courts. She stated: "Openness prevents abuse of the judicial system and fosters public confidence in the fairness and integrity of our system of justice. The press is a positive influence in assuring fair trial."

Not only are judicial proceedings themselves public, but the documents that form a part of a proceeding are also public. Every such document is a public document and, following the principle laid down in the MacIntyre case, should be subject to public access. The problem is that if a court official refuses to give a reporter access to a document,

---

12   (1983), 41 O.R. (2d) 764 (H.C.J.).

that reporter may have to litigate to have the refusal overturned. In most such situations the threat of litigation should be sufficient to overcome official or judicial recalcitrance.

It is not the business of court officials to decide what is proper reporting about judicial proceedings. The law of contempt of court and the law of libel, as we shall see, already address that issue. If a reporter makes a bad job of reporting a particular trial, he may commit the offence of contempt of court. Alternatively, if he gets what is asserted in a particular document all wrong, he may libel somebody. The law already has mechanisms to deal with errors or failings that may occur in reporting. There is no need and no place for administrative officials, or even judges, to attempt to add new ones.

This issue became a matter of controversy in Prince Edward Island in 1995. The province's superior court introduced a rule that prevented members of the public, including reporters, from seeing statements of claim filed by plaintiffs in civil suits. In February 1996 this policy was reversed by a new provincial chief justice. All documents filed with the courts in civil proceedings would henceforth be available to the public, subject to a residual authority in judges to seal confidential documents. This process was entirely a matter of administrative decision making by the province's judges. There was no litigation to test the legality of such action.

1) Cameras and Other Tools

Two specific issues arise in relation to the openness principle. The first has to do with the use of cameras, video recorders, and audio recorders in the courtroom. This has become a vexed issue of late. A standard provision dealing with these matters is found in section 136 of the Ontario *Courts of Justice Act*.[13] It prohibits taking or attempting to take a photograph, motion picture, audio recording, or other record capable of producing visual or oral representations by electronic means or otherwise at a court hearing, during the course of a trial, or of any person entering or leaving a courtroom or of any person inside a court-house who is there for the purpose of taking part in a judicial proceeding. There is an exception to this blanket prohibition, one that it took some time to achieve. Reporters may use audio recorders in courtrooms as a means of taking notes, but not to record material to be broadcast. The clear policy and tradition of the Canadian legal system is against allowing the use of cameras, audio recorders, or video recorders in the courtroom.

---

13   R.S.O. 1990, c. 43.

There are some interesting manifestations of this tradition, one being the unusual 1976 case of *R. v. Rowbotham (No. 3)*.[14] Rowbotham was an American who had been in and out of Canadian courts and in and out of jail regularly. In this instance he had been arrested at Toronto International Airport trying to import an amount of cannabis, and he was put on trial for offences under the *Narcotic Control Act*.[15] An American publication called *High Times* sent a reporter to cover the trial. The simplest way to describe *High Times* is to say that it takes an approach to drugs roughly similar to the approach *Penthouse* takes to sex. It features the High of the Month and so on. The *High Times* reporter, to the horror of the presiding judge, actually went to where the judge's car was parked outside the court-house and tried to photograph him. The judge was having none of it, and made an order that no "person shall take, or attempt to take any photograph, motion picture, or other record capable of producing visual representations by electronic means or otherwise, of any person in any way involved in the case of Regina and . . . Rowbotham . . . either inside the Peel County Court House, or outside the Peel County Court House." Strictly speaking, that meant no one could take a photograph of a witness in the case walking down Yonge Street in Toronto. The reporter for *High Times* became disgusted with the Canadian judicial system and left Peel County, vowing never to return.

A more illuminating case is the prosecution in 1992 of CBC reporter Cathy Squires for photographing something going on inside a courthouse.[16] Squires did not deny having taken the photograph, but based her defence on the *Charter* guarantee of freedom of expression. That guarantee has been interpreted, as we have seen, to mean that the courtroom is open to the public, including reporters. Since reporters have a constitutional right to be inside the courtroom, she argued that there was no justification for imposing limits on the means or tools that reporters might use while there. If the reporter has a right to be in the courtroom, he should have a constitutional right to be there with an audio recorder or a video recorder. Squires was convicted at trial, and the matter eventually went to the Ontario Court of Appeal. Five judges heard the appeal. Three decided that what is now section 136 of the Ontario *Courts of Justice Act* was constitutional, and two decided it was not. All the judges agreed that the section created a limit on the *Charter* guarantee of freedom of expression. "If television journalists are unable to photograph persons entering or leaving a

---

14   (1976), 2 C.R. (3d) 241 (Ont. G.S.P.).

15   Now R.S.C. 1985, c. N-1.

16   *R. v. Squires* (1992), 11 O.R. (3d) 385 (C.A.).

courtroom, their freedom of expression is curtailed." The majority in the court, nonetheless, found this limit to be justified in a free and democratic society. The state's objectives in creating this limit were seen as three-fold:

a. maintaining order and decorum in the courtroom;

b. guaranteeing unimpeded access to the courtroom; and

c. guaranteeing reasonable expectations of privacy.

The means chosen to achieve these objectives were held to be proportionate to them. The general direction of the majority's reasoning was summed up in the judgment of Mr. Justice Houlden: "The fair and impartial administration of justice requires a calm, dignified atmosphere. If photographing and televising is permitted of persons entering or leaving the courtroom, that atmosphere will, I believe, be disrupted."

In the result, Squires's 1992 conviction and the $500 fine imposed on her were upheld. The Supreme Court denied her leave to appeal. Litigation based on the *Charter* will not, then, succeed in opening Canadian courtrooms to television cameras.

A distinction is growing between the actual practice today in trial courts and in appellate courts. The Federal Court of Appeal now regularly allows video recordings of its proceedings, and the Supreme Court has allowed them on a number of occasions. The Ontario Court of Appeal appears ready to adopt a similar practice. Nobody seems to care seriously about whether journalists record proceedings before appellate courts, largely because these proceedings are not very interesting. The reason, of course, is that there are no ordinary people there, no witnesses. All that happens before appellate courts is lawyers arguing points of law.

Should video recorders be allowed in trial courts? My own view has changed substantially since I watched the O.J. Simpson proceedings in California. I was once convinced that it was simply a matter of time until we had television in Canadian courtrooms, but watching the circus surrounding the O.J. Simpson trial has made me rethink the matter. The real issue may not be simply the question of guaranteeing a fair trial or decorum and dignity inside the courtroom. It may be a matter of maintaining the integrity of the judicial process, of ensuring that the judicial process is not swallowed by the entertainment industry. What was often lost sight of during the O.J. Simpson proceeding was that it was a real trial of a real person who was charged with murdering two other real people. The whole business was not staged as yet another means of providing titillation for television viewers.

Any serious proposals that have been put forward for allowing television into Canadian courtrooms have been based on an understanding that there will not be scrums in the courtroom, but fixed cameras that will provide videotape on a pool basis equally to all news agencies. It has never been seriously suggested that individual reporters be allowed to bring video cameras into the courtroom.

How would television affect judicial proceedings? Many have suggested that since television has not destroyed our legislatures, it will not destroy our courts. But there are many significant differences between televising what goes on in the legislature and what goes on in the courtroom. One is that members of legislatures are elected, and one of the ways they got elected was by creating a certain image. A crucial thing in the life of a politician today is to be a good television personality and to establish a good public image, primarily through television. Considerations like this are not only foreign to judicial proceedings but are subversive of them. There is no benefit to the legal system from encouraging lawyers, and above all judges, to become media stars.

A paper produced by the Law Reform Commission of Canada in 1987 makes at least one sound assertion — that there is little empirical information about these matters.[17] On the other hand, I am not sure how one would get such information. There is empirical information that allowing reporters to use audio recorders as a means of taking notes in the courtroom has dramatically increased the accuracy of court reporting.[18] In other words, there is evidence that the use of contemporary technology will improve reporting, but there is no information about the effect that allowing video recorders into Canadian courtrooms will have on the integrity of the judicial process.

It may be inevitable that we will have television coverage of judicial proceedings. Once the foot in the door of video coverage of appellate proceedings has been accepted, it becomes more difficult to argue in favour of restricting video coverage of trial court proceedings. The current practice is hard to justify. Reporters are permitted to use video recorders to cover the dull proceedings; they may not use them to cover the interesting ones.

---

17   Law Reform Commission of Canada, *Public and Media Access to the Criminal Process* (Working Paper 56) (Ottawa: The Commission, 1987).

18   P. Calamai, "Discrepancies in News Quotes from the Colin Thatcher Trial" in *Trials and Tribulations* (Regina: University of Regina, 1986).

2) Preventing Embarrassment

To what extent can limitations on the openness of the courts be justified in order to protect parties from embarrassment? *R. v. Unnamed Person*[19] is an example. In this case a seventeen-year-old woman was charged with infanticide, and the trial judge had issued an order prohibiting publication of her identity.

The judge did so to spare her public embarrassment. As Mr. Justice Zuber of the Ontario Court of Appeal made clear, there is no basis whatsoever for such orders. The power of judges to place limits on the openness of the courts or on public access to the courts has to do solely with protecting the process of the courts, with guaranteeing the due administration of justice. It has nothing to do with avoiding embarrassment. There is no authority for limiting publicity surrounding any judicial proceeding solely in order to protect anyone from embarrassment.

3) Legislative Proceedings

Discussion of the openness principle includes media coverage of the proceedings of Parliament or a provincial legislature. Quite different considerations apply.

Although the courts have decided that section 2(b) of the *Charter* creates a broad right of public and media access to judicial proceedings, this has not been the result in the case of legislative proceedings. The Supreme Court of Canada dealt with this question in *New Brunswick Broadcasting Co. v. Nova Scotia (Speaker of the House of Assembly)*.[20] The Nova Scotia House of Assembly had prohibited television coverage of its proceedings. A number of media organizations sought a judicial order to the effect that this prohibition was an unjustifiable limit on freedom of expression. The Court rejected this claim. It held that Canadian legislatures possessed such inherent privileges as are necessary to ensure their proper functioning. Legislative privilege was, further, a part of the unwritten constitutional law of Canada. The Court went on to say that no one principle of the constitution could be applied so as to negate any other principle. More specifically, the judges decided that the manner in which a particular legislature chose to exercise its privileges, which clearly included the authority to exclude "strangers" — that is, anyone who is not a member of the legislature — could not be subject to judicial

---

19   (1985), 22 C.C.C. (3d) 284 (Ont. C.A.).
20   [1993] 1 S.C.R. 319.

review. Thus, if the legislature of Nova Scotia wished to prohibit television coverage of its proceedings, that was entirely up to the legislature of Nova Scotia.

B. CONTEMPT OF COURT

The most significant limitations on the openness principle are found in the law of contempt of court. There is civil contempt of court and criminal contempt of court. We will say nothing about civil contempt, as it is of no particular relevance to the mass media. The Canadian law of contempt of court is a strange, anomalous, and, most important of all, unclear element of our criminal law.

A useful place to begin is in contrasting how reporters and editors should look at contempt of court with the way lawyers tend to look at it. Lawyers are told from the start of their careers that their primary responsibility is to keep their clients out of trouble. One of the forms of trouble that lawyers are especially concerned to keep their clients out of is criminal prosecutions. Contempt of court is a crime. Lawyers, by their deepest instincts, want to advise their clients not to commit crimes. Thus, they are going to be careful and attempt to steer clients who are journalists away from committing, or running the risk of committing, contempt of court.

Journalists, in contrast, should put contempt in perspective. One way to do that is to realize that there are different levels of crimes. To be convicted of contempt of court is not the same thing as being convicted of molesting children. Contempt does not carry with it the moral opprobrium that attaches to many other crimes.

The most common punishment awarded upon conviction for contempt of court is a fine. Seldom is a reporter sent to jail for contempt of court. And where a journalist has committed a contempt of court in good faith and in the course of his work, it is overwhelmingly likely that his employer will pay his fine. A person who has been convicted of contempt of court will have, in popular language, a "criminal record." Once again, it is important to be clear that there are criminal records and there are criminal records. Having a criminal record for contempt of court is not like having a criminal record for fraud. A contempt conviction is not going to prevent someone being bonded. It is not going to prevent someone travelling outside Canada.

I am not suggesting that journalists be carefree about committing the offence of contempt of court. I am simply saying that lawyers often take a more cataclysmic view of these matters than is always justified.

There is a further problem with contempt of court in Canada, one that makes lawyers even more cautious. Contempt is the only crime that is not defined in the *Criminal Code*. Our criminal law was inherited from and is based on English criminal law. In England the criminal law is part of the amorphous common law. There are statutes that define particular crimes, but England has no general criminal code. One of the reasons we adopted a *Criminal Code* in 1892 was a feeling that the English approach was not adequate.[21] Criminal law has serious consequences for individuals. You can go to jail, you can be fined, your life can be ruined, and, of course, in 1892 you could be hanged. The view was that if the state was going to impose serious consequences like these on individuals who breached the criminal law and, at the same time, was going to reject any defence based on not knowing the law, the state was under an obligation to make the criminal law as knowable as possible. This is the main argument in favour of having a *Criminal Code*. Of course, the average Canadian does not spend much time reading the *Criminal Code* and, even if he did, it is by and large incomprehensible to anyone who is not a lawyer.

One logical result of the adoption of the *Criminal Code* was that the whole common law of crimes was abolished in Canada. The *Criminal Code* says in section 8 that it is a complete statement of the criminal law of Canada. The *Charter*, in section 11, reinforces this stand by providing that persons can only be punished for offences that already exist in law. However, section 9 of the *Criminal Code* exempts the law of contempt of court from this basic principle. Contempt of court is thus preserved as the one common law crime still enforced in Canada.[22]

The major result is that nobody knows for sure what the law of contempt of court is. Lawyers will admit that they do not know its precise boundaries. The vagueness and uncertainty compound the problems with contempt of court by reinforcing the caution of lawyers.

The final point to address is the likely affect on a journalist's career of a conviction for contempt of court. If, in good faith and in the course of serious professional reporting, someone ends up writing or broadcasting something that leads to him being convicted for contempt of court, it is unlikely that this conviction will result in his career being ruined. It might well make someone's reputation.

---

21   See D.H. Brown, *The Genesis of the Criminal Code of 1892* (Toronto: University of Toronto Press, 1989).

22   The Ontario Court of Appeal has held that the existing law of contempt of court meets the standards required by the *Charter*. See *R. v. Cohn* (1984), 48 O.R. (2d) 65 (C.A.).

1) Defining Contempt

Turning to the substance of the matter, the first question to ask and to which we cannot find an answer in the *Criminal Code* is, What is contempt of court? If someone asks what is theft, a lawyer can point to the sections in the *Criminal Code* which define it. But not with contempt of court. So what, in a general sense, is involved? Useful guidance can be found in a 1979 decision of the UK House of Lords, *A.G.* v. *Leveller Magazines Ltd.*[23] This case, as is true of a fair amount of English media law, emerged from one of the periodic spy scandals that are such an entertaining feature of English life. There had been a prosecution under the *Official Secrets Act* during which the judicial officer presiding had to deal with two witnesses who were serving officers in the British Army and who did not want their identities made public. The judicial officer directed that in the course of these proceedings the one officer was to be referred to as Colonel A and the other as Colonel B. However, while giving evidence, Colonel B revealed two facts. First, he gave the name of the army unit to which he belonged and, second, he mentioned that information about his posting to that unit was to be found in a particular issue of an army publication. A reporter did not have to be an investigative genius to figure out that all he had to do was get that issue, look up information about the posting to the unit named of a colonel, and he would have Colonel B's real name. A number of publications did so and published the name. The judge presiding at the original proceeding was mightily offended by this outcome. Contempt of court proceedings were instituted. The question that the House of Lords had to address was whether the publication of Colonel B's identity amounted to a contempt of court. The order made by the judicial officer at the trial was to the effect that *during the course of the proceeding* this person should be referred to as Colonel B. The judge's ego was bruised, the judge's feelings were hurt, the judge was angry, but was this a contempt of court?

The House of Lords said that criminal contempts of court share a common characteristic. They all involve interference with the due administration of justice. The reason the offence exists, the House of Lords emphasized, is to provide a legal mechanism to prevent interference with the administration of justice. Thus, contempt addresses behaviour, actions, and, more to the point, publications that interfere with, or create a real risk of interfering with, the due administration of justice.

What is meant by interference? It is something that will frustrate the operation of the courts, something that will make it impossible, either

---

23   [1979] A.C. 440 (H.L.).

generally or in a particular case, for the judicial system to operate the way it is supposed to. Contempt is not, then, a matter of the egos or the whims of judges. Its purpose is to ensure that the judicial system operates the way it was intended. Thus, it is only when behaviour amounts to an interference with the due administration of justice that it becomes a contempt of court.

Contempt of court has to be balanced with the openness principle. Justice and the due administration of justice both require that the courts operate in public. As a result, fair and accurate reports of what happens in the courtroom are an integral part of the due administration of justice. Contempt of court deals with other kinds of behaviour, acts that interfere with, rather than complement, the due administration of justice.

Figure 2 sketches out a general structure for understanding contempt of court. It is an attempt to give some order and coherence to the law. From the outset, a distinction is made between two broad categories of criminal contempt. The distinction is expressed in Latin: there are contempts that are committed *ex facie* — outside the courtroom; and there are contempts that are committed *in facie* — inside the courtroom.

Figure 2   The Law of Contempt of Court

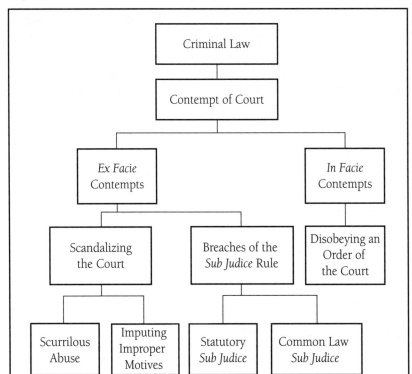

2) *Ex Facie* Contempts

We will focus on two forms of *ex facie* contempt: on scandalizing the court and on breaches of the *sub judice* rule.

a) Scandalizing the Court

Scandalizing the court is a long-winded way of describing contempts committed through saying nasty things in public about judges. This is odd. If you say mean, hurtful, horrible things about me in public, I may well be able to sue you civilly for libel, but that is a matter between you and me. But judges, and only judges, have enjoyed this special protection that, under certain circumstances, it can be a crime to be publicly critical of them. Scandalizing the court derives, as does our entire law of contempt, from English law. There have, over the last few decades, been prosecutions in England for scandalizing the court, but no one has been convicted since 1930. In Canada there were convictions until well into the 1980s.

i) *Scurrilous Abuse*

There are said to be two subbranches of scandalizing the court. The first subbranch is described as directing scurrilous abuse at a judge. It is difficult to define what is meant by scurrilous abuse, but some examples can be found in Canadian cases: describing a judge and a jury at a murder trial as themselves murderers and adding that the judge was a torturer;[24] saying that a judicial decision was silly and could not have been made by a sane judge;[25] saying that a court was a mockery of justice;[26] writing of a particular trial that the "whole thing stinks from the word go";[27] accusing a court of intimidation and "iron curtain" tactics;[28] and, finally, saying of a particular magistrate, "If that bastard hears the case I will see to it that he is defrocked and debarred."[29] So, what exactly is scurrilous abuse? It is using language about a judge or the judiciary which is vulgar, abusive, and threatening. In the 1980s a court in New Brunswick said that any criticism that was "ungentlemanly" amounted to scandalizing the court.[30]

---

24   R. v. *Vancouver (City)*, [1954] 3 D.L.R. 690 (B.C.S.C.).

25   *Re Ouellet (Nos. 1 & 2)* (1976), 72 D.L.R. (3d) 95 (Que. C.A.).

26   R. v. *Murphy* (1969), 1 N.B.R. (2d) 297 (C.A.).

27   *Re Landers* (1980), 31 N.B.R. (2d) 113 at 115 (Q.B.).

28   R. v. *Western Printing & Publishing Ltd.* (1954), 111 C.C.C. 122 at 123 (Nfld. T.D.).

29   *Anger v. Borowski*, [1971] 3 W.W.R. 434 at 437 (Man. Q.B.).

30   *Re Landers, supra* note 27 at 116.

ii) Imputing Improper Motives

The other branch of scandalizing the court, which is called imputing improper motives, is easier to define. Imputing improper motives means alleging that a judge takes bribes. It embraces any allegation that a judge is biased, that a judge is partial.[31] The astonishing thing about the law of scandalizing the court as it was applied in Canada is that the truth was no defence. Even if you had a videotape of an intimidating looking individual dressed in a pinstriped suit handing over an attaché case full of money to a judge, you could not introduce that in your defence. The offence consisted solely in saying publicly that the judge took bribes. The truth or falsity of that statement was irrelevant.

The most famous Canadian case involving scandalizing the court was a 1954 prosecution from British Columbia, *R. v. Vancouver (City).*[32] Eric Nicol was a well-known journalist who wrote for the Vancouver *Province*. The story in question involved a particularly tragic murder prosecution. The accused was a young man called William Gash. He was nineteen years old, married, and had one child. He and his wife and child were living with his parents because he was out of work. In order to get money, Gash was persuaded to take part in the robbery of a shop. In the course of the robbery the proprietor of the shop was murdered. Gash was charged with murder and convicted. At that time, a trial judge had no discretion as to sentence when someone was convicted of murder. The judge was obliged to sentence the convicted person to death. Gash was sentenced to death by hanging.

Nicol's story was an allegorical fantasy. In it, Nicol had died and now stood before the eternal judgment seat, accounting for his life on earth. William Gash had been hanged, and Nicol was accused of murder. Because Nicol was a Canadian citizen and Gash had been put to death by the Canadian state, Nicol was responsible for Gash's death. Nicol attempted to defend himself in the following words: "Although I did not myself spring the trap that caused my victim to be strangled in cold blood, I admit that the man who put the rope around his neck was in my employ. Also serving me were the 12 people who planned the murder, and the judge who chose the time and place and caused the victim to suffer the exquisite torture of anticipation." Thus, he described the members of the jury and the judge as murderers, and added that the judge was a torturer.

It is important to grasp that these assertions about the judge and the members of the jury amounted to civil defamation. A number of mem-

---

31   *Re Duncan*, [1958] S.C.R. 41.
32   *Supra* note 24.

bers of the jury did sue Nicol and the *Province* civilly for libel and won.[33] But the issue before the court in this case was whether, in addition, Nicol's comments amounted to a crime. The BC Supreme Court held that it was necessary, in order to ensure the due administration of justice, to punish people who made assertions like this about the courts and the process of the courts. The judge said:

> No wrong is committed by anyone who criticises the Courts or a Judge in good faith, but it is of vital importance to the public that the authority and dignity of the Courts should be maintained. . . . To refer to the jurors in this case as criminals and to describe the Judge as causing exquisite torture is calculated to lower the dignity of the Court and destroy public confidence in the administration of justice.

Nicol and the *Province* were convicted. Nicol was fined $250, and the paper $2500.

The most significant recent prosecution for scandalizing the court is the case of *R. v. Kopyto*.[34] Harry Kopyto used to be a lawyer in Toronto. In this instance he had been representing a person named Ross Dowson. In the 1960s and 1970s Dowson had been involved with the League for Socialist Action, a Trotskyite group in Toronto. Dowson claimed to be the object of the RCMP dirty tricks, and, in the 1970s, he began an attempt to gain legal redress against the police. He tried civil actions, private prosecutions, and a variety of legal remedies. They all failed. His last attempt ran out in December 1985 and there were no further legal avenues open to him. As Dowson's lawyer, Kopyto made a public statement about this last proceeding which was subsequently reported in the *Globe and Mail*. He said:

> This decision is a mockery of justice. It stinks to high hell. It says it is okay to break the law and you are immune so long as someone above you said to do it. Mr. Dowson and I have lost faith in the judicial system to render justice. We're wondering what is the point of appealing and continuing this charade of the courts in this country which are warped in favour of protecting the police. The courts and the RCMP are sticking so close together you'd think they were put together with Krazy Glue.

Kopyto was convicted of scandalizing the court. The *Globe and Mail* might well also have been convicted for publishing Kopyto's remarks,

---

33   *MacKay v. Southam Co.* (1955), 1 D.L.R. (2d) 1 (B.C.C.A.).
34   (1987), 62 O.R. (2d) 449 (C.A.).

but no proceeding was instituted against it. Kopyto appealed to the Ontario Court of Appeal. The court had no doubt that under the existing law of scandalizing the court, Kopyto had committed the offence. But the crucial issue before it was whether the existing offence of scandalizing was a justifiable limit on the freedom of expression guaranteed in the *Charter*. The court held that comment by citizens about the courts must come within the protection of section 2(b) of the *Charter*.

> As a result of their importance the courts are bound to be the subject of comment and criticism. Not all will be sweetly reasoned. An unsuccessful litigant may well make comments after the decision is rendered that are not felicitously worded. Some criticism may be well founded, some suggestions for change worth adopting. But the courts are not fragile flowers that will wither in the hot heat of controversy.

This approach is similar to the attitude the English courts have adopted towards scandalizing the court for the last thirty years. In one English prosecution where the accused was acquitted, the judge said, "[I]f a judge is going to be affected by what is written or said, he is not fit to be a judge."[35] The majority in the Court of Appeal took the view that the existing offence of scandalizing the court limited freedom of expression and that, further, this was a limit which could not be justified in a free and democratic society. In its view, the existing offence of scandalizing was too broad and infringed freedom of expression far more than was necessary to protect the administration of justice.

Five judges heard the *Kopyto* appeal. Three of them decided that the offence of scandalizing the court could not be justified in a free and democratic society, and two decided that it could. The decision, strictly speaking, is only a precedent in Ontario. But since this decision was released in 1988 and since there do not appear to have been any further prosecutions in Canada, I think that we can take it that scandalizing the court is effectively dead in Canada. Its burial was long overdue. Judges have always had exactly the same right as anybody else to sue civilly for defamation. The additional protection of the criminal law was unnecessary.

b) Breaching the *Sub Judice* Rule

We will now look at another kind of *ex facie* contempt, one that involves breaches of the *sub judice* rule. The *sub judice* rule is that branch of the law of contempt of court which does not seek to *prohibit* the publication of information, but merely to *delay* its publication until such time as

---

35   See U.K., *Report of the Committee on Contempt of Court*, 1974, Cmnd. 5794 at 98.

there is no longer a risk of prejudicing the outcome of proceedings before the courts. The implicit major premise underlying the *sub judice* rule is that there is certain information which, if published while judicial proceedings are pending or actually before a court, could have the effect of prejudicing the outcome of those proceedings. It is useful to subject some of the elements of and some of the assumptions underlying the *sub judice* rule to analysis.

First, while a lawyer would describe the *sub judice* rule as delaying, rather than prohibiting, the publication of information, that distinction is substantially less meaningful to a journalist. The newsworthiness of information is very often a function of its timeliness, and to delay the publication of information can often amount in practice to prohibiting its publication.

The purpose of the *sub judice* rule, as with the law of contempt of court generally, is to protect the integrity of the judicial process. Freedom of expression is, as a general principle, to be respected, but the *sub judice* rule limits that freedom whenever a real risk of prejudice to the administration of justice arises.

But what effect does the *sub judice* rule actually have on the media? The following is a completely fictional story written a number of years ago by an English journalist. The point of the story is to show how the *sub judice* rule distorts reporting. The *sub judice* rule is much stricter in England, but the story gives a clear idea of the flavour of these things and how the *sub judice* rule often operates to distort news stories.

> Stout balding Mr John Jones, cashier to a firm of textile converters, was missing yesterday from his home in Cemetery Avenue, Openshaw.
>
> Round the corner in Funeral Street, Mr Henry Brown said he had not seen his blonde attractive wife Mamie since the week-end.
>
> A director of the firm which employs Mr Jones said yesterday that the firm's books would have been due for audit next week. Mr Jones was also treasurer of the local Working Men's Holiday Fund.
>
> Neighbours described Mrs Brown as a gay girl. It is understood that she and Mr Jones were close friends.
>
> At a flat in Southpool, stout balding Mr Arthur Smith said he had never heard of Mr Jones of Openshaw. Blonde attractive Mrs Dolly Smith said she had never been known as Mamie Brown. Early yesterday police were seeking to interview a stout, bald-headed man whom they believed could be of assistance to them in their inquiries into a case of fraudulent conversion.

A man accompanied police to Southpool police station. Blows were exchanged in Southpool's High Street after a man ran at high speed along the street. Police ran at high speed along the street after a man. Later a man was detained. A man will appear in court today.[36]

That example is much exaggerated, but it is designed to highlight some of the effects of the *sub judice* rule. In England the press still does not actually report that somebody has been arrested. Someone is simply said to be "assisting police with their inquiries." Everyone, of course, knows exactly what that means, but it is done to avoid publishing anything that might, even conceivably, create a risk of prejudicing subsequent proceedings.

The difficulty with the *sub judice* rule, as is the case with much of the law of contempt of court, is that there is little empirical foundation for it. There is no factual basis for saying that certain information, or indeed any information, will actually prejudice the outcome of proceedings. It is difficult to imagine how anyone would test such a thing. In this context it is useful to quote two statements made by Canadian judges about two highly publicized judicial proceedings.

The first was the *Keegstra* trial. The James Keegstra affair received an enormous amount of publicity, especially in Alberta. One of the things Keegstra's lawyer argued before the courts was that the whole proceedings should be adjourned *sine die* — that is, indefinitely. He argued there had been so much publicity that it would be impossible for James Keegstra to receive a fair trial anywhere in Alberta. The trial judge said:

> You know, I do not buy that argument. I do not buy the argument that people in high places, or the newspapers or television necessarily have the influence you readily give them. As a matter of fact, you know, there is another school of thought that they used to teach us when I was younger, that you only believed about ten percent of what you read.[37]

Implicit in the *sub judice* rule are the assumptions, first, that people believe everything they see on television or hear on the radio or read in the newspapers and, second, that they are going to be influenced by what they see or hear or read. I suspect that jurors are far more capable of putting extraneous influences out of their minds than the Canadian legal system has often given them credit for.

---

36   J. Townsend, quoted in Australia, Law Reform Commission, *Reform of Contempt Law* (Issues Paper No. 4) (Sydney: The Commission, 1984) at 14–15.

37   Transcript of unreported pre-trial hearing (*R. v. Keegstra*) (10 October 1994), (Alta. Q.B.).

The second example has to do with a murder prosecution in Winnipeg in the 1980s. Somebody came into a small shop on the outskirts of the city and murdered the person working there. It was a particularly nasty murder and there was a tremendous public clamour to arrest someone and put that individual on trial. A young man called Sophonow was arrested and charged with the murder. He went on trial, and everything that happened at this trial was reported in great detail. At the end of the trial Sophonow was convicted of murder. He appealed to the Manitoba Court of Appeal. The Manitoba Court of Appeal ordered a new trial. The second trial was reported as extensively as the first and, at the end of this trial, Sophonow was again convicted of murder. He appealed again to the Manitoba Court of Appeal and that court ordered a new trial, a third trial. By this time there could not have been a man, woman, or child in the province of Manitoba who was not intimately familiar with every detail of the whole business. Nonetheless, a jury was assembled for the third trial. This time, Sophonow was acquitted. The Crown appealed to the Manitoba Court of Appeal, but the court decided enough was enough. Before the second trial was to take place, an application had been made for an indefinite adjournment on the ground that there had been so much publicity, so much reporting about the first trial, that it would be impossible to assemble an unbiased jury for the second trial. The Chief Justice of Manitoba said in response to this argument:

> The mere fact that a previous trial . . . has been reported at length in the media should not ordinarily provide a case of probable bias or prejudice on the part of the jurors at the second trial for the same offence. It is most unfair to prospective jurors and contrary to the jury system to assume that since these prospective jurors may have some prior knowledge of the case by virtue of the media they are probably biased or prejudiced.[38]

The interesting thing about that statement, if it is accurate, is that it undercuts much of the basis for the *sub judice* rule. The rule, as we have noted, is based on the assumption that certain kinds of information can have the effect of prejudicing the minds of potential jurors and, more generally, prejudicing the entire community. The Chief Justice seemed to dismiss those possibilities.

---

38   The Chief Justice was in dissent. See *R. v. Sophonow* (1984), 11 D.L.R. (4th) 24 at 56 (Man. C.A.). As an example of a case where it was held that publicity had destroyed the possibility of a fair trial, see *R. v. Vermette*, [1988] 1 S.C.R. 985.

We will now look in detail at the *sub judice* rule under two headings. We will look, first, at statutory examples and then at the common law of *sub judice*. While, as has been noted, the major parts of the law of contempt of court remain uncodified, some elements have been put in statutory form.

i) *Statutory* Sub Judice

a. Sexual Offences

We begin the discussion of statutory *sub judice* by looking at what the *Criminal Code* says about sexual offences. In 1983 and in 1992, major reforms were made to the *Criminal Code* provisions dealing with sexual offences.[39] The 1983 reforms did a number of things. First, they removed the offence of rape from the *Criminal Code* and substituted for it two new offences — sexual assault and aggravated sexual assault. Strangely, the *Code* did not define sexual assault. One objective of the reforms was to abandon certain limitations found in the offence of rape — in particular, that rape could only be committed by a man against a woman, that a husband could not rape his wife, and that nothing short of non-consensual intercourse could constitute the offence. The 1983 amendments made it clear that sexual assault could be committed by a person of either sex against a person of either sex, that a husband could sexually assault his wife, and that various forms of conduct short of intercourse might constitute the offence. The details were left to be worked out by the courts, which have broadly defined sexual assault as any assault of a sexual nature.

Second, procedural changes were also made to provisions dealing with sexual offences in 1983. These changes were designed to address what was seen to be a major problem in the application of the law dealing with sexual offences: underreporting by victims. Sexual offences were thought to be occurring in greater numbers than were actually being reported to the police. The 1983 reforms aimed to remove two legal obstacles to the reporting of sexual assaults by victims.

In the first place, since the trial of a sexual offence took place in open court, the name of the victim could be published in the mass media. One of the factors that was identified as inhibiting the reporting of sexual assaults was the knowledge on the part of the victim that her name could be made public. It was believed that limiting the ability of

---

39   For general background, see (1993) 42 U.N.B.L.J., and J.V. Roberts & R.M. Mohr, eds. *Confronting Sexual Assualt: A Decade of Legal and Social Change* (Toronto: University of Toronto Press, 1994).

the media to report the identity of the victim would remove one legal obstacle to the reporting of the offence.

The second obstacle had to do with the nature of rape trials. It was perceived that they often turned into a trial of the woman who was the victim rather than of the man who was the accused. How did this happen? In most sexual offence proceedings the key witness for the Crown is the victim herself. She clearly has the most substantial, most direct, evidence concerning the commission of the offence. Prior to 1983, and consistent with the general procedure in all criminal prosecutions, counsel for the accused was free to fully cross-examine all the Crown's witnesses. One of the matters with respect to which the accused's counsel could cross-examine the victim in a rape prosecution was her previous sexual history. At the time, the law was based on the view that previous sexual history went to the credibility of the victim as a witness. The implicit assumption was that the more sexual experience a women had had throughout her life, the less likely it was that she would tell the truth. That assumption was both sexist and illogical. More to the point, there was an apprehension that a woman who reported a rape could be subjected to a humiliating and, of course, public cross-examination. There was a general sense that many victims of sexual assaults were not reporting them in order to avoid this experience. As a result, the second procedural element in the 1983 reforms substantially limited the ability of the accused to cross-examine the victim about her previous sexual history.

Turning to the specifics of the law, we begin with the question of identifying the victim. The relevant provision is section 486(3) of the *Criminal Code*. It provides that where the accused is charged with a sexual offence — sexual assault, aggravated sexual assault, and some other offences — the presiding judge has the authority to make an order banning publication of the identity of the complainant, the victim. The subsection says that if either the Crown or, more important, the victim applies for the banning order, the trial judge *must* make it. The judge has no discretion. Alternatively, if neither the Crown nor the victim applies for an order, the trial judge *may* make such an order on his own initiative. Section 486(3) achieves one of the important aims of the 1983 reforms, which was to give to the victim herself the power to determine whether her identity will be made public.

If an order is made, it does not simply prohibit the publication of the name of the victim. It is an order, to use the words of the *Criminal Code*, banning the publication of any information that could disclose the identity of the complainant. This can mean serious constraints on reporting about sexual offences. Take one example that has actually arisen on a number of occasions. As has been noted, by definition, a husband could not rape his wife, but it is now legally possible for a husband to sexually assault his wife. Thus, in a case where a husband was charged with sexually assaulting his wife, a publication ban would make it impossible to name the accused. In the circumstances of such a case, the accused's name would clearly be information that could disclose the identity of the complainant. The same would also likely be true if the accused happened to be a relative of the victim, especially if they had the same surname.

What makes this provision problematic is that it does not simply prohibit the publication of any information that *does* disclose the identity of the complainant, but any information that *could* disclose her identity. This means that, in difficult cases, reporters and editors would have to consider such factors as the precise relationship between the complainant and the accused, any institutional connection between them, the size of the community in question, and the particular details of the offence.

The *Criminal Code* does not contain a specific offence of breaching an order made under section 486(3). Any breach would, then, be dealt with as a contempt of court. There have, in fact, been few prosecutions for breaches of this provision. One reason is that the very existence of the section has occasioned considerable caution on the part of reporters and editors. Another is that there has been a general reluctance, except in the most blatant of cases, to prosecute. If it were to be clear from a story that the reporter was simply trying to provide as much information about the accused as possible without actually identifying the victim, then I think it is unlikely there would be a prosecution.

R.(L.) v. *Nyp*[40] is one of the few reported examples of a breach of such an order. An undercover police officer was sexually assaulted. A ban under section 486(3) was made on 12 May 1992 at the trial of her assailant. Despite this ban, the Kitchener-Waterloo *Record* three days later published an article that described the assault and identified the police officer by name. The reporter who wrote the article had been present in court when the publication ban was made by the trial judge. The reporter, Gary Nyp, was brought before the same judge in a contempt proceeding. He was acquitted on the ground that the breach of the publication ban was "inadvertent." Subsequently, however, the police officer sued Nyp and the owner of the *Record*, Southam Inc., civilly for negligence. The court held that the conduct of the reporter in publishing the plaintiff's name had not met the standard expected of a "reasonably prudent reporter." The court awarded general damages of $12,000 each against Nyp and Southam. A further $5000 in punitive

---

40   (1995), 25 C.C.L.T. (2d) 309 (Ont. Gen. Div.).

damages was awarded against Southam for "contemptuous disregard of the plaintiff's rights."

The banning order does not operate retrospectively. It acquires legal force only from the moment that it is made. If no publication ban is made, however, there is no legal obstacle to the identification of the victim.

In 1988 the Thomson chain challenged what is now section 486(3) of the *Criminal Code* as an infringement of the *Charter* guarantee of freedom of expression.[41] Clearly, it is a limit. If the state says you cannot report certain information about a judicial proceeding, the state has beyond doubt limited freedom of expression. But is this a limit that can be justified in a free and democratic society? What was the state's objective? The Supreme Court said it was to encourage the reporting of sexual assaults. Was that objective pressing and substantial? Did it seek to uphold social values of superordinate importance? Beyond any doubt, said the Court. Was there a rational connection between limiting publication of the identity of the victim and encouraging the reporting of sexual assaults? Yes, said the Court. The real problem before the Court was the issue of minimal impairment. The argument was made that the minimal impairment standard required that some degree of discretion be retained in the trial judge to decide in the context of each case whether or not to impose a ban. The Court disagreed and said that under the special circumstances of sexual assault the total absence of discretion in the trial judge was justifiable. Section 486(3) was upheld in its entirety.

While we are dealing with section 486, mention should also be made of subsection (1). It gives the judge presiding at a sexual offence trial a broad authority to "exclude all or any members of the public from the courtroom for all or part of the proceedings" when he is of the opinion that it is in the interest of "public morals, the maintenance of order or the proper administration of justice" to do so. This provision is clearly a substantial limitation on the openness principle and on freedom of expression. Nonetheless, the Supreme Court of Canada held in 1996 that it is constitutional.[42] The Court has not yet released its reasons, but since it upheld a decision by the New Brunswick Court of Appeal, some instruction can be gained from the judgments of that court. The sexual assaults in this case involved young female victims. The court concluded that the need to protect these victims was sufficient to justify the limit on freedom of expression. This reasoning

41   *Canadian Newspapers Co. v. Canada (A.G.)*, [1988] 2 S.C.R. 122.
42   *Canadian Broadcasting Corp. v. New Brunswick (A.G.)* (1996), (S.C.C.) [reasons not yet released]. The decision of the New Brunswick Court of Appeal is reported at (1994), 148 N.B.R. (2d) 161 (C.A.).

appears to miss the point. The issue is not whether the particular way the trial judge exercised the discretion created by section 486(1) can be justified, but whether section 486(1) itself can be justified.

Turning to the second procedural element of the 1983 reforms, not only were limits placed on the ability of the accused to cross-examine the victim about her previous sexual history but the freedom of the mass media to report on such matters was also limited. Before addressing these matters in detail, it must be noted that further changes were made in the *Criminal Code* provisions dealing with sexual assault in 1992.

There was concern that the 1983 reforms were a substantial interference with the right of accused persons to defend themselves fully. This issue went before the Supreme Court in 1991 in a case called *R. v. Seaboyer*.[43] Seaboyer argued that his *Charter* right to a fair trial had been infringed because he was limited in his ability to cross-examine the complainant. The Court accepted his argument and struck down the existing provisions in the *Criminal Code*. So from 1991 to 1992 there was a hiatus where there were no statutory rules on the question. Then in 1992 further amendments to the *Criminal Code* created a new set of limitations — sections 276.1 to 276.4 — on the ability of accused persons to cross-examine victims about previous sexual history.[44] What does the *Criminal Code* now say about reporting on such matters?

The *Code* sets out a procedure that the accused must follow before he will be permitted to exercise his still limited right to cross-examine the victim about her previous sexual history. He must make an application in writing to the trial judge to be allowed to do so. The application must set out the purpose of the proposed cross-examination and its relevance to whatever defence is being raised. The judge will then hold a hearing in his chambers. The judge, the prosecutor, and counsel for the accused will be present at this hearing. The judge will decide whether to permit the limited cross-examination. If the judge decides to allow it, the cross-examination takes place in open court and can be fully reported, subject, of course, to any ban that may have been made on disclosing the identity of the complainant. The other possibility is that the judge will refuse to allow the cross-examination. If this happens, the *Criminal Code* prohibits any reporting whatsoever about the whole business. It may not be reported that the accused applied to be allowed to cross-examine the victim. No one may report any of the evidence or arguments that the accused presented, nor that there was a hearing in

---

43   [1991] 2 S.C.R. 577.
44   *An Act to amend the Criminal Code (sexual assault)*, S.C. 1992, c. 38, amending R.S.C. 1985, c. 46.

the judge's chambers, nor anything that may have happened at that hearing. If the judge says there is to be no cross-examination of the victim about her previous sexual history, then not a word can be published about the whole matter.

As a final point, a provision of this nature is often referred to journalistically as a "rape shield law." This phrase suggests that it is a law that exists to shield rapists. The phrase is misleading and should be abandoned.

b. Young Offenders

The Canadian legal system, like all legal systems, recognizes that below a certain age persons should not be held criminally responsible for their acts. There is room for debate in any society as to what that precise age should be. In our system it is twelve. We make a basic distinction between persons over twelve and persons under twelve. Persons over twelve are criminally responsible, persons under twelve are not. Having made that distinction, we go on to make a further distinction. We have created two subclasses of persons who are criminally responsible for their acts. One is persons between twelve and eighteen, and the other is persons over eighteen. Persons over eighteen are regarded as fully responsible for their acts and are dealt with through the normal court system. Persons between twelve and eighteen stand in a grey area. They are criminally responsible for their acts, but not as responsible as persons over eighteen. Thus, as a general principle, persons between twelve and eighteen are dealt with in different courts and according to different rules from persons over eighteen. These matters are the subject of a much-criticized federal statute called the *Young Offenders Act*.[45]

The important parts of the *Young Offenders Act* for reporting purposes are sections 38 and 39. The Act states that these sections deal with the protection of privacy of young persons. Section 38 sets out a prohibition on the publication of certain information. Before looking at this prohibition in detail, it is important to understand a distinction between section 38 of the *Young Offenders Act* and section 486(3) of the *Criminal Code*, the section dealing with the publication of the identity of victims of sexual assaults. Section 486(3) gives a judge the authority to make an order banning the publication of certain information. That is not the case with section 38 of the *Young Offenders Act*. Under the *Young Offenders Act*, a judge does not have to do anything. The publication ban is imposed directly by the statute itself.

---

45   *YOA, supra* note 5.

Section 38 prohibits the publication of any report in which there is any information serving to identify a young offender — the person who is charged with an offence. But the section goes further and prohibits the publication of any information that would serve to identify a young *victim* or a young *witness*. Much like section 486(3) of the *Criminal Code*, the prohibition is not just on naming but on identifying. The section itself provides that it is an offence to breach the prohibition it imposes.

The *Juvenile Delinquents Act*, the predecessor to the *Young Offenders Act*, contained a similar prohibition against identifying the juvenile delinquent, but the *Young Offenders Act* added two further classes of persons who may not be identified. If it is considered legitimate to take special steps to protect the identity or the privacy of young offenders, what is the justification for creating similar protection with respect to young victims or even young witnesses? If a young person — a person under eighteen — is the victim of an offence committed by an adult, there is no special protection for that individual's identity, nor is there any special protection for the identity of any young person who appears as a witness before an adult court.

Section 39 is a further and substantial compromise on the principle of the openness of the courts. Section 39 gives a judge hearing a young offender proceeding a broad discretion either to close the courtroom or to exclude particular persons from the courtroom. If the trial judge thinks that evidence or information presented would be seriously injurious or seriously prejudicial to the young offender, a young witness, or a young victim, or if it would be in the interest of public morals or the maintenance of order, he may exclude the public generally, or any section of the public, from the proceedings. This seems odd, because in any criminal proceeding most of the evidence presented by the Crown is going to be prejudicial to the accused.

Sections 38 and 39 were the objects of a constitutional challenge by Southam Inc., once again through the Ottawa *Citizen*.[46] In 1984 the Ontario High Court upheld their constitutionality. It must be obvious that both sections limit freedom of expression. The question, therefore, is whether these limits can be justified in a free and democratic society. What was the state's objective in creating them? According to the Court, it was to promote the rehabilitation of young offenders. As the means to achieve that objective, the state chose to protect young offenders from the harmful effects of publicity.

---

46   *Southam Inc. v. R.* (1984), 48 O.R. (2d) 678 (H.C.J.).

This concern raises a problem, however, one that the court did not address. Even if the state's objective and the means it has chosen can be justified — promoting the rehabilitation of young *offenders* by protecting them from the harmful effects of publicity — what have either of these got to do with protecting young *witnesses* and young *victims*? There is no need to rehabilitate, at least in the sense in which the court used the word, a witness or a victim.

There must also be some question about the matter of promoting the rehabilitation of young offenders by protecting them from the harmful effects of publicity. Does society not have an equal interest in promoting the rehabilitation of adult offenders? If the rehabilitation of young offenders is prejudiced by the harmful effects of publicity, why should we not create a similar protection for adult offenders? Are not adult offenders going to be affected by publicity? What is lacking in this judgment is an empirical foundation. The reasons given by the court must stand or fall on a comparison of the recidivism rates for young offenders and the recidivism rates for adult offenders. If it turned out that the recidivism rate for young offenders was substantially lower than that for adult offenders, it could be concluded that the *Young Offenders Act* was indeed working and, presumably, the limits it imposes on expression could be justified in a free and democratic society. But if there was no difference in the two rates, there would be no basis for upholding the Act. Unfortunately, the comprehensive statistics that would make such a comparison possible do not exist.

Section 38 appears to say that the mass media cannot ever publish any information serving to identify the young offender. In its own terms, section 38(1) applies forever. However, once a young offender has passed the age of eighteen and has, in addition, been charged with a subsequent offence that is being heard before an adult court, there is little danger of being prosecuted for breaching section 38 if one were to publish a report about the earlier proceeding under the *Young Offenders Act*.

To avoid any problems, it would be preferable to report that "a person is being prosecuted under the *Young Offenders Act*," rather than "a young offender is being prosecuted." The individual being prosecuted is not, strictly speaking, a young offender until he is convicted.

Amendments were made to the Act in 1986 after tremendous public, and especially police, outcry.[47] Subsections 38(1.1) to (1.4) allow a police officer to apply to a youth court for an order allowing publication

---

47   *An Act to Amend the Young Offenders Act, the Criminal Code, the Penitentiary Act and the Prisons and Reformatories Act*, R.S.C. 1985 (2d Supp.), c. 24, amending R.S.C. 1985, c. Y-1.

of the identity of the young offender, if there is reason to believe that the young person is dangerous to others and that the publication of the report will assist in apprehending him. This publication is to be used solely for police purposes. The order permitting publication is effective for only two days.

c. Preliminary Inquiries

The *Criminal Code* contains two broad categories of offences. They derive from the old distinction in English law between felonies and misdemeanours. Felonies were the more serious offences; misdemeanours were the less serious. The distinction was important, because when English criminal law was at its most barbaric there was only one punishment possible on conviction of a felony and that was death. A felony trial was a serious business and, thus, a special procedure was adopted to precede the trial itself. The point was to determine whether there was sufficient evidence against the person accused of a felony to justify putting him on trial. Even though we no longer have the death penalty, we maintain this distinction between less serious offences and more serious offences, except that we now call the more serious ones "indictable" offences and the less serious ones "summary conviction" offences. In fact, we have three categories of offences. We also have something called "hybrid" offences. These can be either indictable or summary conviction offences.

If someone is charged with a summary conviction offence, that person goes straight to trial. If, however, someone is charged with an indictable offence, there must be a preliminary inquiry before a trial can be held. The purpose of the preliminary inquiry is, once again, not to determine whether this individual is guilty or innocent. It is to determine whether there is sufficient evidence against him to justify holding a trial. A preliminary inquiry is normally conducted by a justice of the peace. For present purposes, the point about a preliminary inquiry is that some of the evidence introduced may never be introduced at the trial or may be held to be inadmissible. Publication of this evidence might prejudice the outcome of the subsequent trial.

The preliminary inquiry takes place in open court. Reporters are entitled to be there and are entitled to take notes. There are, however, certain limitations on what may be published about a preliminary inquiry. Section 539 of the *Criminal Code* provides that prior to the preliminary inquiry actually beginning, the prosecution, or the accused, or any one of the accused if there is more than one, may ask for a publication ban. If the prosecution asks for a ban, the justice *may* make it. If an accused person asks for the ban, the justice *must* make it.

What is the result of an order banning publication? It is that the evidence given at the preliminary inquiry may not be published until such time as it is no longer possible to prejudice the outcome of the subsequent trial. When is that? At the end of a preliminary inquiry there are two possibilities. The justice holding the inquiry may discharge the accused on the ground that there is not sufficient evidence to justify holding a trial. If there is not going to be a trial, clearly its outcome cannot be prejudiced. Thus, if the accused is discharged at the end of the preliminary inquiry, the publication ban is spent. The other alternative is that the justice may commit the accused for trial. If the accused is committed for trial, it is still possible to prejudice the outcome of the trial. When will it no longer be possible to prejudice the outcome of the trial? Obviously, when the trial is completed. At that point, once again, the ban is spent. Whether there is subsequently an appeal is irrelevant.

A number of points about a publication ban made at a preliminary inquiry should be noted. First, it is a ban on publication. It is not a ban on reporters being present in the courtroom, nor is it a ban on their taking notes. There is a significant practical point in this distinction. A number of reporters who have written books about well-publicized criminal trials have used the preliminary inquiry as the basis for their books. They have written the book from their notes taken at the preliminary inquiry and had the manuscript ready in proof form. When the actual trial began, they checked the proofs each day against what happened at the trial. Thus, the instant the trial was completed, the book could be printed. Taking notes at the preliminary inquiry, even though they cannot be published at that time, can also be useful for other reasons, such as checking the evidence that is subsequently given at the trial. To repeat, once the trial is completed, information from the preliminary inquiry may be published.

The application for the publication ban must be made before the taking of evidence at the preliminary inquiry starts. Once the preliminary inquiry is under way the opportunity to apply for the ban has passed. If the accused is not represented by counsel, the presiding justice must inform the accused of his right to apply for a publication ban. Nonetheless, if the commencement of the inquiry passes without an application being made for a ban, it is too late. Here again is a contrast with section 486(3) of the *Criminal Code*, the section that deals with an order banning publication of the identity of the victim in a sexual offence proceeding. An application under section 486(3) can be made at any time during the proceeding.

Section 539(3) makes it an offence to fail to comply with a publication ban. A reporter covering a preliminary inquiry should assume, until the contrary is established beyond any doubt, that the publication ban has been made. There is no rule in the *Criminal Code* about the form of a publication ban and it is sufficient for the justice to say, "I hereby order that none of the evidence to be given at this preliminary inquiry shall be published." The onus is on a reporter to find out whether a ban has been made.

The constitutionality of publication bans at preliminary inquiries has been challenged. Such a ban is obviously a limit on freedom of expression, so is it a limit that can be justified in a free and democratic society? What is the state's objective? It is, obviously, to ensure that the accused receives a fair trial, something that is, itself, guaranteed in section 11 of the *Charter*. The only decision on this ban is from the New Brunswick Court of Queen's Bench in 1983.[48] The court upheld the constitutionality of section 539 of the *Criminal Code*. The basis for its decision was the traditional Canadian approach that whenever there is an apparent conflict between an accused person's right to a fair trial and freedom of expression, freedom of expression must give way and the accused's right to a fair trial must take precedence. That used to be the approach, but, in *Dagenais v. Canadian Broadcasting Corp.* in 1994,[49] the Supreme Court that it would not continue to follow this approach. The Court said that judges should attempt to "balance" the right to a fair trial and free expression, with neither taking precedence over the other. One of the results of the *Dagenais* decision is that the constitutionality of section 539 of the *Criminal Code* must now be open to doubt.

Whether a publication ban is made or not, section 552 of the *Criminal Code* creates an absolute prohibition against publishing anything about the fact that the prosecution may have sought to have a confession entered into evidence during a preliminary inquiry. The obvious point of this rule is that information that the accused may have confessed is, in and of itself, highly prejudicial. Further, even if the preliminary inquiry accepts the admissibility of a confession, it is perfectly conceivable that the trial court will not. This is an absolute statutory ban and it operates regardless of whether a publication ban has been made under section 539. Once again, this prohibition lapses at the point at which it is no longer possible to prejudice the outcome of the trial — either when the accused is discharged or, if the accused is committed for trial, when the trial is completed.

---

48   *R. v. Banville* (1983), 45 N.B.R. (2d) 134 (Q.B.)
49   *Supra* note 10.

d. Bail Hearings

Under the *Criminal Code* and under section 11 of the *Charter*, a person who is simply charged with an offence is an innocent person, a constitutionally innocent person. Such a person has a basic right to liberty — to move about freely, undisturbed by the state. There is no constitutional or theoretical problem with locking up someone who has actually been convicted of a crime by a court. But it is difficult in principle to justify locking up a constitutionally innocent person. Our criminal law recognizes that a person accused of a crime should *prima facie* be at liberty until such time as he may be convicted. However, the *Criminal Code* also recognizes that there can be exceptional circumstances where an accused person should, nonetheless, be held in custody until his trial. In order to allow these issues to be addressed, section 515 of the *Criminal Code* makes provision for bail hearings to be held before a justice of the peace. At this hearing the Crown will argue in favour of having the accused remanded in custody. Section 515 sets out a *primary* and a *secondary* ground on which the justice's decision to do so may be based. The primary ground is that the detention of this accused is necessary in order to ensure his attendance at his trial. Clearly the state has an overriding interest in ensuring that someone accused of a crime does show up for his trial. The secondary ground set out is that the detention of this accused is necessary for the protection or safety of the public. The section also allowed for detention that was necessary in "the public interest," but in 1992 the Supreme Court found that this phrase was a vague and, therefore, unjustifiable limit on the freedom of the individual.[50]

The point is that a bail hearing is held for the sole reason of determining whether an exception should be made in a particular case and a still innocent person locked up. The eventual question of guilt or innocence is not in issue at a bail hearing. It must be obvious that the Crown, in order to persuade the justice conducting the bail hearing to remand someone in custody, may introduce all sorts of highly prejudicial information. The accused's previous record and the accused's propensity to violence are among the sorts of things that might be introduced. They are probably not relevant to the question of guilt or innocence and would likely be inadmissible at the trial.

Section 517 allows a publication ban to be made at a bail hearing. The specific rules are very similar to those concerning a preliminary inquiry. If the Crown asks for a publication ban, the justice *may* make it; if the accused asks for a publication ban, the justice *must* make it. The

---

50   *R. v. Morales*, [1992] 3 S.C.R. 711.

application for a ban, in contrast to the rule about preliminary inquiries, can be made at any time during the bail hearing. If the ban is made, there is a complete prohibition on publishing any information or any evidence presented at a bail hearing. Not even the reasons given by the justice for his decision may be published. Nonetheless, the bail hearing takes place in open court, so reporters can be there and take notes, but nothing can be published while the ban remains in effect. As with the ban issued at a preliminary inquiry, the bail hearing ban stays in operation until it is no longer possible to prejudice the outcome of a subsequent trial. If the accused is charged with an indictable offence and is discharged at the preliminary inquiry, there will be no trial to be prejudiced and the ban is spent. Alternatively, if the accused goes to trial, whether it is a summary conviction offence or an indictable offence, the publication ban is spent at the end of the trial — at the point at which it is no longer possible to prejudice the trial.

Section 517(2) makes it an offence not to comply with an order made under section 517(1). The constitutionality of this section has been challenged on the basis of the *Charter*. Once again, a clear limit on freedom of expression has been created. In 1984 a Canadian woman called Kathy Smith was charged in California with the murder of John Belushi. The United States applied for her extradition to be tried on this charge. She was remanded in custody pending the outcome of the extradition proceedings, and a banning order was made in connection with the bail hearing. The Ontario Court of Appeal held that the state's purpose in limiting expression was to guarantee the accused's right to a fair trial. It further held that whenever there is a conflict between the accused's right to a fair trial and freedom of expression, freedom of expression must give way.[51] This decision was also made before the Supreme Court's decision in *Dagenais*, so there may be doubt today as to the constitutionality of section 517.

e. Jury Trials
A jury can be directed in one of two ways in a criminal trial when it is not actually sitting in the courtroom hearing evidence or deliberating — that is, when the court is not in session. One is that the jury may be given permission to separate: the jurors may go home and live their normal lives and, most important for our purposes, read newspapers, watch television, listen to the radio, and so on. The other is that the jury may be sequestered: members, when they are not sitting in court, are, in

---

51   *Global Communications Ltd.* v. *Canada (A.G.)* (1984), 44 O.R. (2d) 609 (C.A.).

effect, imprisoned in a hotel. The television and the telephone are taken out of their rooms, they cannot get newspapers, and the sheriff provides their food from a local restaurant. This is an unreasonable burden to inflict on citizens who are already undergoing considerable inconvenience in order to perform a public duty. One of the great strengths of the Canadian legal system is that juries are seldom sequestered, something that is common in the United States. This difference is one of the benefits of the more restrictive rules in Canada about reporting judicial proceedings. The more controlled position for juries in the United States results from their laxer reporting rules.

Section 648 of the *Criminal Code* addresses the issue of reporting about things that happen during the course of a criminal trial when the jury is not in the courtroom. A variety of proceedings may go on during a criminal trial which require that the jury be sent out of the courtroom. The most common has to do with the admissibility of a confession. The Crown wants to introduce a confession, ostensibly made by the accused, into evidence. At that point the jury is sent out of the room and a hearing called a *voir dire* is held to determine whether or not the confession was made voluntarily. If the judge decides the confession was made voluntarily, then the confession is admitted. The jury is called back and they get to know about the confession. If the judge decides the confession was not made voluntarily, it is not admissible. The jury is called back and nothing more is said about the confession. The *Criminal Code* provides that if the members of the jury have been sequestered, reporters are free to report about things that happen in the courtroom when they are not there; there is obviously no way jurors are going to find these things out. But if the jury has been given permission to separate, no one may report on anything that happened when jurors were out of the courtroom. Subsection (2) of section 648 makes it an offence to breach this prohibition.

A serious drawback to the Supreme Court's decision in *Dagenais* is that the Chief Justice actually recommended sequestering juries. He said there were many means short of publication bans which could be used to guarantee the fairness of a trial. One of them was sequestering juries. It is not clear on reading the judgment that the Chief Justice understood that sequestration seldom happens in Canada, or, more important, that it would be a major imposition on jurors.

Section 649 makes it an offence for a juror, except in an investigation of possible jury tampering or perjury offences, to disclose to anyone any information about what went on in the jury room. What is interesting about this offence is that it can only be committed by the juror or ex-juror who makes the disclosure. It is not specifically stated that a reporter commits an offence if he asks a juror to tell him what happened in the jury room. While a reporter should not be running a risk by *asking*, he should avoid encouraging, cajoling, or browbeating. Nonetheless, if the juror is foolish enough to tell the reporter, no offence would be committed by publishing that information. However, in the real world no juror is likely to tell a reporter anything, because the last thing judges do with jurors at the end of a trial, before they discharge them, is give them a lecture and put the fear of God into them. They suggest to jurors that if they ever breathe a syllable about anything specific that happened in the jury room, or during any of their deliberations, they could face severe penalties.

It may be possible to ask jurors very general and non-specific questions — about their feelings, for example. "Did you find it difficult? Were there psychological strains?" A juror would probably not be committing an offence by answering questions like that.

ii) *Common Law* Sub Judice

We turn now to the common law of *sub judice*, the undefined, vague, amorphous parts of *sub judice*. The aim is to try to extract from the cases some principles that can be followed or that can operate as guidelines in dealing with these kinds of issues. We begin with a 1973 decision of the English House of Lords in what is undoubtedly the most famous decision on *sub judice*: *A.G.* v. *Times Newspapers Ltd.*[52] We will discuss only the judgments given in the House of Lords. Although that body's decision was overruled by the European Court of Human Rights in 1979, it is the reasoning of the House of Lords which has been consistently cited in Canadian courts. In 1958 a drug called thalidomide was developed and marketed in a number of countries. At the time, thalidomide was prescribed to women in the early stages of pregnancy and was supposed to be effective in controlling some of the difficulties experienced in those months — morning sickness, general debilitation, and so on. The drug was apparently effective at doing this. Unfortunately, it had a tragic, but unexpected, side effect. Many of the children of women who had taken thalidomide were born without limbs. They had hands and feet, but in many cases either their hands or their feet, or in some cases both, were attached directly to their torsos. Thalidomide was immediately withdrawn from circulation. It had been marketed in the United Kingdom by a subsidiary of the Seagram's empire, a corporation called Distillers (Biochemicals) Limited. The families of these children obviously wanted

---

52   [1973] 3 All E.R. 54 (H.L.).

compensation, and sought it from Distillers. As a legal matter, the families of the thalidomide children sued Distillers for negligence.

The litigation, therefore, involved the law of torts — the law of civil wrongs, or non-criminal injuries. In English law each tort has its own special rules and its own special peculiarities. To understand what happened in this case, it is necessary to know something about the tort of negligence. A plaintiff in a negligence action cannot ordinarily ask a court to infer negligence from results. Thus, a woman who had taken thalidomide could not simply point to her armless or legless child and say that the people who marketed this drug must have been negligent. The plaintiff must prove actual negligence on the part of the defendant. In this case, that meant requiring the plaintiff to show that somewhere in the process of research, development, testing, manufacture, and marketing of thalidomide, somewhere in that complicated series of events, there was actual negligence on the part of Distillers. This was the difficulty facing these families in their lawsuits. They had to identify the specific points at which Distillers had been negligent and, further, show that this negligence caused their children's deformities. These difficulties were compounded by the fact that Distillers was a wealthy multinational and could afford the best lawyers available. Although these lawyers did not do anything unlawful or unethical, they certainly raised every possible defence or legal obstacle that Distillers had available in resisting the claims against it. Offers to settle were made to the families, but these offers were generally regarded as inadequate.

We now move forward to 1972. The thalidomide children were not babies any more. Some of them were teenagers, but there was still no compensation from Distillers. The various lawsuits were inching their way along, but little had happened for fourteen years. Along came the *Sunday Times*. It had an Insight Team — a permanent group of investigative reporters who were given the resources and the time to work on complicated and difficult stories. The *Sunday Times* Insight Team was assigned to work on the thalidomide story and the litigation with Distillers.

Two stories were eventually prepared. The first was a history of the litigation between the families of the thalidomide children and Distillers. It talked about the foot dragging that Distillers' lawyers had engaged in and was critical of both Distillers and its lawyers. At the end of the piece, the *Sunday Times* urged Distillers to do the right thing and make a fair, indeed generous, offer of settlement to these families. The first piece was actually published. This story made reference to the second piece, which was to come later and was promised to be a review of the research, development, testing, manufacturing, and marketing of thalidomide. It was going to explain how the whole tragedy happened. That piece had not actually been published when the litigation began.

The response to the publication of the first story was that the attorney general moved to have the *Sunday Times* cited for contempt of court. The attorney general further sought an order prohibiting the publication of the second piece on the ground that its publication would amount to a contempt. The matter eventually ended up before the House of Lords. In its judgment the court dealt with the two articles separately.

With respect to the first piece, the judges said there was no contempt of court in commenting critically, but in fair and temperate language, on the conduct of litigation. It was not contempt to comment critically, nor was it contempt to urge specific courses of action on litigants. The metaphor used was that it would not be a contempt of court to suggest to Shylock that he forgo his pound of flesh.

There is little critical writing in the Canadian media about the way people conduct themselves in litigation and the behaviour of parties and their lawyers. The judgment in the *Sunday Times* case made it clear that as long as the parties to litigation are not subjected to public ridicule or public contempt, there is no contempt.

The second article, however, led to a different result. The court said that what must be avoided in this area of contempt of court was what it described as trial by newspaper. On this basis, the judges concluded that the second piece would amount to a contempt of court and, thus, could not be published. Why? Because, said the House of Lords, the *Sunday Times* had taken it upon itself to resolve precisely the issue that would be before the court when, if ever, this matter actually went to trial. The issue before the court would be, Was Distillers negligent? That was exactly the question the *Sunday Times* addressed in the second article. Whenever the media purport to resolve an issue that will be before the courts, they are acting in breach of the *sub judice* rule. The essence of the breach in this case lay in *prejudging* an issue that would eventually have to be resolved by the courts.

The House of Lords said:

> The law on this subject is and must be founded entirely on public policy. It is not there to protect the private rights of parties to a litigation or prosecution. It is there to prevent interference with the administration of justice and it should in my judgment be limited to what is reasonably necessary for that purpose. Public policy generally requires a balancing of interests which may conflict. Freedom of speech should not be limited to any greater extent than is necessary but it cannot be allowed where there would be real prejudice to the administration of justice.

The court went on, however, to conclude that it would find a breach of the *sub judice* rule only when a particular publication created a real risk of prejudice to the administration of justice, as opposed to a remote possibility. It also held that there must be strong evidence to satisfy a court that a particular publication would indeed create a real risk of prejudice. In the end, the House of Lords upheld an order prohibiting publication of the second article. This has been a much criticized decision, but it is a decision that has been quoted over and over in Canadian courts.

The House of Lords asserted that the *sub judice* rule did not prevent publication, but merely postponed it. The implication was that the second piece could be published sometime in the future after the eventual trial had ended. The interesting result of this litigation and the attention that was focused on it was that the Distillers Corporation made a more generous offer to the families of the thalidomide children and settlements were reached.

Having a general sense of the scope of the *sub judice* rule, we can turn to specific concerns that arise in its application. The first one has to do with prejudicing the outcome of a trial and can be exemplified by the case of one-time corporal Denis Lortie. In 1984 he was a member of the Canadian Armed Forces stationed at Valcartier. He took an automatic weapon to the National Assembly in Quebec City. Once inside the legislative building, he began shooting indiscriminately, killing a number of people and wounding others. Given the place he picked to go on his rampage, not only were there permanent videotaping facilities in the building, but there were many reporters around. The result was that many media agencies had videotape of Lortie firing his weapon — that is to say, actually committing some of these murders. There was much debate as to whether these tapes could be aired. The worry was that airing them might amount to a breach of the *sub judice* rule.

When we reflect concretely on the notion of creating a real risk of prejudice to the outcome of a pending trial, it must mean creating a real risk of prejudicing the resolution of a specific issue that will actually be before the court. Lortie was charged with murder. If we think about his trial, it must be clear what would be in issue and what would not be. It is evident, given the circumstances of this crime, that identity could not be an issue. It was inconceivable that Lortie would go before the court and deny that he committed the killings or attempt to argue that the police had arrested the wrong man. The point here is simple, but requires some judgment. It is not a matter of editors or news directors deciding that nothing can be published about a particular pending trial. It is a matter of familiarizing oneself with the specific circumstances of the trial and attempting to determine, in consultation with lawyers if necessary, what will be the specific issues the trial court is going to have to address and resolve. There should have been no risk in airing those videotapes. It must be clear that sanity, not identity, would have been the only issue before the court. If something is not in issue, then, by definition, the media cannot prejudice its resolution.[53]

The second question about the application of the *sub judice* rule concerns the time at which it begins to operate. There is little in the way of clear direction or guidance that can be given here because of the vagueness and uncertainty of the law. In Ontario a decision in a civil libel action called *Bielek* v. *Ristimaki* points up this uncertainly.[54] (The *sub judice* rule does not apply simply to criminal matters but to civil ones as well.) In this case, both the plaintiff and the defendant were members of the municipal council in Timmins, Ontario, and were involved in a perfectly straightforward civil libel action. One of the documents a plaintiff files with a court in order to commence a civil action is a statement of claim; here he sets out what he is upset about, how the defendant has wronged him, and how much money he wants. The plaintiff in this case had filed a statement of claim asking for half a million dollars in damages. The statement of claim, as a court document, was a public document, and reporters were entitled to look at it and write stories about it. The *Timmins Daily Press*, the local paper, had done a story about this litigation. The newspaper had not only printed what the action was all about, but also how much money the plaintiff was asking for in his statement of claim. The article appeared in the paper and there were no legal problems. Time passed and about a year later the trial was set to begin.

One of the peculiarities of civil libel actions is that they are the last refuge of the civil jury. This was to be a jury trial. The jury had been picked and the trial was set to begin. Because the trial was starting that day, the *Timmins Daily Press* did another story about it and repeated the fact that the plaintiff was asking for half a million dollars. This time the reporter and the paper were brought before the court on contempt citations and convicted.

A year previously the identical information had been published and there was no problem, but to publish it the day the trial began was to commit a contempt of court. But when, exactly, did the *sub judice* rule begin to operate? All the trial judge could say on the issue was, "[I]t's a question of timing." The closer you get to the date of the trial, the greater the risk. The reason the newspaper could publish the amount

---

53   The Quebec Court of Appeal differed with the analysis presented here. See *Lortie* v.
     R., [1985] C.A. 451 (Que.) [hereinafter *Lortie*].

54   (21 June 1979), (Ont. H.C.J.) [unreported]. See S.M. Robertson, *Courts and the Media* (Toronto: Butterworths, 1981) at 287–292.

the plaintiff wanted when the statement of claim was first issued is that at that point no one could be certain there would ever be a trial at all. And even if there was going to be a trial, it would happen at some time in the future. A newspaper or broadcaster can be confident about publishing this information when a statement of claim is first issued, but as the trial draws closer one has to be more cautious.

We must note here a basic practical difference between civil proceedings and criminal proceedings. With civil proceedings, in the majority of cases where a statement of claim is issued, there is probably not going to be a trial. Equally, in most cases where criminal charges are laid, there is likely going to be a trial.

The third point about the *sub judice* rule is that the rigour with which it is applied varies according to the court that will deal with the particular case. Built into the *sub judice* rule is a certain distrust of juries and an assumption that juries, which are made up not of lawyers but of ordinary human beings, are fickle and much influenced by what they read in the newspapers or see on television. The *sub judice* rule is applied with the greatest rigour in dealing with a trial that is to be held with a jury. It is applied with less rigour when the trial is to be conducted by a judge alone.

Fourth, at what point does the *sub judice* rule cease to apply? It seems that its application ends when the trial ends, when it is no longer possible to prejudice the outcome of the trial. The general view in Canada is that there is no *sub judice* rule with respect to appellate proceedings. There are two reasons. First, there are ordinarily no factual issues in dispute before appellate courts; they accept the findings of fact reached by trial courts, and they deal only with legal issues. Second, appellate courts are always composed exclusively of judges and tend to operate in a much more rarefied and abstract atmosphere than do trial courts.[55]

A fifth, and crucial, point about *sub judice*, and about contempt generally, is that culpability may depend on the language and tone used in a particular story. This can be seen in *Zehr v. McIsaac*,[56] a case that involved a dangerous offender proceeding before a single judge in Toronto. On the day the proceeding was actually under way before that judge, the *Globe and Mail* published, on page 5, a piece with the heading, "Fed Up With Deciding on Confining Criminals Indefinitely, MD Says." There was no reference in the heading to the actual person who was the subject of the dangerous offender application. The story began:

---

55   *Bellitti v. Canadian Broadcasting Corp.* (1973), 2 O.R. (2d) 232 (H.C.J.). *Lortie*, supra note 52, takes a different view.

56   (1982), 39 O.R. (2d) 237 (H.C.J.).

A director at the Penetanguishene Mental Health Centre says he is fed up with being asked to decide whether criminals should be designated dangerous offenders and thus incarcerated indefinitely. The courts should stop foisting the question on psychiatrists and instead make the dangerous offender designation automatic if a crime is repeated a certain number of times, said Russel Fleming, director of the centre's forensic science unit.

The story continued in this vein until the bottom third of the article, where it read: "Dr. Fleming's remarks came after he testified in the Supreme Court of Ontario concerning a Crown application to have a convicted rapist designated a dangerous offender." The story was saying that this person had a criminal record. It went on:

A 24-year-old man with a long record of breaking and entering was convicted in December of raping a woman while holding a knife to her throat. He had one previous conviction, but the Ontario Court of Appeal ordered another trial at which the man was found not guilty. "We and the police are satisfied he has done it twice anyway," John McIsaac, the Crown attorney handling the case, said.

Contempt of court proceedings were instituted, but both the paper and the writer were acquitted. Why? First, the judge made reference to the "type and tenor" of the article. Clearly the subject-matter of the article was not this particular alleged dangerous offender, but dangerous offender proceedings generally. As far as the tenor was concerned, the story was written in straightforward and dispassionate language. The position of the article in the newspaper, on page 5, was also significant. The absence of the offender's name from the article was important. There was material that tended to identify the individual in question, but his name was not included. There was no sensationalism. This piece came as close as possible to breaching the *sub judice* rule, but the way it was written, the way it was placed in the paper, the heading, the lead, and everything about it was such that the judge was induced to acquit. This decision can be seen as illustrating the general principle that the way you do something may be just as important as whether you do it.

The sixth point about *sub judice* has to do with *mens rea*. In order for someone to be convicted of a crime, the Crown must first establish that he has committed the *actus reus* — the guilty act constituting the particular offence. Not only does the Crown have to show that the accused performed the guilty act, but that, in addition, the accused did so with the required *mens rea* — with the necessary degree of mental culpability. The basic difference between murder and manslaughter has to do with *mens rea*. The *actus reus*, causing another person's death, is the same for both offences, but it is the mental element that makes murder 1 different from murder 2 and murder 2 different from manslaughter.

Turning to contempt of court, the *actus reus* involved in breaching the *sub judice* rule is the publication of material that creates a real risk of prejudice to the outcome of proceedings before a court. What is the *mens rea*? The crucial question here is whether the Crown has to establish that the accused published the material in question with the intention of either prejudicing or creating a risk of prejudicing the outcome of a matter before the courts or, simply, that the accused published it intentionally. In *R. v. CHEK TV Ltd.*,[57] a television station in Victoria aired some videotape about a person who was at the time on trial for murder. The videotape came from a story the station had broadcast a year earlier when there had been a hostage incident and a riot at a BC penitentiary. It showed an artist's impression of this same person who was now standing trial for murder holding a knife to the throat of a prison guard. This was, of course, highly prejudicial, since it not only suggested that he was a violent individual, but made clear that he had a criminal record. The station's defence was that airing this tape had been a mistake, that it had been done by a junior and inexperienced employee, and that there had been no intention of prejudicing the outcome of proceedings before the court. The court said that the *mens rea* required was not an actual intention to interfere with proceedings before the court, but simply an intention to publish material that had that tendency. The only question, then, was whether the station had intentionally aired the tape. Since the answer to that question was clearly yes, the station was found to have committed contempt.

The last issue to deal with in relation to *sub judice* is that of publication bans. When a general publication ban is made, as in the thalidomide case, the court is issuing an injunction. An injunction is an order made by a court with the purpose of preventing the commission of an unlawful act. The unlawful act the court is concerned with preventing in these cases is a breach of the *sub judice* rule. Now, generally speaking, individuals are free to choose whether they will obey the law or not. Anyone is free to break the law as long as he is prepared to accept the consequences of so doing. An injunction should only be issued to restrain a breach of the law when the injury to someone which would result from that breach would be irreparable. The injury that would result from a breach of the *sub judice* rule is the prejudicing of a proceed-

---

57   (1985), 23 C.C.C. (3d) 395 (B.C.S.C.).

ing that is pending or before the court. That injury is seen as irreparable. Thus, the point of the injunction, of the publication ban, is to prevent that injury occurring.

The leading case on publication bans is *Dagenais* v. *Canadian Broadcasting Corp.*[58] The CBC, together with the National Film Board, prepared a so-called docudrama entitled "The Boys of St. Vincent." It purported to be a fictional account of the abuse of boys at a Roman Catholic–run institution. It was to air in December 1992. At that time, however, there were several real trials pending or before the courts of real men charged with real abuse of real boys in real institutions. A number of these men, Dagenais being one of them, applied for an order to delay the broadcasting of "The Boys of St. Vincent" until such time as their trials had been completed. Clearly, once the trials were completed, there could be no possibility of prejudicing their outcome.

An application for an injunction was made to a single judge of the Ontario Court of Justice without giving notice to the CBC. One of the peculiarities of these sorts of injunctions was that they could be made without both sides being present at the hearing. The judge made an order that the docudrama not be aired anywhere in Canada and that no information about the injunction itself be broadcast. The very next day the CBC appealed this order to the Ontario Court of Appeal. That court amended the original order to say that the ban would apply only in Ontario and to a particular television station in Montreal. The basis for generally sustaining the injunction was the court's conclusion that the airing of this docudrama would create a real and substantial risk of prejudice to criminal trials that were pending or under way before the courts. The CBC and the National Film Board appealed further to the Supreme Court of Canada.

The Supreme Court's judgment may indicate a significant change in direction in Canadian law in the whole area of reporting about judicial proceedings. Chief Justice Antonio Lamer asserted, as we have seen, that the traditional notion that the right to a fair trial must always take precedence over free expression should be abandoned. He said further that there was no hierarchy of rights in the *Charter*, so that no single right was to be preferred over any other right. Instead of freedom of expression giving way to the right to a fair trial, the two, he said, must be "balanced." He also said that the American approach — called the "clash model" — of free press versus fair trial must be abandoned, because the two are not necessarily always in conflict. A judge hearing

---

58 *Supra* note 10.

an application for a publication ban must attempt to balance the two rights and should issue a ban only when he is satisfied that: (a) the publication in question will create a real and substantial risk of prejudice to judicial proceedings; and (b) there is no reasonable alternative means of preventing that risk.

What did the Chief Justice mean by reasonable alternative means? He talked of sequestering juries. He talked about adjourning proceedings. He also spoke about change of venue — changing the location of a trial. He referred to challenges for cause during jury selection. And, finally, he said that when the judge charges the jury at the end of the trial, or possibly even during a trial, he should give strong directions to the jurors to put certain things out of their minds.

The problem with this analysis lies in the notion of "balancing." How is it possible in an adversarial system to *balance* competing claims? At the end of the day the judge has to make a choice. In the final instance the judge must choose either freedom of expression or the right to a fair trial. The Chief Justice's judgment in *Dagenais* suggests that the judge can somehow simultaneously choose both.

Another problem with the *Dagenais* decision is that it casts doubt on a great deal of existing case-law. Many of the issues discussed in this chapter had once appeared to be resolved, but they may now have to be revisited, case by case.

3) *In Facie* Contempts

The one form of *in facie* contempt which can be committed by journalists is disobeying an order of a court. *In facie* contempts are most often committed by lawyers. Lawyers show up late for court, they do not show up, they show up drunk, or they engage in abusive arguments with the judge. The one time that a journalist can commit this form of contempt occurs when he is called as a witness and is asked either to reveal the identity of a source or to reveal information received in confidence from a source. If the journalist refuses to be sworn as a witness or, having been sworn, refuses to answer a question properly put to him, he commits a contempt of court. This is an issue that looms far larger in movies and television dramas than in real life. Nonetheless, it is an issue of some interest.

What we are talking about in legal terminology is the question of whether there exists, or should exist, a privilege in journalists — a legal right in journalists — to refuse to disclose certain information to courts. A privilege, in this context, means a legal right to say, "I do not want to tell you that and, more to the point, I am under no legal obligation to tell you. I have a right to refuse to disclose that information." Does Canadian law recognize any privilege in journalists to refuse to disclose information received in confidence from a source, including the identity of the source? The simple answer is no, but it is necessary to investigate how that answer has been reached.[59]

The older approach that Canadian courts took to the question of privilege was described as the category approach. There were certain fixed categories of relations that were recognized as giving rise to privilege in respect of communications made during the course of those relations. Their number was limited and included the solicitor-client relation, the relation of husband and wife, communications with and among high officers of state, and jury deliberations. The law was quite mechanical. If you were party to one of those relations, communications made within it were privileged. If you were not, you had no basis for claiming privilege. If a solicitor had received information from a client during the course of the solicitor-client relationship, the solicitor could claim a privilege to refuse to divulge that information. But since the journalist-source relation did not fit within any of the recognized categories, no basis existed for such a claim by a journalist.

In recent years Canadian courts have moved away from the category approach and have adopted a more flexible approach that is not confined to categories, but is based on a step by step analysis of the relation in question. This analysis is borrowed from an American writer called Wigmore, who wrote an eleven-volume treatise on the law of evidence.[60] Wigmore laid out four criteria which he said should be applied, and which Canadian courts have adopted,[61] in order to determine whether a particular relation gives rise to privilege. I will set out Wigmore's criteria and then determine whether any of them is satisfied with respect to the journalist-source relationship.

Wigmore's first criterion was that the communications must originate in a confidence that they will not be disclosed. Certainly the journalist-source relationship satisfies that criterion. When a source discloses confidential information to a journalist, the expectation is that at least one important part of that information — the source's identity — will not be further disclosed.

---

59 A very full survey of the entire question is found in S.N. Lederman, P. O'Kelly & M. Grottenthaler, "Confidentiality of News Sources" in P. Anisman & A.M. Linden, eds., *The Media, The Courts, and The Charter* (Toronto: Carswell, 1986) 227.

60 See J.H. Wigmore, *Evidence in Trials at Common Law*, vol. 8, 3d ed., rev. by J.T. McNaughton (Boston: Little, Brown, 1961).

61 The first case was *Slavutych v. Baker*, [1976] 1 S.C.R. 254.

Wigmore's language is somewhat stultified, so I will set out what he said and then try to put it in ordinary words. He formulated his second criterion: "The element of *confidentiality must be essential* to the full and satisfactory maintenance of the relation between the parties." He was saying that not only must the relation originate in confidence but it must continue on that basis. Confidence must be essential to the continuation of the relation. Here, again, the journalist-source relation passes muster.

Turning to Wigmore's third criterion, he stated that the relation must be one "which in the opinion of the community ought to be sedulously fostered." This statement simply means that it is a socially legitimate and valuable relation and, generally speaking, although not always, Canadian courts have accepted that the journalist-source relation satisfies the third criterion.

It is with Wigmore's fourth criterion that the journalist-source relation has failed to measure up. "The *injury* that would inure to the relation by the disclosure of the communications must be *greater than the benefit* thereby gained for the correct disposal of litigation." [Footnotes omitted]. What he is saying is that a court weighing this question must do a balancing act. What is the benefit gained in resolving the case before the court of getting the information as weighed against the injury to the relation that would result from forcing its disclosure? Which is more valuable — getting the information before the court or harming the relation through the forced disclosure of that information? Canadian courts have said that the nature of the journalist-source relation is such that it will not satisfy Wigmore's fourth criterion. Judges have agreed that disclosure will result in injury to the relation between the journalist and the source, but the benefit of getting the information before the court has consistently been taken to outweigh that injury.

In the era of the *Charter* it has been argued that the guarantee of freedom of expression in section 2(b) should be interpreted as creating a degree of journalistic privilege. It has been asserted that freedom of expression, or freedom of the press, demands recognition of such a privilege. This is not an assertion all Canadian journalists would necessarily agree with. The issue was litigated before the Supreme Court in 1989 in *Moysa* v. *Alberta (Labour Relations Board).*[62] It was an unusual case.

Moysa was a reporter with the Edmonton *Journal*. She did a story about some employees of Hudson's Bay Company outlets in Edmonton trying to organize themselves into unions. One of the largest unorganized sectors in the Canadian economy is retail distribution, and for a

---

62   [1989] 1 S.C.R. 1572.

long time the labour movement has been trying to do something about this and failing. The precise facts, at least what one can glean of them from the Supreme Court judgment, are not clear, but, allowing for a certain amount of surmise, it seems that roughly the following happened. Moysa, in preparing her story, talked to some of the employees at one Hudson's Bay outlet who were active in the organizing drive. She also talked to management. A reasonable inference is that Moysa, whether advertently or not, communicated the names of these employees to someone in management. Management then sacked six employees, presumably the ones whose names it got from Moysa. The now former employees of the Bay filed complaints before the Alberta Labour Relations Board that they had been fired for trying to organize a union. The Bay denied this. Since the employees had brought the complaints, they had the burden of proving that they were true. They called Moysa as a witness. She was subpoenaed and appeared before the Labour Relations Board; she was asked whether she had spoken with management. She responded that she could not reveal that information and claimed journalistic privilege.

In this case the issue was backwards. Moysa was not claiming a privilege in respect of information she had received from a source. She was trying to claim a privilege in respect of information that, in so far as I understand the facts, she gave to a source. It was not the case to take to the Supreme Court to argue in favour of journalistic privilege. The issue of privilege did not even arise on these facts.

The Court denied the claim to privilege. The judges said, further, although not very strongly, that there might be some basis in section 2(b) of the *Charter* for a claim to journalistic privilege, but the Court could decide that only when it got a real case. In my opinion, however, you do not have to read far between the lines to conclude that the Court did not hold out much hope that, even in a proper case, it would find the existence of a privilege. In my view, the correct conclusion is that in Canadian law there is no privilege as such.

An important question underlying the *Moysa* decision is whether the *Charter*'s guarantee of freedom of expression and freedom of the press can be regarded as creating any special legal status for journalists. The Supreme Court's decision suggests that it cannot.

Moysa, however, is not the end of the matter for a journalist called as a witness. We turn to an English decision called *A.G. v. Mulholland*.[63] It arose out of a spy scandal. Two reporters for the *Daily Telegraph* wrote a story about Soviet spies in the British Admiralty. As a result, a tribunal

---

63   [1963] 2 Q.B. 477 (C.A.).

of inquiry was set up to look into the question. Inevitably, the reporters who wrote the story that led to the tribunal being established were the first witnesses called before it. They were asked to tell the tribunal the sources for their story, but they refused. They were cited for contempt of court, convicted, and then appealed to the Court of Appeal. The court accepted that there was no such thing as a privilege in law, but it did not say that journalists could be subpoenaed and questioned at will or whimsically. The court said that journalism was an "honourable" profession and that the confidences members of honourable professions receive in the course of their work should be respected. As a result, a journalist who was called as a witness should not be subjected to a fishing expedition. Practically speaking, it was held that a journalist witness should be required to reveal information received in confidence from a source only when the party seeking that information is able to satisfy the court as to two matters. First, it must be shown that the information sought is *relevant*, that it bears directly on the resolution of an issue actually before the court. It is not, then, simply a matter of a party saying I would like to know this, or I think it is interesting, or I would like to find out. Second, it must also be shown that the information sought is *necessary*. Necessary here means that the issue that is before the court cannot be resolved unless the court has this information.

The decision in *Mulholland* has been accepted in Canadian courts, so that before a journalist can be required to reveal information received in confidence, the court must be satisfied that the information sought is both relevant and necessary. And only when the court is so satisfied can the journalist who is a witness be required to disclose that information.

But even at this point all is not lost. Even if the court decides that the information sought is relevant and necessary, the journalist witness, or his lawyer, may ask the judge to use the "moral authority" of the court to suggest to counsel asking the question that the question "not be pressed."[64] This is what has happened traditionally in the cases of priests and penitents, physicians and patients, and so on. None of these relations gives rise to a legal privilege to refuse to disclose information received during its course, but at the end of the day counsel would say to the trial judge, "I ask you to use the moral authority of the court to suggest that the question not be pressed," and the judge would say to the lawyer posing the question, "I ask you not to press the question." A wise lawyer would know the right response.

---

64   *Reference Re Legislative Privilege* (1978), 18 O.R. (2d) 529 at 540 (C.A.).

So, summing up, what is the practical position? *Moysa* resolved the basic issue. There is no privilege to allow a journalist legally to refuse to divulge information. If a journalist is subpoenaed, he is surely going to know why. That journalist should go to court with a lawyer and, when he goes into the witness box and is sworn, remembering that it is an offence under the *Criminal Code* to refuse to be sworn,[65] and the fateful question is asked, the lawyer representing him will stand up and request that counsel asking the question be required to satisfy the court that the information sought is both relevant and necessary. If counsel is not successful in both endeavours, the journalist should not be required to answer the question. If, however, the court is satisfied that the information is relevant and necessary, then the lawyer representing the journalist should ask the court to use its moral authority to suggest that the question not be pressed. The court may accede to that request. If, however, the judge declines to exercise the moral authority of the court, the journalist is on his own. If he refuses to answer the question, by that refusal he has committed a contempt of court.

One of the unfortunate things about contempt of court is that in a superior court, at any rate, the trial judge can punish summarily — right there and then. The judge can say, "I find you guilty of contempt of court and I sentence you to three days in jail." After the journalist has had a chance to reflect on things for three days, he can be brought back to the court and asked the question again, and, if he refuses to answer, he would commit a fresh offence and could be summarily punished again. This, in theory, could go on forever. It has never happened to a journalist in a Canadian courtroom and, in the unlikely case that it did, everybody involved would probably go to extraordinary lengths to find some way out of what would be an embarrassing situation. It is worth noting that, because contempt of court is a common law crime, the maximum punishment that may be awarded is nowhere specified, but is at the discretion of the judge.

The final point on the issue of privilege has to do with something called the newspaper rule. This rule is of limited application as it arises only in civil libel proceedings and only at the pre-trial stage of examination for discovery. The newspaper rule says that a media defendant in a libel action cannot be required at discovery to reveal the source of the allegedly libellous statements. Why would the plaintiff's lawyer want to know where the defendant got the allegedly libellous material from?

---

65   See *Criminal Code of Canada*, R.S.C. 1985, c. 46, s. 545 [hereinafter *Criminal Code*].

Presumably, because it would give that lawyer a much better idea of how strong a defence the defendant might be able to mount. The newspaper rule has been upheld in Ontario,[66] but rejected in other provinces.[67]

4) Conclusion

Before leaving our discussion of contempt of court, it is worthwhile to stress again the unsatisfactory state of Canadian law on the subject. Reform and codification of the law are both long overdue. In 1982 the then Law Reform Commission of Canada produced proposals for codifying the law of contempt.[68] Although the idea of reducing the uncertain common law of contempt to a statutory form was desirable, the substance of what was proposed was a disaster. It would have made an unnecessarily restrictive offence even more restrictive. The report died. In 1984 an omnibus Criminal Law Reform Bill[69] was introduced in Parliament. Part of this bill would have codified much of the law of contempt. The bill was not enacted. Nothing has happened since. It would seem that much of the existing law of contempt of court denies a number of the rights set out in the *Charter*. Despite this restriction, there has not been a systematic challenge, based on the *Charter*, to the existing law. One of the difficulties in the way of such a challenge has been uncertainty about whether the *Charter* can apply to purely judicial acts, which the judge-created, non-statutory law of contempt is. The Supreme Court's decision in *Dagenais*[70] may have made it procedurally easier to make such a challenge.

Nevertheless, the Ontario Court of Appeal in *Kopyto*[71] was able effectively to jettison scandalizing the court. But in an earlier decision, *R. v. Cohn*[72] in 1984, the Court of Appeal found no contradictions between the *Charter* and the essentials of the law of contempt of court.

---

66   See *McInnis v. University Students' Council of the University of Western Ontario* (1984), 48 O.R. (2d) 542 (H.C.J.).
67   See, for example, *Baxter v. Canadian Broadcasting Corp.* (1978), 22 N.B.R. (2d) 307 (Q.B.).
68   Law Reform Commission of Canada, *Contempt of Court*, (Report 17) (Ottawa: Minister of Supply & Services, 1982).
69   Bill C-19, 2d Sess., 32d Parl., 1984.
70   *Supra* note 10.
71   *Supra* note 34.
72   *Supra* note 22. The Supreme Court of Canada refused leave to appeal, suggesting that, at this time, it agreed with the Ontario Court of Appeal.

C. DEALING WITH MATERIAL THAT MIGHT BECOME EVIDENCE IN A LEGAL PROCEEDING

1) General Considerations

What are the legal responsibilities of journalists who have in their possession information that they know, or ought reasonably to know, might be sought to be used as evidence in a subsequent proceeding before the courts?

The law is really quite simple and consists of two principles. They are best understood as two poles. The first is that no one is under any legal obligation to assist the police or other authorities in the investigation of any matter. Even if someone was an eye-witness to an absolutely horrifying murder, that person is under no legal obligation to tell anybody about it. That is one pole. The other is that no one may in any way obstruct the police or other authorities in carrying out their duties, including the gathering of evidence during an investigation. It is an indictable offence to obstruct, pervert, or defeat the course of justice.[73]

Let us make this example as concrete as possible. Someone who has a videotape that clearly shows the commission of a serious criminal offence is under no obligation to bring the existence or contents of that videotape to anyone's attention. If, however, that person destroys the videotape in order to prevent its becoming used as evidence in a subsequent proceeding, he has committed the offence of obstructing the course of justice.

This issue arises in a number of contexts. One that occurs with some regularity has to do with the use of video out-takes. No legal question can arise with respect to videotape that has been aired, since it thereby enters the public domain. But out-takes, by definition, are not aired.

We could, of course, just as easily be talking about material on audiotapes which is not aired; or photographs, either negatives or contact sheets, which are not actually printed in a newspaper or magazine; or material in notebooks which does not form part of a published story; or obviously, and more and more commonly, information stored in computers which has not been used in stories.

What are a journalist's obligations with respect to all these types of material? To repeat, there is no obligation to inform anybody or bring it

---

73 *Criminal Code, supra* note 65, s. 139.

to anyone's attention. But what must be avoided is destroying or erasing such material under circumstances where it could be alleged that this was done with the purpose of preventing it becoming evidence in a judicial proceeding. How can problems be avoided? The simple answer is to have a standard course of conduct. A standard operating procedure must be established, always followed, and never deviated from. Thus, one would keep video out-takes for a specified period of time and erase them or reuse the tape. If there is a standard course of conduct and it is well known and everybody follows it, then whenever a question is raised about why a videotape was erased, the answer will be: That is the way it is always done. The management of any media organization should establish clear rules and clear procedures and make sure all employees follow them.

It is worth raising a question about the moral and social, and not simply legal, obligations of journalists. Something that Global Television did in Toronto in 1979 is of interest. There was a demonstration at the headquarters of the Workers' Compensation Board organized by a group called the Union of Injured Workers. For one reason or another the demonstration got out of hand. It turned into a riot and many people were arrested and charged with assaulting police, obstructing police, and so on. A Global cameraperson shot the riot and, while a fair amount of videotape was aired, a lot of out-takes remained. The network was not clear what to do with them. What it finally decided to do, after much soul-searching and discussion, was organize a public screening. It let this fact be known to everyone who had an interest in the matter, both the police and the accused. People in the media are often reluctant to make material like out-takes generally available because they do not want to be seen as agents of the police, as a part of the investigative apparatus of the state. The interesting thing in the Global case was that, by and large, the video out-takes were more useful to the accused as a means of establishing their innocence than they were to the police.

2) Searches of Newsrooms

The police can ask permission to search a newsroom and, if someone with the necessary authority agrees to allow them to do so, that is fine. If, however, an organization or an individual is not prepared to assist the police by consenting to a search, the police can apply for a search warrant. Although searches may be authorized for specific purposes under certain federal and provincial statutes, as a general principle in the investigation of a criminal offence, a non-consensual search by the police of business or residential premises may only be conducted under the authority of a search warrant.[74] A warrant is a document issued by a judicial officer — a justice of the peace — authorizing the search of named premises. It is to be issued only when the justice is satisfied by information given by police on oath that there is in those premises material that is directly relevant to the investigation of an offence.[75] There is considerable case-law that repeats the phrase that search warrants are not to be issued to permit "fishing expeditions." It is definitely not sufficient for the police to go before a justice and say, "We don't really know what is in there, but we would like to go inside and have a look around."

What are the rights and duties of someone working in a newsroom when the police arrive with a search warrant? When executing a warrant to search business premises, the police should initially request entry. If entry is denied, they may force their way in. It is a convention that searches of residential premises should ordinarily be conducted in daylight. However, in the case of a newsroom that operates twenty-four hours a day, it probably does not matter whether the search is conducted in daylight or otherwise.

The person who greets the police officers at the door is entitled to ask to see the search warrant and it should be produced. It is permissible to check the warrant for any obvious defects, such as, for example, the police being at the wrong premises. If, however, there are no patent defects and it appears to be a valid search warrant, there is a legal obligation to get out of the way and let the police proceed with their search. Any attempt after that to oppose or interfere in any way with the officers conducting the search may amount to obstructing. As with the general rule already noted, no one is under any obligation whatsoever to assist the police with their search; but it is unlawful to obstruct them.

A number of suggestions may be made about searches. If it is a television newsroom that is being searched, someone should videotape the search. Whoever is doing this taping should stay physically as far away from the police officers as possible, to avoid any possibility of being charged with assault or obstruction. If the police tell the person videotaping the search to turn the camera off, he is not obliged to comply, so long as he is in no way physically obstructing the search. In the case of a newspaper, it is going to be difficult to videotape a search, but there should be people with cameras around. Somebody should take photographs of the search, again staying as far away from the police officers as possible.

---

74 See *Canada (Director of Investigation & Research, Combines Investigation Branch)* v. *Southam Inc.*, [1984] 2 S.C.R. 145, and J.A. Fontana, *The Law of Search and Seizure in Canada*, 3d ed. (Toronto: Butterworths, 1992).

75 *Criminal Code, supra* note 65, s. 487.

Problems can arise when the police ask for assistance during the course of a search. The first example is a bit dated, but makes the point. The police come to a locked filing cabinet and ask someone to open it. No one is obliged to produce a key and unlock the cabinet. However, the police are entitled, as a general rule, to use reasonable force in executing the search warrant. In these circumstances, that would mean using a crowbar to break open the filing cabinet. To take another example, there may be a room where video out-takes are kept and the police might ask to see the out-takes from, say, the demonstration that occurred outside the minister's office yesterday. If no one helps the police, they are entitled to use reasonable force to find those out-takes and, if the room ends up trashed, so be it. A more vexed issue, one that has not yet been litigated, could arise if the police were searching for information stored in a computer. Let us say they ask a particular reporter for his access code. Once again he is not obliged to assist. But if the reporter refuses to divulge his access code, the police would be entitled to take the computer with them to allow their technical experts to attempt to figure out the code.

This is the core of the problem. How much inconvenience are principles worth?

What about the constitutionality of searches of newsrooms? One of the effects of the *Charter* has been to turn almost everything into a constitutional issue. In 1991 the Supreme Court decided a case about searches of newsrooms called *Canadian Broadcasting Corp.* v. *New Brunswick (A.G.)*.[76] The CBC argued two things about such searches, both based on section 2(b) of the *Charter* and its constitutional protection for freedom of the press. The first, and more extreme, position was that newsrooms should be regarded from the perspective of police searches as constitutional no-go areas. Logically, the CBC was arguing that there should be certain premises that are beyond the authority of the state, that the newsroom be regarded as the equivalent of the sanctuary of the medieval church. The Court said no. It is hard to imagine how it could have said anything else. How can any territory in Canada be beyond the jurisdiction of the Canadian state?

The second and more plausible argument the CBC made was based on the 1977 decision of the British Columbia Supreme Court in *Pacific Press Ltd.* v. *R.*[77] Pacific Press is the organization that publishes both the Vancouver *Sun* and the Vancouver *Province*. A warrant had been issued

---

76   [1991] 3 S.C.R. 459.
77   [1977] 5 W.W.R. 507 (B.C.S.C.).

authorizing a search of its premises. Lawyers for Pacific Press subsequently challenged the warrant before a court and, as a result, the court laid down two principles about searches of newsrooms. The first was that before a warrant is to be issued authorizing the search of a newsroom, the justice of the peace should be satisfied that there is no reasonable alternative source from which the police might discover the information being sought. This meant that the justice is supposed to be satisfied that the newsroom has to be searched because it is the only place where this particular evidence can be found. The second principle was that if there is an alternative source, an attempt must already have been made to obtain the information from that source and the attempt had failed. The apparent result of this decision was that a warrant to search a newsroom would only be issued as a last recourse. But the *Pacific Press* decision was a decision of a trial court. It had been followed occasionally by other courts, and in *Canadian Broadcasting Corp.* v. *New Brunswick (A.G.)* the Supreme Court was asked to decide that it should be the general rule throughout Canada. The Court declined to do so. The judges said that, while a search of a newsroom gave "rise to special concerns," a newsroom was, at the end of the day, as amenable to a lawful search as any other workplace or, for that matter, residence in Canada.

The *Criminal Code* was recently amended to allow for the issuance of what is called a tele-warrant.[78] This means that the police do not have to be physically present before the justice of the peace for a warrant to be issued. They can telephone a justice and tell him the basis on which they are seeking a warrant. Furthermore, since the justice is not able physically to issue the warrant, what results is not a traditional warrant signed and sealed by the justice, but something called a *facsimile* warrant. People working in newsrooms are entitled to ask to see the warrant, but what they are shown may be a facsimile warrant. That is still a real warrant.

Tele-warrants were devised to deal with organized crime and with drug trafficking, when it is a matter of every second counting, when the police know that if they have to wait two hours to get into a certain place, the evidence they are looking for might be destroyed. It seems difficult to imagine those considerations applying to the search of a newsroom. An attempt might be made to litigate whether or not newsrooms can properly be searched on the basis of tele-warrants.

---

78 *Criminal Code, supra* note 65, ss. 487.1 and 487.2, as am. by S.C. 1995, c. 44.

3) Taking Photographs or Videotapes against the Instructions of the Police

Section 129(a) of the *Criminal Code* makes it an offence to wilfully obstruct "a public officer or peace officer in the execution of his duty or any person lawfully acting in aid of such an officer." For someone to be convicted of this offence, the Crown must show that there was an obstruction that to some degree interfered with a police officer in carrying out the task he was engaged in and, further, that the accused did the obstructing intentionally. Persons taking photographs for the media have been convicted of this offence for refusing to obey police instructions. In one case the conviction seems to have been based largely on the fact that the photographer entered an area from which the public had been excluded as a security measure during the visit of the leader of another state.[79] In another the police asked a photographer to stop taking pictures of a psychiatric patient they were moving to hospital. He continued taking photographs. He was convicted of obstructing largely because his presence was causing the patient to become agitated, thereby making the task of the police more difficult.[80] These cases suggest that some degree of direct or indirect physical interference with the police will be necessary before a conviction can result. The obvious answer for photographers in such situations is to stay physically well away from the police.

FURTHER READINGS

No Canadian monograph deals exclusively and systematically with contempt of court. Two useful works that provide general background are S. M. Robertson, *Courts and the Media* (Toronto: Butterworths, 1981), and P. Anisman & A. M. Linden, eds, *The Media, the Courts, and the Charter.* (Toronto: Carswell, 1986). Both are somewhat dated, particularly the Robertson book, which was published before the *Charter* became part of the Constitution.

79   *Knowlton v. R.*, [1974] S.C.R. 443.
80   *R. v. Kalnins* (1978), 41 C.C.C. (2d) 524 (Ont. Co. Ct.).

CHAPTER 4

FREE EXPRESSION AND PRIVATE RIGHTS

So far we have looked at limitations on freedom of expression which are imposed by the state to further some state purpose. In this chapter we change the focus, at least somewhat. Although the limitations we will look at arise out of the law of the state, they exist as means whereby individuals can enforce private rights against other individuals. We will spend the bulk of the chapter investigating the law of civil libel and then analyse the extent, if any, to which an individual right to privacy is recognized.

A. CIVIL LIBEL

In the Canadian legal system there is both civil libel and criminal libel. We have already noted the three forms of criminal libel (see chapter 2 (C)). The law of civil libel is part of the law of torts. Torts addresses civil wrongs, or, to put it slightly differently, non-criminal injuries. By and large the law of torts consists of legal mechanisms whereby people can seek redress for losses they have suffered as a result of the unlawful conduct of others. In a practical sense, the law of torts today is very much the law of car accidents.

The English law of torts is called torts with an "s" for a reason. There is a series of different torts, each of which has different rules and its own complexities. This is especially true of libel, which is a complicated business and often difficult to understand. It is also a matter about which most lawyers do not know a great deal, for the simple reason that libel actions are not a common occurrence.

What are the effects on individual journalists of being involved in a libel action? Many lawyers would regard publishing a contempt of court as a far more serious matter than publishing a libel, but from the perspective of an individual reporter or editor the reverse may be true. Few things do more to ruin a journalist's reputation than to write stories that lead to libel actions, especially libel actions that employers lose. The journalist gets a reputation as someone who is not thorough, who is sloppy, who is inaccurate, and so on. Libel can have exceedingly serious consequences for the career of a journalist.

Traditionally, the broad tort we are dealing with has been called defamation. Defamation was subdivided into two further categories called slander and libel. In the traditional definition, slander consisted of purely spoken words — words that emerged from someone's mouth, but were never reduced to any other form; libel, in contrast, was said to consist of written or printed words. That distinction has been overtaken by technological change. Although slander still means purely spoken words, libel embraces words or images that have been reduced to a permanent or potentially permanent form. Permanent or potentially permanent form includes not only written or printed words but material on film (both movie film and still film), audiotape, videotape, computer disks, and hard drives. Quite different rules govern libel actions and slander actions. We will say nothing more about slander as such, because anyone can slander anyone else and the tort is thus of no particular interest to journalists.

Some of the common law provinces — Manitoba, for example — have abolished the distinction between libel and slander and simply have one tort called defamation. Other common law provinces, such as Ontario, maintain the distinction. Henceforth we will deal purely with libel, although the words "libel" and "defamation," or "libellous" and "defamatory," may be used as if they were interchangeable.

Two broad introductory points must be made about libel law. The first is that it applies to everything that a newspaper or broadcaster publishes, publish being used in the widest possible sense. With newspapers for example, the law of libel applies not only to news stories or editorial columns, but to literally everything that is in the newspaper. It applies to letters to the editor, to editorial cartoons, to classified advertisements. It applies to material that comes from sources outside the paper — wire stories, syndicated columns, and syndicated features. The law of libel can even apply to the way a newspaper is laid out. If someone puts the wrong cut line on a photograph, he may have thereby created a libel. You might have a story that is perfectly harmless and a head that is also perfectly accurate and harmless, but the way the page is laid out may create a libellous impression. Let us say there is a story on page 1 about a pillar of the community, loved, honoured, and respected and, in particular, the retirement dinner held to honour this noble human being. There is an accompanying photograph of this person. On the same page, with a much bigger head, there is a story about a convicted child molester. The page is, unfortunately, laid out so that the huge head about the molester looks as if it refers to the photograph depicting the pillar of the community. That is a libel. Even though each constituent element on the page, viewed independently of every other element, may be fine, the way the whole page has been put together can create an impression that is libellous. The same principle, slightly amended, applies to television. The words in a script may be absolutely innocent and no libellous imputation would be conveyed to anyone who read those words to himself. But the announcer who actually reads the script over the air may deliver it in a tone of voice that creates a libel. The visuals, or the music that is used, or the background, or the way different parts of a television story have been edited together may, nonetheless, create a libellous impression. Whether you are talking about broadcasting or newspapers, every single element of what has been published or any combination of those elements can become the subject of a libel action.

The second important general point to be noted is that, regardless of the source of a piece of information or an opinion, whoever publishes it is responsible for it. A radio station is responsible for everything that is aired by that station. A newspaper is responsible for everything that appears in its pages. Let us say that there is a libel in a wire story supplied by a news service. It may well be that the person who claims to have been libelled could sue the news service, but that is not the point. Any newspaper that publishes the story is responsible. The same is true for letters to the editor. The newspaper that publishes the letter can be held accountable in a libel action. A plaintiff may have choices about whom to sue, but that is not relevant now. The simple point is that anyone who publishes libellous material is legally responsible for it.

How would a libel action actually unfold? The first actor in a libel action, as indeed in any civil action, is the plaintiff. In civil actions the plaintiff not only instigates the proceeding but has the burden of proof — the obligation of proving the case. In that sense, civil actions are analogous to criminal actions, though in criminal actions it is the Crown that initiates proceedings and that has the burden of proving that the accused is guilty. In libel cases, the plaintiff, the person who claims to have been libelled, initiates the action and has the burden of proving that he was indeed libelled.

1) The Plaintiff's Case

In a libel action the plaintiff has to prove three things: that the material complained of is defamatory; that it refers to the plaintiff; and that it was published. We will deal with each element in turn.

a) Defamatory

The first thing the plaintiff has to prove is that the material in question — the novel, the classified ad, the letter to the editor, the news story — was defamatory. What does that mean? I will quickly run through four definitions that are found in the cases, suggest that these definitions are not really helpful, and set out what I think is a more useful practical definition. Material is said, first, to be defamatory if it would tend to lower the plaintiff in the estimation of right-thinking people generally. Second, material is said to be defamatory if it would tend to cause the plaintiff to be shunned or avoided. Material is, on the third definition, defamatory if it would tend to expose the plaintiff to hatred, ridicule, or contempt. Notice the use of the verb "tend" in all those definitions. It points up an integral feature of libel actions — the plaintiff is not required to prove any actual injury. The plaintiff does not have to prove he was *actually* lowered in the estimation of right-thinking people generally, which would, presumably, involve getting a host of right-thinking people and bringing them into the courtroom as witnesses to say: "I saw that piece and it lowered the plaintiff in my estimation." The plaintiff is required to establish only that the material at the basis of the action has that tendency. This is a remarkable feature of libel actions, as compared with other tort actions where the plaintiff is required to prove injury. Once it is established that the material is libellous, injury to the plaintiff is assumed.

The fourth definition, which takes a different tack, is that a libel is a false statement about a person to that person's discredit. It is not merely that a statement about someone is untrue, but that it is untrue and to that person's discredit.

All these definitions are far too abstract. I want to suggest a more practical approach, practical in the sense that it can be helpful in alerting working journalists early on that there might be a problem with a particular story. A libel on this approach is simply something you would not like to see said in public about yourself. If a journalist is going to say something in print or over the air about somebody else which he would not like to have said about himself, then the first early warning bell should go off. This warning says there is a need to be careful with this story, to devote special care or attention to it.

We now turn to some decided cases that may assist in giving a better sense of when material is defamatory and when it is not. The first of these is *Brannigan* v. *S.I.U.*,[1] a case from British Columbia. One of the many interesting points about Canadian libel law is that the bulk of the reported cases come from British Columbia, which appears to be the country's libel capital. In the 1960s, Canada still had an ocean-going merchant marine. Canadian vessels carried Canadian flags as they sailed the seas. The sailors who sailed in these ships belonged to a union called the Canadian Seamen's Union, a radical union with ties to the Labour Progressive Party, the communist party of the day. The government of Canada decided to smash this union and invited an American gangster, Hal Banks, to come to Canada to carry out the task. He arrived in Canada ostensibly to promote his own union, the Seafarers' International Union. A struggle ensued between the SIU and CSU. There was a great deal of violence and unpleasantness, but by the early 1960s it was over. The Canadian Seamen's Union was crushed, the SIU was dominant, and in the process the Canadian merchant marine largely disappeared. *Brannigan* is a minor footnote to the whole business. The Seafarers' International Union published a magazine called *Canadian Sailor*. Brannigan, the plaintiff, belonged, not to the Canadian Seamen's Union, but to a union with close ties to the Canadian Seamen's Union and itself a radical union, the Canadian Brotherhood of Railroad, Transport and General Workers. In the August 1961 edition of *Canadian Sailor* there was a piece about Brannigan. The sting of the piece was that Brannigan was a communist. He sued the SIU for libel. The key issue was whether it was libellous to call Brannigan a communist. The difficulty in answering this question arises out of the fact that there have been times and places where not only was it not libellous to call a trade unionist a communist, but it was positively complimentary. So how does one resolve the issue?

The court said that the question must not be addressed in the air, in the abstract. It must be addressed concretely. The court looked at the time, the place, and the circumstances under which these statements were published to determine whether they were defamatory or not. The context had to be looked at. What was the context in which these statements were made about Brannigan? It was Canada in 1961 when the Cold War was raging. More particularly, there was a battle going on between two hostile trade unions. The court concluded, looking at the time, the place, and the circumstances, that it was libellous to call Brannigan a communist. To put the same issue in a contemporary perspective, would it be libellous in 1996 to say that someone was gay or lesbian?

---

1   (1963), 42 D.L.R. (2d) 249 (B.C.S.C.).

Libel is said to be a tort of strict liability. The defendant's intention as to whether the statements complained of were to be interpreted as defamatory or not is irrelevant. It is absolutely beside the point for the defendant to argue that he did not intend the statements to be defamatory. This is illustrated in another case from British Columbia, *Murphy* v. *LaMarsh*.[2] Judy LaMarsh was a minister in various Pearson governments throughout the 1960s. In 1968 she published a book of political reminiscences, *Memoirs of a Bird in a Gilded Cage*. In her book she made certain references to Ed Murphy, a journalist whom she obviously did not like. The assertion that led to the libel action was the following: "[a] brash young radio reporter, named Ed Murphy (heartily detested by most of the Press Gallery and the members)." At the material time Murphy was a member of the Parliamentary Press Gallery in Ottawa. LaMarsh was asserting that he was "heartily detested" by most of the reporters with whom he worked in the Gallery and by the members of Parliament. Murphy sued. The court decided that it was not libellous to call someone "brash." The central issue was whether it was libellous to say that Murphy was "heartily detested" by most of the Press Gallery and the MPs.

LaMarsh was crafty and called as expert witnesses at the trial two well-known Canadian journalists of the time, Charles Lynch and Jack Webster. Each testified that neither of these assertions was libellous and, in fact, that both were complimentary. Why was Murphy heartily detested by most of the reporters with whom he worked in the Press Gallery? Well, obviously, because they spent all their time drinking in the Press Club and schmoozing with politicians. They were not doing their work, but Murphy was constantly out getting the good stories and so his fellow reporters were jealous of him. Likewise, MPs heartily detested Murphy because they knew that he was always producing the great stories, finding the skeletons in the closets, and so on. Both expert witnesses said that whatever they might look like on the surface, neither statement was libellous of Murphy.

The court disagreed. The court said the proper perspective to adopt was not that of the defendant. In fact, it was quite beside the point what the defendant might have intended. Equally, the standpoint was not that of someone like Lynch or Webster, with specialized or inside knowledge. The standard by which to measure whether these assertions were defamatory was that of the ordinary reader. The court said the question to be asked was, What would an ordinary person, reading that Ed Murphy was heartily detested by most of his fellow workers and the people about

---

2   (1970), 13 D.L.R. (3d) 484 (B.C.S.C.), aff'd [1971] 18 D.L.R. (3d) 208 (B.C.C.A.).

whom he wrote, think of Ed Murphy? Phrased that way, the answer to the question is obvious. The ordinary reader would think there was something wrong with him. It is not the intention of the defendant that determines whether statements are defamatory or not, it is the way the ordinary listener or ordinary viewer would interpret them.

Thomas v. Canadian Broadcasting Corp.[3] had to do with an investigative report aired on CBC Radio. The background was that Dome Petroleum had been exploring for oil in the Arctic under the Beaufort Sea. Exploring for oil under the seabed was, and is, a complicated and expensive business. First, in order to be permitted to carry out exploration, Dome Petroleum had to have a licence from what was then the Department of Indian Affairs and Northern Development. The licence was quite specific and, in particular, it dealt with what was called "[s]ecuring the [drill] casing." Exploring for oil in this fashion did not simply involve sticking the drill bit into the seabed and making a hole. It was necessary to secure the sides of the hole in order to give it stability. Dome's initial licence said that it had to secure the hole by creating a concrete sleeve around it down to a depth of 10,000 feet below the seabed. Obviously, that would have been extremely expensive, and after Dome had begun drilling it applied for an amendment to its original licence so that it would be required to secure the casing down to only 4000 feet. The amendment was approved. Some time later there was an explosion at the site and, as a result, one worker was killed. Those are the basic facts. CBC Radio did some investigation and produced a piece. The point of this piece, and what the case addresses, is that the CBC strongly suspected that the villain in the whole affair was a civil servant working for the Department of Indian Affairs and Northern Development, Maurice Thomas, but it did not quite have proof. In the report, the CBC hinted at certain conclusions about Thomas, without coming out and saying them directly.

In its script the CBC set out the basic background to the story and then, with regard to the amendment to the drilling authority, said that it was approved "without any long examination." It is interesting to think about those words. What exactly does the phrase "without any long examination" mean? It does not mean anything, in fact, but seems to carry a sinister implication. The script continued. Reference was made to the explosion: "Securing the casing with cement all the way down to 10,000 feet would also likely have prevented the gas problems which led to the explosion that killed data engineer, George Ross

---

3 (1981), 27 A.R. 547 (N.W.T.S.C.).

MacKay." And a bit further on the script noted that there had been an inquest into the whole matter, but stated, "None of these facts were presented to the inquest jury last month." Then the script quoted somebody from an organization called the Committee for Original Peoples Entitlement saying, "[T]he government is not able to regulate Dome." If you take those four statements — approved "without any long examination," "would also likely have prevented the gas problems," "none of these facts were presented to the inquest," "the government is not able to regulate Dome" — none of them directly asserts anything libellous about Maurice Thomas. But what is being implied is that Thomas was at best incompetent and more likely on the payroll of Dome Petroleum while he was supposed to be working for the government of Canada. His corruption or incompetence was the direct cause of the explosion that led to someone's death, and then he tried to cover the whole thing up. Though unpleasant implications are suggested about Thomas, nowhere does the script actually say anything bad about him. In libel, implications of this kind are called innuendo — beating around the bush, hinting at things. The simple point, which this case makes clear, is that hinting at something is just as culpable as coming right out and saying it. Journalists should never waste their time beating around the bush or coyly suggesting conclusions. If a reporter does not have all the details of the story verified, he should not try to make up for the gaps in it by hinting at things. Either have the story and say it straight out, or stick to the material that is actually available.

b) Reference to the Plaintiff

The second element in the plaintiff's case is that he must prove that the allegedly defamatory material refers to him. Libel is said to be a personal action. A plaintiff sues because his personal reputation has been attacked. The plaintiff is thus legally obliged to establish that the libel specifically identifies him. We will look now at some of the complications that can arise.

We begin with a charming old English case, *E. Hulton & Co. v. Jones*,[4] from 1910. This had to do with a provincial newspaper, the *Sunday Chronicle*, which did a piece about the scandalous behaviour of English tourists holidaying at Dieppe. This is what the paper said about the behaviour of some of these tourists.

> Upon the terrace marches the world, attracted by the motor races — a world immensely pleased with itself, and minded to draw a wealth of inspiration — and, incidentally, of golden cocktails — from any

---

4   [1910] A.C. 22 (H.L.).

scheme to speed the passing hour. . . . 'Whist! there is Artemus Jones with a woman who is not his wife, who must be, you know — the other thing!' whispers a fair neighbour of mine excitedly into her bosom friend's ear. Really, is it not surprising how certain of our fellow-countrymen behave when they come abroad? Who would suppose, by his goings on, that he was a churchwarden at Peckham?

The clear suggestion in the story is that Artemus Jones is a fictitious name, but, unfortunately for the paper, a real person called Artemus Jones came along and sued it. (In 1996 in Canada it would probably not be regarded as libellous to say these things about someone, but clearly in England in 1910 it was libellous.)

The paper's response was to say to the plaintiff, "We were not talking about you. We did not mean to refer to you." But the defendant ran into the problem of libel being a tort of strict liability. The defendant could not argue that it did not mean to refer to this plaintiff. The question was not the intention of the defendant, but rather whether readers of the *Sunday Chronicle* who knew Artemus Jones could reasonably conclude that he was the one being referred to in this article. The court took the view that, since there were not many people called Artemus Jones, people who did know the real Artemus Jones could reasonably conclude that he was the one referred to.

There is a standard disclaimer always seen in movies and novels — "All characters and events depicted in this novel (or film) are fictitious, no reference to any person living or dead is intended" — and so on. This disclaimer is meaningless. It is an attempt on the part of publishers of novels and producers of movies to unilaterally absolve themselves of any liability.

A well-known decision in this regard is a 1934 English case, *Youssoupoff* v. *Metro-Goldwyn-Mayer Pictures Ltd.*[5] MGM made a movie about an ostensibly fictional kingdom that existed in eastern Europe before and during the First World War. In this fictional kingdom there was a fictional royal family that lived in a fictional palace. The fictional queen had a fictional son who suffered from haemophilia. The queen spent an inordinate amount of time worrying about the survival of her son and tried all sorts of devices and remedies to cure him of this disease. She became a bit crazy as a result and, at one point, a fictional mad monk appeared and moved into the royal family's palace, claiming he could cure the son. While he was living in the palace, this mad monk spent an evening in the company of a fictional grand duchess to whom he fed

---

5   (1934), 50 T.L.R. 581 (C.A.).

large amounts of alcohol and whom he eventually seduced. A real grand duchess who had been a member of a real royal family in a real kingdom in eastern Europe saw the movie and sued MGM. MGM said the movie was just a work of fiction, a fairytale. The English court, however, said that what MGM might have intended was beside the point. Persons who knew this real grand duchess could reasonably conclude that she was the one being depicted. Thus, she had been sufficiently identified and could maintain a libel action.

An interesting question of social and legal policy which arises here involves the extent to which Canadian law does and should recognize group defamation. If you assert that all lawyers are thieves and scoundrels, can I, as a lawyer, sue you? Does your assertion identify me to a sufficient degree to permit me to maintain a libel action against you? The answer is no. Simply belonging to a group about which defamatory statements have been made is not sufficient to entitle any individual member of that group to maintain an action. The plaintiff must be personally identified. If you say that all Fantasians are horse-thieves, the mere fact that I happen to be a Fantasian is not enough. The obvious question, then, is what degree of identification is required?

A case from British Columbia illustrates the point nicely.[6] In the early 1980s BCTV did a public affairs piece about street crime in Vancouver. As part of this piece there were various interviews with people on the streets — "streeters" in the jargon of the trade. In one of these interviews, reporters talked to someone whom they identified as a prostitute and asked her about police corruption. The key question put to her was whether she could name police officers actually involved in corruption. Her response, which was aired, was:

> Oh I could — yeah — but I'm not gonna name them — cause that would just get me up a creek without a paddle — but there is, I'd say three on the Morality Squad that are quite high for payoffs and I know two on the Narc Squad that are high up — right up on top that take payoffs, and there's a few other ones on — like Traffic — you know they're special squads that take some.

These words led to a libel action. In order to understand what happened, we have to know the organization of the narcotics squad of the Vancouver police force. The squad was organized into two groups, one called the "undercover subgroup" and the other the "trafficking sub-

---

6   *Booth v. British Columbia Television Broadcasting System* (1983), 139 D.L.R. (3d) 88 (B.C.C.A.).

group." Each group was headed by a senior police officer, and then within it were various ordinary police officers. Eleven members of the narcotics squad of the Vancouver police force sued BCTV. Of these, one was the head of the undercover street group, one was the head of the trafficking group, and the other nine plaintiffs were ordinary police officers. The court dismissed the actions of these nine ordinary officers on the ground that none of them had been sufficiently identified as an individual, but upheld the actions of the head of the undercover group and the head of the trafficking group. Why? — because of the words: "I know *two* on the Narc Squad that are high up — right up on top." The court said these words were sufficient to identify these two plaintiffs as individuals; that reasonable persons who knew them could conclude that they were the ones being referred to.

Ten years ago a libel action was started at the Carleton University Journalism School. A group of female journalism students held a press conference and said that male professors in the journalism school were sexually harassing female students. There were at the time about a dozen male professors in the school. Three of them launched a libel action. It was eventually settled, but had it gone to trial the issue would have been whether the assertion that male journalism professors sexually harassed female students sufficiently identified any individual plaintiff. One of the crucial factors with this question is going to be the size of the group referred to. If there had been only three male journalism professors at Carleton and all three had sued, they probably would have succeeded, but on the facts of this case the group was likely too large and there was insufficient identification of any individual for him to be able to maintain an action. The larger the group being referred to, the less likely it is that any individual member of that group will have been sufficiently identified.

The general policy of Canadian law is against the recognition of group defamation. That is why the courts dismissed a libel action arising out of the CBC television series *The Valour and the Horror*. One of the episodes in the series appeared to imply that Canadians who flew with RAF Bomber Command during the Second World War were war criminals. A number of people who had been in the RCAF during the Second World War were annoyed and launched an action against the CBC. The action was dismissed on the basis that, even if the assertions in the program were libellous, the group referred to was far too large to permit the identification of any individual plaintiff.

What is the position with respect to libels directed at organizations? There are, in law, two kinds of persons — real persons and artificial persons. Corporations, artificial persons, have many of the legal attributes of human beings. One result is that a corporation has roughly the same rights to its reputation as does an individual. Thus, a corporation can sue for a libel just as an individual can. But an unincorporated organization cannot, because it does not have legal personality.

The trick in doing stories about organizations is to avoid identifying any of their individual members or officers or directors. The law is clear that a libellous statement about an organization is not in and of itself a libel about any member of that organization, unless, of course, that member is identified as an individual.

The last point to note is that it is not possible to libel a dead person. Since libel is a personal action, it must be maintained by the person who claims to have been libelled. If a plaintiff were to drop dead an hour before judgment was to be given in his favour, that would be the end of his libel action. If, on the other hand, judgment has already been given, that judgment becomes part of the dead person's estate. But an estate cannot proceed with a libel action. The important thing to remember is that, while anyone can say anything he likes about a dead person, a degree of caution must be exercised so that in the course of making critical statements about a dead person one does not also libel a living person: "X was a lunatic and has no doubt passed on those defective genes to his two children."

c) **Publication**

The third, and final, element in the plaintiff's case requires him to establish that the defamatory statements about him were published — that is, communicated to a third party. Strictly speaking, even one third party will do. If there are two people alone in a room and one calls the other all sorts of names or questions his ancestry and intelligence, there is no libel. The statements must be communicated to a third party. Insults or abuse as such are not libellous.

Legislation in every province makes the third element easier for the plaintiff. All the legislation deems that material which has been printed in a newspaper or broadcast over radio or television has been published.[7] It is reasonable to assume that, for example, somebody must read the *London Free Press*. It used to be the case in libel actions that the plaintiff would have to bring a parade of witnesses to court who would say, "Yes I read the *London Free Press* last Saturday and I read that story" or "I watched the CBC prime time news and I saw the libellous asser-

---

7   See, for example, the Ontario *Libel and Slander Act*, R.S.O. 1990, c. L.12, s. 2 [hereinafter *LSA*].

tions about the plaintiff." That, surely, is silly and a waste of time and money. The legislation makes it unnecessary.

The Ontario legislation defines broadcasting as follows:

> "Broadcasting" means the dissemination of writing, signs, signals, pictures and sounds of all kinds, intended to be received by the public either directly or through the medium of relay stations, by means of, (a) any form of wireless radioelectric communication utilising Hertzian waves, (b) including radiotelegraph and radio-telephone, or cables, wires, fibre-optic linkages or laser beams.[8]

That definition, I assume, would be broad enough to cover libellous material disseminated through online computer services.

If the statements were not contained in a newspaper or broadcast over radio or television, the plaintiff would have to prove that they had actually been published. In so far as the plaintiff's case is concerned, it is sufficient that the libel has been published to one other person. How many people in fact saw or read the libel is relevant to the question of damages, but not to the basic issue of liability.

The final point to look at is the question of republication. If I am the initial publisher of a libel, to what extent and under what circumstances can I be held responsible for subsequent republications of that libel by other persons or organizations? As a general matter, any republication is a fresh libel and the original publisher cannot be held liable. There is only one circumstance under which the initial publisher might be held liable for subsequent republication and that is when the republication is a natural and probable consequence of the initial publication.[9] This circumstance could arise with a news service. The news service publishes material by putting stories out on the wire. It does this so that subscribers will pick the stories up and republish them. Clearly, for example, any republication of a Canadian Press story by a CP subscriber is a natural and probable consequence of the initial publication by CP, assuming, of course, that the subscriber had republished the story exactly as it came over the wire and without making any changes to it. The simple point is that if a plaintiff is suing a news service for having published a libel, it may be able to hold the news service responsible not just for what went out on the wire, but for subsequent republications by its subscribers.

What about the phenomenon known as "rip and read," in which it is alleged that some radio stations simply take stories from newspapers and

---

8   *Ibid.* s. 1(1).
9   *Basse v. Toronto Star Newspapers Ltd.* (1983), 44 O.R. (2d) 164 (H.C.J.).

read them over the air? A newspaper should not be liable in respect of what the radio station broadcasts, since "rip and read" would not be regarded as a natural and probable consequence of the initial publication.

Defamation, identification, and publication are the three elements that the plaintiff has to prove. Proof of actual injury is not part of the plaintiff's case. As has been noted, if the plaintiff can establish the three elements required, injury to reputation is assumed.

If the plaintiff is successful in proving these elements, the plaintiff is said to have established a *prima facie* case. Having done that, the plaintiff will win if the defendant does nothing — that is, unless the defendant attempts to raise a defence. Alternatively, if the plaintiff does not establish a *prima facie* case, the defendant can move the court to have the action dismissed on the ground that there is no case to answer. The plaintiff has not discharged the basic burden that rests with him.

2) The Defendant's Case

We turn now to the defendant's case, to the defences available to a libel action. The law recognizes four defences, and we will deal with each in turn. The defendant is in no way required to look the four possible defences over, select one, and reject the other three. He could, in an appropriate case, plead all four. In civil actions there is no general principle that prevents a defendant from pleading a multiplicity of defences, from pleading overlapping defences, or, even under certain circumstances, from pleading contradictory defences.

Although we address the various defences primarily as legal phenomena, underlying this approach is a commitment to the notion that, in a practical journalistic sense, the best defences to a libel action are good reporting and good editing.

a) Justification
The first defence is called justification. In ordinary language that means truth. A number of observations may be made about this defence. The first is that the law presumes defamatory statements to be false and thus requires the defendant to prove their truth. The plaintiff is not obliged to prove that the defamatory assertions are false. This approach has occasioned a certain amount of concern about "libel chill." It has been argued that requiring the defendant to prove the truth of defamatory statements amounts to creating a "reverse onus." This is misleading, because the notion of reverse onus belongs exclusively to the criminal law. The plaintiff in a libel action has the burden of proof. The plaintiff, as we have seen, has to prove the three elements that make up a *prima*

facie case. Only when the plaintiff has satisfactorily established those three elements is any obligation cast on the defendant. Turning to the general policy question of whether the plaintiff should have to prove that the defamatory assertions are false or whether the defendant should have to prove they are true, there is a number of significant considerations that argue in favour of requiring the defendant to do so. The first is the problem that anyone who has done an undergraduate course in philosophy or logic will be familiar with: It is impossible to prove a negative. If the defamatory statement is that I molest little children, I cannot prove that I have never molested a child. I can prove that I have not molested this child, or that child, or some other named child. I can prove that I did not molest a child last Wednesday, but, as a matter of logic, I cannot prove that I have never on any occasion molested a child. But more to the point, the requirement that the defendant prove the truth of the statements in question is entirely consistent with the demands of good journalism. If a newspaper or broadcaster is going to publish damaging statements about someone, then before it actually does so it should have sufficient factual underpinning for those statements to satisfy itself that they are true. And if it did not have sufficient factual underpinning to satisfy itself that the assertions were true, then it should not have published them. Knowledge of the truth or falsity of statements that have been published is, and should be, peculiarly the province of the media. Who else is going to know better whether statements are true or false than the newspaper or broadcaster that published them? Indeed, in a 1995 decision, the Supreme Court of Canada not only rejected the notion of "libel chill," but expressly accepted the legitimacy of the current position: "Surely it is not requiring too much of individuals that they ascertain the truth of the allegations they publish."[10]

It is important in understanding the requirements of proving the truth of the allegedly defamatory statements to grasp some of the distinctions between civil and criminal proceedings. Two different, but related, phrases are used in law — "burden of proof" and "standard of proof." We have seen that the plaintiff in a libel action initially bears the burden of proof. Standard of proof addresses the issue of how well a party has to prove the things it is obliged to prove. In criminal cases the Crown has the burden of proving that the accused is guilty. How well does the Crown have to prove the accused's guilt? Beyond a reasonable doubt. Beyond a reasonable doubt does not mean absolute certainty, but if we were to put it in arithmetical terms, we would be talking about

---

10   *Hill v. Church of Scientology of Toronto*, [1995] 2 S.C.R. 1130 at 1187.

something around 90 percent certainty. The standard of proof in civil proceedings is "on a balance of probabilities." That means that a fact is taken to have been proved if the court accepts that it is *more likely than not*. Arithmetically, more likely than not means 51 percent. The simple point is that it is far less demanding to have to prove something in a civil proceeding than it is in a criminal proceeding. There is another important distinction. Libel actions are the last bastion of the jury in civil proceedings in Canada. But the way civil juries work is different from the way criminal juries work. Criminal juries operate on the basis of unanimity. If an accused is to be convicted, twelve jurors out of twelve must be persuaded beyond a reasonable doubt that he is guilty. Civil juries, in contrast, act on the basis of majorities. In Ontario a civil jury consists of six people. Five out of six members of a civil jury can reach a verdict. In Saskatchewan a civil jury consists of twelve people, and ten out of twelve is sufficient to reach a verdict. Thus, for a defendant to prove that ostensibly libellous assertions are true, all he has to do, in Ontario, is persuade five jurors out of six that the assertions are more likely to be true than not.[11]

The normal method of proving facts in Canadian courtrooms is through the evidence of witnesses. There is scope for the use of documentary evidence, but litigants rely primarily on the oral testimony of live witnesses to prove facts. This practice leads to some important considerations about raising the defence of truth, considerations that have to do with sources. A crucial matter in libel actions has to do with a feature of the law of evidence called the hearsay rule. This rule, or at least the exceptions to it, is exceedingly complicated, but its basic principle is easy to state: the only person who can testify as to the existence of a fact is someone who has direct knowledge of that fact through his own senses. That means, most commonly, someone who can say, "I saw it happen." The hearsay rule means a witness cannot seek to prove the truth of something by saying that someone else told him it happened. The response would be that if somebody told you it happened, get that somebody here as a witness. Thus, if a defendant wants to establish the truth of ostensibly libellous assertions, he must have a witness or witnesses who can give direct personal evidence as to their truth.

We now address four issues that can arise in relation to sources. The first is generally referred to as the problem of the disappearing source. A defendant is very much at the mercy of its sources in a libel action.

---

11   See Ontario, *Juries Act*, R.S.O. 1990, c. J.3, and Saskatchewan, *The Jury Act, 1981*, S.S. 1980–81, c. J-4.1.

The defendant is going to have to rely on a source going into the witness box, taking an oath, and saying in open court the same things that that person said to a reporter some time ago, possibly in confidence. Once the source steps into the witness box and starts giving evidence, the defendant has no control over what is being said. A crucial thing about sources that a reporter has to address and an editor may have to address and, eventually, a lawyer, is making a judgment whether this source, if it comes to it, will truthfully recount his information in court under oath. That judgment is crucial, because if a reporter has only one source, and his judgment and an editor's judgment is that they are not confident this person will tell the truth in court, then the story may have to be recast. The only means of eventually proving the truth of a particular assertion in the story may prove not to be reliable. This is one of the reasons reporters should try to have more than one source. The great virtue of having a number of sources is that if source A proves unreliable, the defendant will have source B and source C to fall back on.

The second, and related, problem with sources has to do with their credibility. The point of raising the defence of truth is not to argue that in some abstract philosophical or moral sense a story is true. The concrete point is to prove to the satisfaction of a court that it is true. A crucial element in doing this, of course, is to persuade the court to believe the defendant's witnesses — that is, the sources. The issue here is not whether the source is telling the truth, but whether the court believes that the source is telling the truth. A good example of this problem is a Newfoundland case, *Drost* v. *Sunday Herald Ltd.*[12] The facts were simple. A man was driving along a road outside St John's. Two RCMP constables allegedly came along, pulled him over to the side of the road, dragged him out of his car, and beat him up. The man went to a newspaper reporter and told him what had happened. Obviously, the reporter believed the man because his story appeared in the newspaper. One of the police officers sued the paper for libel. The paper's defence was truth, but, of course, its only witness was the man who claimed he had been beaten up. It turned out that this man had an impressive criminal record and was a well-known ne'er-do-well. What happened at the trial? Two sterling members of the RCMP said none of this ever happened, and one man who had a criminal record said it did. Who did the court believe? The paper lost the libel action.

Judgments will have to be made as to whether the sources for the story will be credible witnesses. Once again, if the conclusion is that the

---

12   (1976), 11 Nfld. & P.E.I.R. 342 (Nfld. T.D.).

source or sources are unlikely to be credible witnesses, then it may be necessary to recast the story. This is another reason for trying to have more than one source. If a particular source is not going to be a credible witness, perhaps others will be.

These judgments about the reliability and credibility of sources cannot be made solely by the reporter who is working on the story. They should also be made by editors and, if necessary, by lawyers. That means that in certain cases an editor and the newspaper or the station's lawyer will have to interview the sources and reach conclusions about their reliability and credibility.

The third problem with sources is the unfortunate fact that they may often have their own agendas. Sources do not speak to journalists only because they are motivated by a commitment to truth. A source can have his own purposes and seek to manipulate a reporter or an editor in order to further those purposes. A classic case is *Vogel* v. *Canadian Broadcasting Corp.*[13] The CBC in Vancouver had hired a young journalist and given him the official title of investigative reporter. It appears from the cases that to formally describe someone as an "investigative reporter" is a sure-fire way to destroy that individual's judgment. This person was sitting in the newsroom with his new title, all ready for the investigative pieces he was bound to do, when he received an anonymous phone call. The caller would not give his name, but said he had a great story. The story was about someone called Richard Vogel, who happened to be the deputy attorney general of British Columbia. The caller, although the reporter did not know it at the time, was actually a lawyer who worked in the Attorney General's Department and did not like Richard Vogel. More to the point, the caller wanted to get Vogel and had figured out that a good way to do so would be to induce CBC television to do a critical story about him. The caller's story was appealing to the investigative reporter because he claimed to know of three instances where the deputy attorney general had interfered with cases actually before the courts, interfered with the administration of justice, in order to benefit his friends. This was a wonderful story, except for the fact that it wasn't true. The source's stories were not complete fabrications. There was a grain of truth in each, enough certainly to provide sufficient basis for persuading a credulous reporter. The source also embellished his stories with certain theatrical flourishes that had the effect of further persuading the reporter. The source put out the bait. The reporter rose to it and was then skilfully played and landed. The

---

13   [1982] 3 W.W.R. 97 (B.C.S.C.) [hereinafter *Vogel*].

reporter did make some effort to confirm the stories. There were indeed three cases before the courts. And there were facts about them which the source had accurately recounted and which the reporter confirmed. But the fundamental fact — that Richard Vogel had interfered in all three cases in order to help his friends out — was just not there.

The CBC went to air with this story in 1981 and eventually paid Vogel $125,000 in damages.

Reporters must approach sources, especially ones who are telling spectacular stories, with a certain amount of scepticism. There should be documents that back up what a particular source is saying. It would be useful for reporters to ask themselves why a source is giving them this information. What are the source's motives? Reporters should never forget the fundamental stricture that you do not believe everything people tell you. Everyone in some way or other has an axe to grind. Finally, the traditional reluctance of reporters to rely on material from sources who refuse to let their names be used in a story should be revived. If a source says he does not want his name used in a story, that fact must raise questions about the source's motives and, most important, about whether he is telling the truth.

The fourth and final problem in relation to sources arises when there aren't any, when reporters simply fabricate stories. This is precisely what happened in one of the more spectacular Canadian libel cases, *Munro* v. *Toronto Sun Publishing Corp.*[14] John Munro was a member of Parliament from Hamilton, Ontario, and a minister in several Trudeau governments. The Toronto *Sun* hired someone and made the same mistake as had been made by the CBC in Vancouver of calling him an investigative reporter. In fact it compounded its error and called two people investigative reporters. It took a young reporter who was eager to get his career going and teamed him with an older reporter whose career had not been doing much for about twenty years. This was a fatal combination.

In the 1970s PetroCanada, which originally was started as a state oil holding company, got into the service station business. PetroCanada acquired all the service stations in Canada first of PetroFina, then of British Petroleum, and turned them into PetroCanada stations. In order to do this, a range of corporate regalia had to be designed and manufactured — colours for the pumps, flags, uniforms for the people working in the service stations, credit cards, and so on.

The supposed story was that John Munro had used his position as a federal minister to ensure that the PetroCanada contract went to a com-

---

14   (1982), 39 O.R. (2d) 100 (H.C.J.) [hereinafter *Munro*].

pany in which he had an interest. He was, thus, accused of serious corruption. The problem with the story was that it had been made up. The younger reporter made it up and then sold it to his partner. It was easy to do so because the older reporter wanted to believe the story, just as the CBC reporter in *Vogel* wanted to believe what the source was telling him. But the older reporter did have some residual scepticism and suggested he should talk to the younger reporter's sources. There ensued a great deal of cloak and daggerish toing and froing, with the predictable result that the older reporter never quite managed to speak to any of the sources.

There was a certain amount of concern about this story in the *Sun* newsroom, especially since the plan was to run it on page 1. The reporters had a meeting with the editor, the publisher, and a lawyer to talk about the story. During the course of this meeting someone asked the younger reporter if he had any documents to support the story. The reporter said he once had the original documents, but had somehow lost them. He told the others not to worry and held up a microfiche saying, of the documents, "They are all here." No one at that meeting asked to look at the microfiche. The *Sun* published the story.

John Munro sued immediately. The *Sun* did a bit of further investigation, discovered the story was a fabrication, and issued a belated apology.

The trial judge made a number of observations about avoiding libel actions. These observations are nothing more than a lawyer's way of formulating some of the basic rules of good reporting and good editing.

> [T]here *must* be a separation of functions between the reporter and the editor, it being the responsibility of the editor to confirm the accuracy of the contents of a story before publication. . . . [T]here must be constant supervision maintained by the editor over the reporter, with a regular reporting requirement. . . . [I]t is the editor's responsibility to know in detail before publication, the documentation to support the story and the reliability of the sources and so ensure its accuracy.

If a reporter says to an editor, "I cannot tell you the identity of my source," the only reply the editor can make is, "In that case we cannot run the story." If the reporter says, "Trust me on this one," an editor's response and what an editor is paid to say is, "It's nothing personal, but it's not my job to trust you. I want to know who the sources are and I want to talk to the sources myself and in fact I think I want to arrange for our lawyer to talk to the sources." If the reporter refuses to divulge the identity of the sources, then the only course open to someone in an editorial position is to refuse to publish the story. The main reason the story in *Munro* v. *Toronto Sun Publishing Corp.* was printed is that when the editor asked the reporters who their sources were, they replied,

"You're going to have to trust us on this one." And the editor made the mistake of agreeing.

If a reporter files copy that says that a federal minister is guilty of gross corruption or that the deputy attorney general of a province has on three separate occasions interfered with cases actually before the courts in order to help his friends, then an editor is under a clear obligation to review every detail of such a story carefully. There cannot be any other course of action.

Reporters should never give their word to sources that they will under no circumstances reveal their identity. Reporters should be honest with sources. They should say to sources, "I will do my very best to protect your identity, but you have to understand some things about the way this business operates. I cannot give you an absolute guarantee." If necessary, the reporter should explain why he cannot give an absolute guarantee. To say anything else is to mislead the source. It is also important to remember what should be the response of the lawyer if it is decided that a particular story should be lawyered before being published. Whatever the editor says to the reporter, the lawyer must make clear to the editor and the reporter that he has to know who the sources are. If a lawyer were to review a story like the one in *Munro* v. *Toronto Sun Publishing Corp.*, the very first question he should ask would be the identity of the sources. If the reporter refused to divulge this information, the only advice the lawyer could give his client, the newspaper or broadcaster, would be not to run the story.

Other points in the judgment in *Munro* are worth noting — and it is remarkable that a judge would feel it necessary to say these things to people who work for a large urban daily newspaper. The judge added, "[W]here important documentation has been obtained it is good practice to put it in a safe place and to thereafter work from a copy." The idea that there could be an editor who, on asking a reporter to produce the documentation a story was based on, would accept the statement that the reporter had lost it and would further accept an assurance that it was on microfiche, but not demand to actually look at that microfiche, is also astonishing.

The final point the judge made may be controversial. "[W]hen the story is prepared — and the paper has the 'goods' on the person targeted in the story it is basic and necessary that that person be confronted with the story so that his reaction be obtained." It seems clear that had the *Sun* contacted John Munro and told him the nature of the story it was planning to publish, Munro's reaction might have led to some rethinking. Some newspapers and broadcasters are reluctant to do this check as a matter of principle. I do not agree with this approach. I believe there is a professional obligation to apprise the person targeted of the story and, more to the point, it can help avoid a great deal of trouble.

What *Vogel* and *Munro* make clear above all is the value of good reporting and good editing as practical defences to a libel action. If there has been good reporting and good editing, you may still get sued, because there is, of course, no way to control such action. But, even if you are sued, if there has been good reporting and good editing, you are going to win. And where there has been bad reporting or bad editing, or both, you stand a good chance of losing.

Good reporting and good editing are directly relevant to other concerns that can arise when truth is raised as a defence. First, when the defence of justification is argued, a court may demand that the defendant prove the truth of precisely what was published. The court may give a strict interpretation to the allegedly defamatory words and then require the defendant to prove the literal truth of that interpretation. This is what happened in *Baxter* v. *Canadian Broadcasting Corp.*[15] This case had to do with a report broadcast on *the fifth estate* in April 1977 about certain activities of John Baxter, a former minister of justice in New Brunswick. Rumours had been circulating in the province about kickbacks being made to a secret Conservative Party fund. The RCMP began an investigation, but, according to the CBC, was ordered by Baxter to desist. The crucial words from the script were:

> In an internal police memo written in September, 1973, an R.C.M.P. sergeant reported that a man under investigation for another matter makes many references to kickbacks to a Conservative Party fund. The police wanted to follow that lead, but then a week later they were stopped by the then Minister of Justice, John Baxter, and their own superiors.

So the CBC said that Baxter, as minister of justice, had stopped an RCMP investigation into *kickbacks* made to his own party. Baxter sued. The CBC relied on the defence of justification. It lost.

The New Brunswick Court of Appeal concluded that the RCMP had been directed to stop its investigation of *political contributions* to the Conservative Party. Political contributions, the judges said, are not the same as kickbacks. The CBC's story was not, therefore, strictly true and the defence of justification failed.

A moment's reflection reveals the flaw in the court's reasoning. Political parties do not keep separate accounts for kickbacks; special receipts marked "kickback" are not given. A kickback is, on its face, a

---

15   (1980), 30 N.B.R. (2d) 102 (C.A.).

lawful political contribution. It is only after investigation that an ostensibly lawful contribution may be revealed to be a kickback. Thus, an order to stop investigating lawful political contributions would have the effect of frustrating the investigation of kickbacks.

The point is that the statement broadcast by the CBC expressed the inevitable result of the order which Baxter, it was conceded, actually gave to the police. But because the matter was not stated with absolute precision, the defence of justification failed. One further sentence added to the script would probably have allowed the CBC to avoid liability. The practical result is that stories, and especially stories that make serious allegations of corruption or impropriety, must be meticulously reviewed. The question to be asked of each sentence, each phrase, indeed, each word is: Can we prove precisely what this is saying? If the answer is not an immediate "Yes," the story may need more work.

The case of *Brannigan* v. *S.I.U.*,[16] dealing as we have seen with a bitter struggle between two unions, raises the question of circumstantial evidence. The defendant, it will be recalled, had asserted that Brannigan, the plaintiff, was a communist. The defendant sought to prove the truth of this assertion. It introduced evidence that Brannigan had belonged to a communist-dominated union, that he had friends who were communists, and that he had marched in May Day parades. It asked the court to infer from these facts that Brannigan was a communist. The court, correctly, refused. Evidence of surrounding circumstances will only be taken as proof of a particular inference if that inference is the only one that can reasonably be drawn from the evidence. Good journalism would suggest that negative conclusions should not be asserted about individuals on the basis of circumstantial evidence alone.

As with all useful things in life, there is a risk involved in raising justification as a defence. If a defendant relies on the defence of truth and sticks to it right to the bitter end and loses, then, unfortunately, that defendant is going to pay even more in damages. The theory is that by maintaining to the bitter end that your nasty little story was true, you have worsened the injury to the plaintiff. A defendant must be confident of success when raising the defence of truth.

Commentators on libel law often note that the defence of truth is seldom raised in actual libel actions. This is correct — and for a very good reason. If the story is true, no one is going to sue. If we reflect on what happens in a libel action, it must be obvious that the plaintiff, or the potential plaintiff, is going to know whether the story is true or not.

---

16   *Supra* note 1.

If anyone is going to know for certain that the story is accurate, it must be the person about whom it was written. John Munro knew whether he had in fact been engaged in the kind of corrupt behaviour that the *Sun* accused him of. If the potential plaintiff knows what was published about him is true, it is unlikely he will sue. Why would anyone go to all the expense and bother if he knows that it will come out in court that the statements made about him were indeed accurate? Truth is a pre-emptive defence; the truth of a story ensures that there will not be a libel action.

b) Fair Comment

The next defence to consider is fair comment. It is important to understand the distinction between the use of justification, the defence of "truth," and the defence of "fair comment." If you are sued in respect of assertions of fact, you defend those assertions by attempting to prove that they are true. If you are sued in respect of an expression of an opinion, then you defend your opinion by seeking to establish that it was fair comment made in good faith and without malice on a matter of public interest. The law makes a distinction, then, between assertions of fact and expressions of opinion. As we shall see, this distinction can cause difficulties.

"Fair comment" can be an extraordinarily useful and broad defence, as was demonstrated in a case called *Pearlman* v. *Canadian Broadcasting Corp.*[17] It arose out of an investigative piece that CBC Radio in Winnipeg did about a local person, Pearlman, who was both a lawyer and a slum landlord. It was a rigorous piece of reporting. Abuse after abuse, deficiency after deficiency, was meticulously catalogued in the report. At the end, the CBC said of Pearlman that he was a person who had "no morals, principles, or conscience." It is difficult to imagine anything worse that could be said about another person. The CBC successfully defended this statement as "fair comment." If fair comment allows you to say that someone has no morals, principles, or conscience and successfully defend that statement, it is an exceedingly useful defence.

We will catalogue the elements that make up the defence and note some of the difficulties that can arise. In the first place, a court must be persuaded that the allegedly libellous statements being defended as fair comment are indeed expressions of an opinion rather than assertions of fact. The difficulty is that, if a defendant tries to raise "fair comment" and the court decides that the libellous statement is not an expression of an opinion but an assertion of a fact, that defence will not be available. The only way to defend factual assertions is to prove that they are

---

17   (1981), 13 Man. R. (2d) 1 (Q.B.).

true. This was the problem in a well-known libel case from British Columbia, *Vander Zalm v. Times Publishers*.[18] The *Times* ran an editorial cartoon about Bill Vander Zalm, later premier of British Columbia, who was at the time the province's minister of human resources. It was a simple, straightforward drawing of Vander Zalm seated at a table, a smile flickering across his lips, pulling the wings off flies. Vander Zalm sued. The paper's defence was "fair comment." But the trial court said the paper could not raise that defence because the cartoon was not an expression of an opinion but an assertion of a fact. What fact? The court said the newspaper was asserting as a fact that Vander Zalm was a cruel person. One would have thought that to say someone is cruel is to express an opinion. How can it be established as a matter of fact that someone is or is not cruel? Nonetheless, that was what the court said. The *Times* could not prove that Vander Zalm was a cruel person and it lost at trial. The newspaper had the good sense, and also, of course, the resources, to appeal to the BC Court of Appeal. The Court of Appeal reversed the trial court's decision and held that, almost by its nature, an editorial cartoon was an expression of opinion. Having decided that this cartoon was an expression of an opinion, the court had no difficulty in concluding further that it was "fair comment."

It is crucial to ensure that assertions of fact are clearly set out as such, that expressions of opinion are likewise set out as such, and that the two are demarcated from each other.

The next requirement in establishing the "fair comment" defence, and the next area where there can be some difficulty, is that the matter commented upon must be one of public interest. This makes sense. The law of libel is an ongoing attempt to "strike a fair balance between the protection of reputation and the protection of free speech."[19] There is an inherent tension between the two that manifests itself in libel law. Both are recognized as important — the reputations of individuals should be protected, but expression should also be free. Libel law requires the courts to attempt to find the right balance. Thus, when it comes to matters of public interest, individuals and the mass media will be allowed to comment broadly and, obviously, adversely about other people. The protection of reputation will give way somewhat to the promotion of free expression. The corollary is that fair comment may not be relied upon to defend public attacks on relatives or friends or former friends, or lovers, or associates, because none of these would be matters of public interest.

---

18   (1980), 109 D.L.R. (3d) 531 (B.C.C.A.).
19   *Cherneskey v. Armadale Publishers Ltd.*, [1979] 1 S.C.R. 1067 at 1095.

How is the distinction made? We have another British Columbia case called *Pound* v. *Scott*.[20] Pound was a physician who had left the United Kingdom allegedly out of disgust with its National Health Service. He came to Canada because of his opposition to a system of health care run by the state. He was of the opinion that Canada should not repeat the mistake made by the United Kingdom. Dr. Pound believed this so strongly that he contacted a reporter for the Victoria *Times* to express his point of view. He suggested that the reporter do a story about him and about his views on health care. The reporter agreed and a piece was duly published in the *Times*. Scott, the defendant, was a columnist with the same newspaper and did not like Dr. Pound's views on health care. Scott wrote a column attacking Pound and his opinions. He wrote the following:

> What I am saying is that Dr. Pound, to my own knowledge, was not at all fair in his presentation of these facts. As for his opinion, I find it equally suspect. Any man who describes health as "a commodity" and the doctor's role "as free trade with his customers," is hardly qualified to judge a national medical scheme based on the philosophy that good health is every citizen's right.

He also said a number of other quite critical things about Dr. Pound. Pound sued. The defence raised was fair comment. Dr. Pound's response was that neither the paper nor Scott should be permitted to raise fair comment because this was not a matter of public interest. Pound was, in effect, saying, "I'm not a rock star, I'm not a professional athlete, I'm not a politician, I'm not a public figure; I'm just an ordinary, everyday, private citizen and you can't attack me and my opinions and defend your attack on the basis of fair comment because what I happen to think about health care is simply the personal view of one private citizen and not a matter of public interest." The court disagreed. It accepted that Dr. Pound was an ordinary private citizen, but it also noted that he had himself, and on his own initiative, voluntarily entered the arena of public controversy and public debate. Health care was clearly a matter of public interest. Dr. Pound involved himself as an ostensible expert in a public debate about health care and, therefore, his opinions on that subject were a matter of public interest. Criticism of those opinions could be defended as "fair comment." Fair comment would not have succeeded if, for example, Scott had gone to a purely social gathering, met Dr. Pound and chatted with him concerning his views on a state-operated health-care system, and then written a column attacking Pound and his ideas. Under

20   (1973), 37 D.L.R. (3d) 439 (B.C.S.C.).

those circumstances, Pound's opinions would not have been matters of public interest. But clearly when we talk about rock stars, professional athletes, politicians, and so on, what these people think and do are matters of public interest. The point — that when it comes to matters of public interest, individuals must be prepared to sacrifice some part of their reputations — was well expressed by the trial judge who commented of Dr. Pound: "Like a boxer, having entered the ring, he must accept the blows given him, provided always that none is 'below the belt.'"

The third point about fair comment is that the defendant is required to establish a factual basis for the opinion that is to be expressed. Built into the defence is the notion that opinions do not simply fall from the sky. In order to succeed with fair comment, the defendant must have set out the facts on which the opinion is based or from which it is derived. As was noted in the *Pearlman* case, the Winnipeg slum landlord case, CBC Radio detailed all the salient facts. The factual foundation must be laid in the same piece as the one that contains the opinion. This is always required, except where the facts on which the opinion is based are so well known as to be notorious.

Libel law is simply a formalization of basic rules of good journalism. If you are going to express critical opinions about somebody in public, you should lay out a factual groundwork before you do so. The facts must be set out and, of course, they must be set out accurately. It surely makes sense to require that a person may rely on "fair comment" to defend the expression of his opinion only if the facts on which he claims to base his opinion are accurate and accurately stated.

What is the crucial element in the fair comment defence? Having ensured that you are in fact expressing an opinion, having made sure that it has to do with a matter of public interest, having accurately set out all the facts on which the opinion is based, it becomes simply a matter of honestly expressing your real opinion. A defendant is not required to persuade the court to agree with his opinion. A defendant is not even required to persuade the court that his opinion is reasonable. All a defendant must do is persuade the court that it was his honestly held opinion. The court may think that the opinion is absurd or implausible. The court may be incapable of imagining why anyone would hold such an opinion. All this is beside the point. If it is an honest expression of the defendant's real opinion, it is fair comment. Passages from two old English cases, both of which have been quoted over and over again in Canadian courts, will illustrate this point. The first is from an 1887 decision called *Merivale* v. *Carson*:[21]

---

21   (1887), 20 Q.B.D. 275 at 281–282 (C.A.).

Every latitude must be given to opinion and to prejudice, and then an ordinary set of men with ordinary judgment must say whether any fair man would have made such a comment. . . . Mere exaggeration, or even gross exaggeration, would not make the comment unfair. However wrong the opinion expressed may be in point of truth, or however prejudiced the writer, it may still be within the prescribed limit. The question which the jury must consider is this — would any fair man, however prejudiced he may be, however exaggerated or obstinate his views, have said that which this criticism has said?

And in *Silkin* v. *Beaverbrook Newspapers Ltd.*[22] in 1958 the judge said:

"They must believe what they say, but the question whether they honestly believe it is a question for you to say. If they do believe it, and they are within anything like reasonable bounds they come within the meaning of fair comment. If comments were made which would appear to you to have been exaggerated, it does not follow that they are not perfectly honest comments."
. . . Could a fair-minded man, holding a strong view, holding perhaps an obstinate view, holding perhaps a prejudiced view — could a fair-minded man have been capable of writing this? . . . That is a totally different question from the question: Do you agree with what he said?

The law is saying that when you are honestly trying to say what you really think about a matter of public interest, your exercise of your freedom of expression takes precedence over my reputation. But if you are saying nasty things about me simply because you are motivated by a whim or by a desire to spread scandal about me, then protection of my reputation should take precedence over your freedom of expression.

Recent legislation in a number of the common law provinces has altered this fundamental aspect of fair comment. In 1978 the Supreme Court of Canada decided *Cherneskey* v. *Armadale Publishers Ltd.*[23] This litigation was between a local politician and the Saskatoon *Star-Phoenix* over a letter to the editor that had been highly critical of the politician, claiming he was a "racist." The paper raised fair comment as a defence, but did not join the two writers of the letter as co-defendants or call them as witnesses. The Court trapped itself in a conceptual dead end. Since the evidence given at trial indicated that none of the actual defendants in the action — officials of Armadale, which owned the *Star-*

---

22   [1958] 2 All E.R. 516 at 518–520 (Q.B.), Diplock L.J., quoting from *R.* v. *Russell* (2 December 1905), (Q.B.) [unreported].
23   *Supra* note 19.

Phoenix, and of the paper itself — believed the plaintiff to be a racist, the Court concluded that the defence of fair comment could not be raised. The statement was not an honest expression of the real opinion of any defendant and, as a result, the newspaper lost. This conclusion required the Court to disregard the obvious point that the statements in the letter clearly represented the real opinions of the people who wrote it. Several of the common law provinces amended their legislation to avoid the result in *Cherneskey*. Section 24 of Ontario's *Libel and Slander Act* now reads:

> Where the defendant published defamatory matter that is an opinion expressed by another person, a defence of fair comment by the defendant shall not fail for the reason only that the defendant or the person who expressed the opinion, or both, did not hold the opinion, if a person could honestly hold the opinion.[24]

A media defendant can now successfully raise fair comment with respect to an opinion that neither it, nor the author of the opinion, actually holds. This defence seems strange.

There is one instance where fair comment does not allow such broad latitude for free expression. This is where, to use the legal jargon, the defendant imputes corrupt or dishonourable motives to the plaintiff. We find an example in another case from British Columbia, *Masters v. Fox*.[25] This case had to do with a letter to the editor published in a local newspaper, the *Comox District Free Press*. The letter was written during a local election campaign about two people who were candidates in that election. The letter read as follows:

> Election time is here again with some of the same old types trying to get in on the action. During the past year the Communist Party Action Committee [the plaintiffs actually belonged to something called the Community Planning Action Committee] has managed to belch a lot of bile and in the process make every effort to con the people into believing they are concerned with local issues and the orderly progress of the community — when in point of fact they are much more interested in spreading their particular brand of political venom — all of it under the guise of community interests. . . .
>
> I would not think that the voter has much of a problem in selecting a suitable and worthwhile candidate. With a full time career lay about and an old maid would appear (at a glance) to be an excellent recipe

24   *Supra* note 7. For comment, see R. Martin, "Libel and Letters to the Editor" (1983) 9 Queen's L.J. 188.
25   (1978), 85 D.L.R. (3d) 64 (B.C.S.C.).

for a loser — but in spite of all some of these loud mouth windbags are going to tell and show everyone how to be winners and whatever the problem — you name it and they will cure it. Not one of them could run a peanut stand without a grant or subsidy and I would even suggest that one of them should be careful that the natural vegetation doesn't slowly take over and immobilize all activity.

It would be unfortunate if the voter was misled by some of their published rubbish which might permit (by accident) a few to get their grubby hands onto the tail end of a few more tax dollars.

This letter raises important issues about the proper scope of libel law. It is clearly extreme. On the other hand, it was written to a newspaper during the course of an election campaign. Should individuals be permitted, without any legal sanctions, to write letters like that during an election campaign about candidates in the election? I do not, for example, believe I should be able to write letters to the editor like that about my neighbour. But this was an election and the plaintiffs were candidates.

There were a number of problems with this letter, but the most important, and the reason the plaintiffs won, had to do with this question of imputing corrupt or dishonourable motives. The letter suggested that these people were running as candidates in the election in order to get their hands into the public till and start embezzling the public's money. The statement "might permit (by accident) a few to get their grubby hands onto the tail end of a few more tax dollars" was taken to suggest that the plaintiffs ran for election for the purpose of putting themselves in a position where they could more successfully indulge their inclinations towards corruption.

The law about imputing corrupt or dishonourable motives is clear. If the defendant imputes such motives in the course of expressing an opinion, then the defendant will have to prove that the plaintiffs were indeed motivated in exactly the fashion suggested. In *Masters* v. *Fox* the court said that in order to succeed the defendant would have to prove that the "full time lay about" and the "old maid" were running for public office precisely because they wanted to get their "grubby hands onto the tail end of a few more tax dollars." It must be obvious how difficult it would be to prove that unless, of course, these two defendants had publicly admitted that was why they were running for office. Once again, libel law accords with the requirements of good journalism. As a matter of principle, journalists should not speculate about people's motives. Idle speculation has no place in good journalism. Thus, not only is it bad journalism, but it is dangerous, to speculate about motives. The practical answer is to avoid it.

The final point to note about fair comment is the question of malice. When fair comment is raised, the plaintiff can attempt to show that in expressing his opinion the defendant was motivated by malice. If the plaintiff can successfully persuade the court that this was the case, the defence is lost. The same principle arises in relation to the defence of privilege, so a full discussion of malice will be left until that point.

c) Privilege

We now move to consider the third defence in libel actions — privilege. The defence of privilege is conceptually different from the other two defences of justification and fair comment. When the defence of justification is raised, the defendant is saying to the court that the statements complained of may look as if they are libellous, but they are not. They are not libellous because they are true. Similarly, when the defence of fair comment is raised, the defendant is saying these statements may appear to be libellous, but they are not because they are fair comment made in good faith and without malice on a matter of public interest. Both defences focus on the substance of the allegedly libellous statements. Privilege is different. When the defence of privilege is raised the defendant is, in effect, conceding that the statements complained of are libellous and is basing his defence, not on the substance of those statements, but on the circumstances under which they were made. As the Supreme Court put it in a recent decision: "[P]rivilege attaches to the occasion upon which the communication is made, and not to the communication itself."[26] The obvious implication is that a statement may be defensible if made on an occasion of privilege, but the identical statement might not be defensible if repeated on another occasion, under different circumstances, which were not privileged.

The point about privilege is that, in trying to find the proper balance between protection of reputation and the promotion of free expression, the law recognizes that there are certain situations in which it is so important that people be able to express themselves freely that they require preferring free expression over the protection of reputation. An important illustration is the case of senators or members of Parliament speaking inside the chamber of the Senate or the House of Commons. There is a clear social interest in ensuring that senators and MPs feel free to say whatever they like on any subject. A member of Parliament, speaking inside the chamber of the House of Commons, is absolutely

---

26   *Botiuk v. Toronto Free Press Publications Ltd.*, [1995] 3 S.C.R. 3 at 29 [hereinafter *Botiuk*].

privileged in respect of anything he says. He can stand up in the House of Commons and tell a series of malicious lies about me for no reason other than to damage my reputation. There is nothing I can do because the law takes the view that on this occasion the freedom of the MP to say whatever he wishes to say is more important than my reputation.

The purpose of having the defence of privilege is said traditionally to be the "common convenience and welfare of society."[27] The common convenience and welfare of society require that MPs feel free to express themselves as they choose. As a result, the common convenience and welfare of society also require that, in that circumstance, my reputation take a back seat.

The practical point about privilege as a defence in a libel action is that, under appropriate circumstances, it permits the mass media to report statements made by other people without having to worry whether what is being asserted in those statements is true. If a statement is made by someone else on an occasion of privilege, the only question that will arise in a libel action against a newspaper or broadcaster which reported that statement is whether the statement itself was accurately reported. No issue can arise as to whether the substance of the statement was accurate.

Turning specifically to privilege as a defence to be raised by the media, there are two broad subcategories: absolute privilege and qualified privilege. The structure of privilege is set out in Figure 3.

Figure 3   The Defence of Privilege

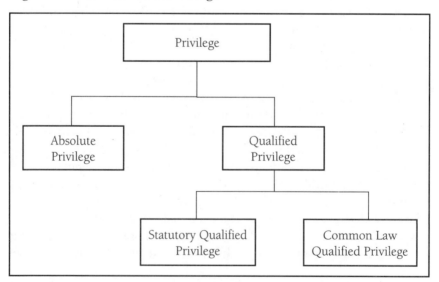

---

27   *Shultz v. Porter and Block Brothers Ltd.* (1979), 9 Alta. L.R. (2d) 381 at 391 (S.C.) [hereinafter *Shultz*].

i) Absolute Privilege

Absolute privilege arises on one occasion and one occasion only: it will apply to a fair and accurate report of the public proceedings of a court. A reporter covering a trial does not have to trouble his mind whether what the witnesses or the judge or the lawyers are saying is true. His only concern is that his report of what they are saying is fair and accurate.

Why does absolute privilege exist? Once again, the answer is that the common convenience and welfare of society require that the public be informed as fully as possible about what is happening in the courts. But this would not be possible if reporters and editors were required to establish the correctness of every assertion made in court before a report could be published. From a slightly different perspective, what we have here is another manifestation of the principle of the openness of the courts.

Absolute privilege results in the common law provinces from either the *Libel and Slander Act* or the *Defamation Act*. Certain difficulties may arise with the defence. First, all the statutes use the adverb "contemporaneously."[28] For the fair and accurate report of the public proceedings of a court to be privileged, it must be published *contemporaneously* with the proceeding in question. None of the statutes defines exactly what is meant by contemporaneously. The usual rule of thumb is that contemporaneously spans three to five days after the actual hearing or, if the publication in question is a weekly or a monthly, extends to the next issue after the proceeding. The general view is that after a week has passed, a report of the particular proceeding will no longer be contemporaneous and will, thus, not qualify for the privilege.

A second and important qualification is that in order to attract the privilege, the report of what went on in the courtroom must be "fair and accurate." The obvious point is that a reporter must get what witnesses and lawyers and judges are saying right. If something is wrongly reported and a story has a witness saying exactly the opposite of what the witness really said, it will not be a fair and accurate report and the defence of privilege will not be available. Once again, good reporting and good editing are the secret. However, it is clear that a fair and accurate report does not have to be verbatim. Nor does a fair and accurate report have to be a precis of what went on in the court. It is perfectly proper to select portions of what happened for reporting, or to focus on one witness or even one statement made by one witness. The report can still be fair and accurate. The standard that has been applied to determine if a particular report is fair and accurate is to ask whether the

---

28   See, for example, the Ontario *LSA, supra* note 7, s. 4(1).

impression created in the mind of a reader or a viewer of the report would be consistent with the impression that would have been created in the mind of somebody who was actually in the courtroom at the time. If the answer to the question is "yes," the report is fair and accurate. If the answer is "no," the report is not.[29]

An interesting issue arises with respect to language in Libel and Slander Acts or Defamation Acts to which few, if any, people have paid attention and whose meaning is, as a result, unclear. For example, section 4(1) of the Ontario Libel and Slander Act requires that, as a condition of raising the defence, the defendant must have been prepared to insert in its newspaper or broadcast a reasonable statement of explanation or contradiction by or on behalf of the plaintiff. This could mean, for example, as bizarre as it might appear, that if a reporter had covered the Paul Bernardo trial and, presumably, written some unpleasant things about Bernardo, that reporter might conceivably be under an obligation to afford some sort of right of reply to Bernardo. This provision has not, as far as I am aware, actually become an issue in litigation.

Why is absolute privilege called *absolute* privilege? Herein lies the basic distinction between absolute privilege and qualified privilege. If the defendant has raised qualified privilege, the plaintiff can attempt to show that the defendant was motivated by malice in publishing the story. If the defendant was motivated by malice, the defence will be lost. By way of contrast, evidence of malice is irrelevant when the defendant relies on absolute privilege. This distinction is not entirely logical. If the defence raised is absolute privilege, it is difficult to see how a report that was motivated by malice could be regarded as fair and accurate. Nonetheless, that is the distinction.

ii) Qualified Privilege
There are two subcategories of qualified privilege — qualified privilege that arises under statute and qualified privilege that arises under common law. We will first deal with qualified privilege under statute and then turn to qualified privilege under common law.

a. Statutory Qualified Privilege
The various Libel and Slander Acts or Defamation Acts create extraordinarily broad bases for qualified privilege. They set out lengthy lists of occasions and circumstances about which the mass media may report and claim a defence of privilege, so long as the report in question is fair and accurate. The most significant of these are as follows. A fair and accurate

---

29   Cook v. Alexander, [1974] Q.B. 279 (C.A.).

report of the proceedings of any legislative body in the Commonwealth, or part or committee thereof that exercises either sovereign law-making power or delegated law-making power, is privileged. The most common example of a body that exercises delegated law-making power is a municipal council. Such a body has had the authority to make laws given or delegated to it by the provincial legislature. Thus, a fair and accurate report of proceedings in Parliament, or of the provincial legislature, or of a city council, or of any committee of Parliament, and so on, is privileged.

There is an interesting paradox here. Members of sovereign legislatures, when they are speaking inside the chamber of the legislature, are speaking on an occasion of privilege. Not only is the MP privileged in respect of what he says, but the media's fair and accurate report of what he said is also privileged. But because municipal councils are not sovereign law-making bodies, members of councils probably do not enjoy the same degree of privilege in respect of what they say during council meetings. So if councillor X stands up and calls the mayor a lying scoundrel, the mayor might successfully sue councillor X, but not the newspaper or broadcaster that published a fair and accurate report about the incident.

A fair and accurate report of the proceedings of any public administrative body in Canada is also privileged. That includes the proceedings, for example, of such bodies as the CRTC, or a provincial Workers' Compensation Board or Labour Relations Board. A fair and accurate report of the proceedings of any public commission of inquiry is privileged. The Dubin Commission into the use of drugs in sport would be a good illustration of the utility for the media of the defence of privilege. It sometimes seemed that every statement made by witnesses before the Commission was a libel of somebody or other. Many witnesses said such things as "he was supplying drugs," "she was using drugs," "someone else was prescribing drugs." If it had not been for the defence of qualified privilege, it would have been impossible to publish reports about the proceedings of the Dubin Commission.

Indeed, a fair and accurate report of the proceedings of any lawful public meeting, whether admission to the meeting is general or restricted, is privileged. This category would include a shareholders meeting from which members of the public were excluded. So, once again, if a reporter were to cover the annual general meeting of the Middlesex County Cat Fanciers' Association and all kinds of outrageous accusations were hurled round the room, that reporter's fair and accurate report would be privileged. This means, to repeat a point made in relation to absolute privilege, that the accuracy of what is being reported must be ensured in the sense that this is indeed what the outgoing president of the Cat

Fanciers' Association said, but the reporter is under no obligation to check that the substantive content of the outgoing president's statement is accurate.

A fair and accurate synopsis of any public statement or press release put out by any public or governmental body in Canada is also privileged. Thus, when the ministry of whatever sends out a press release, the media can report about it and not have to worry whether what is asserted in that press release is correct.

The defence is even broader. A fair and accurate report of any of the decisions, proceedings, or public statements of any association or body in Canada which is dedicated to any art, science, religion, or learning, or any trade, business, industry, or profession, or any game, sport, or pastime is privileged. It is useful again to think back to the Dubin Inquiry. The Canadian Track and Field Association, for example, regularly issued statements disagreeing with what certain witnesses before the Commission had said. Many of its press releases arguably libelled various people. But as long as the media produced fair and accurate reports of what was in one of those press releases, their reports were privileged.

If qualified privilege did not exist, a great deal of reporting would not be possible. How on earth, for example, could a reporter check the accuracy of every statement made by every member of a municipal council at every council meeting?

It is essential that the occasion in question actually be an occasion of privilege. For example, as has been noted, a fair and accurate report of a lawful public meeting is privileged. But it must have been a *bona fide* public meeting. In an old Saskatchewan case an individual rented a hall and invited the public in for no reason other than to give himself a platform from which to rail against various people he did not like. This occasion was held not to be a *bona fide* public meeting and, as a result, reports of it, even though they were fair and accurate, were not privileged.[30]

b. Qualified Privilege at Common Law

The question of qualified privilege under common law is especially interesting because it relates to the broader question of the direction Canadian libel law should be taking and, most important, whether it should become Americanized. At common law, privilege is attached to communications made under the following general circumstances. If the person making the communication was under a moral, social, political, legal, or professional duty to make it and the person to whom it was

---

30   *Hefferman v. Regina Daily Star* (1930), 25 Sask. L.R. 148 (K.B.).

made was under a corresponding obligation to receive it, then the relation between them was one that gave rise to privilege.[31] Privilege would attach to communications made during the course of that relation. For example, let us say a psychiatrist was engaged by a firm that was contemplating hiring someone to give an opinion about that person's emotional stability. The psychiatrist would be under a professional duty to provide that information. Likewise, the firm would be under a corresponding obligation to receive it. Thus, a relation is created between the firm and the psychiatrist which gives rise to a qualified privilege surrounding communications made during the course of the relation. If the firm, having received a letter from the psychiatrist, showed that letter to an outsider, however, no privilege would attach to that communication.

How far can this principle be extended? Can it be argued that the mass media in a democracy are under an obligation to inform the public on matters of public interest and that the public is under a corresponding obligation to be informed? The result of accepting this argument would be that whenever the mass media speak to the public on matters of public interest, a relationship is created that gives rise to privilege. Thus, any plaintiff wishing to sue the mass media over a story that dealt with a matter of public interest would be met by the defence of qualified privilege; the plaintiff could only succeed if he were able to establish that the defendant was motivated by malice. That, in fact, has been the basis of American libel law since a decision of the US Supreme Court in 1964 in a case called *N.Y. Times Co.* v. *Sullivan*.[32] Practically speaking, the result has been that the mass media in the United States are under no legal obligation to check their facts whenever they are dealing with a matter of public interest.

Such an approach was expressly rejected by the Supreme Court of Canada in 1961 in a case called *Banks* v. *Globe & Mail Ltd.*,[33] another piece of litigation arising out of the struggle between the Canadian Seamen's Union and the Seafarers' International Union. But the argument has been revived with the adoption of the *Charter* and, in particular, the guarantees of freedom of expression and freedom of the press in section 2(b).

Basing themselves on *N.Y. Times Co.* v. *Sullivan*, many in this country have argued that the defence of qualified privilege should be expanded to the point where any statement made by the mass media on any matter of public interest would attract a *Charter*-based privilege. This argument was expressly and unequivocally rejected by the Supreme Court in 1995

---

31   *Adam* v. *Ward*, [1917] A.C. 309 (H.L.).
32   376 U.S. 254 (1964).
33   [1961] S.C.R. 474.

in *Hill* v. *Church of Scientology of Toronto.*[34] This decision, while it did not directly involve the mass media, set out important conclusions about the general direction the law of defamation should take in Canada.

The Court noted that the *Sullivan* approach had been widely criticized in the United States and, more important, had not been adopted by either the courts or the legislature of any other country. It further held that there was no compelling evidence to lead it to conclude that existing Canadian defamation law unduly limited freedom of expression. In addition, the Court saw nothing objectionable in the idea that the media should be legally responsible for the accuracy of what they publish. Finally, the court concluded that Canadian law struck an appropriate balance between the competing claims of expression and reputation.

At a more general level, the Supreme Court's decision in *Hill* v. *Church of Scientology of Toronto* can be seen as a definitive affirmation that the law of defamation is consistent with the standards of the *Charter*. Since the *Charter* was adopted in 1982, many people have suggested that Canadian defamation law limited freedom of expression and would have to be altered to bring it into conformity with the *Charter*. *Hill* would seem to have removed most of the basis for such arguments.

This is not to say that there is no common law qualified privilege in Canada. It is simply to say that it is substantially more limited than in the United States. One reason is that Canadian courts have generally been unwilling to accord any special legal status to journalists. As justification for this restriction, the judges have often quoted a 1914 UK decision, *Arnold* v. *R.*: "The freedom of the journalist is an ordinary part of the freedom of the subject, and to whatever lengths the subject in general may go, so also may the journalist, but, apart from statute law, his privilege is no other and no higher."[35] An illustrative, if somewhat unusual, decision is *Camporese* v. *Parton.*[36] Ms. Parton was a reporter for the Vancouver *Province*. Under the heading "Importer Pushes Canning Lids That Could Spell Death," she wrote a story for the *Province* ostensibly to warn the public about the danger of food poisoning through the use of a certain brand of canning lid. There was, in fact, no danger and the assertions about the canning lids which she made in her article were inaccurate. Nonetheless, a trial court upheld her claim to privilege. The court said the question of food poisoning was clearly one of general public interest and, moreover, the defendant was under a duty to communicate the imagined risk to the public. Most important, the defend-

---

34   *Supra* note 10.
35   (1914), 83 L.J.P.C. 299 at 300.
36   (1983), 150 D.L.R. (3d) 208 (B.C.S.C.).

ant had an "honest belief" in the truth of what she had written about the particular brand of canning lid.

Hill v. *Church of Scientology of Toronto* did extend the common law of qualified privilege in one respect. The Supreme Court held that documents prepared for the purposes of litigation do attract the privilege even before they are filed with a court or read out in open court.

iii) Malice

We turn now to the question of malice. If the defendant raises either fair comment or qualified privilege, both these defences can be lost if the plaintiff can show that the defendant was motivated by malice. By way of contrast, malice is irrelevant when the defendant raises the defence of justification. Truth is a complete defence.

It may be useful, since we are addressing questions of motive, to digress slightly and ask whether truth should always be a complete defence in libel actions. Let us take an extreme case and say that there is someone who is a pillar of the community, universally loved, admired, and respected, has enjoyed a wonderful working life and family life, and so on. A reporter discovers that thirty years ago this individual did one despicable thing. This reporter decides, for no other reason than to ruin our mythical character's reputation, career, and family life, to make the information public. The reporter and whoever publishes this story will have a complete defence. Should malice, or motive, which is what is at issue here, also be relevant to the defence of truth? Does it make sense to say that you may not express your opinions maliciously, but as long as you are telling the truth you can be as malicious as you like?

What is malice? The case-law is clear. Malice will be found when the desire to injure is determined to be the dominant motive in publishing the defamatory material.[37] It is important to note that knowledge that publication may have the effect of injuring the plaintiff is not the same thing as the desire to injure. Go back to the *Pearlman* case. One would have to be naive not to know that, when you say that someone has no morals, principles, or conscience, the statement is going to cause some injury. But that is not the issue. The issue is whether the defendant was motivated by the desire to cause injury. If the court is satisfied that the defendant was motivated by such a desire or was reckless whether injury resulted, that is malice, and the defences of fair comment and qualified privilege will be lost.

---

37 *Shultz, supra* note 27.

The case-law makes a distinction between *recklessness* and *carelessness*. With qualified privilege it is essential that the defendant have an honest belief in the truth of what has been published. If it turns out that the assertions made are inaccurate or untrue, the defence will not necessarily be lost. It will be lost if the material was published recklessly, if the defendant neither cared nor considered whether it was true. It will not be lost if the defendant was merely careless — impulsive or irrational — about whether it was true. Recklessness amounts to malice; carelessness does not.[38]

Sloppy reporting may be held to be evidence of malice. The sloppiness, however, may have to be so extreme as to amount to recklessness. In *Camporese* v. *Parton*, despite its conclusion that the defendant had prepared her article "without adequate research and with untimely haste," the trial court was still not prepared to find evidence of express malice on her part. On the other hand, deliberately keeping information favourable to the plaintiff out of a story may be regarded as malicious.

The point about good reporting and good editing is worth repeating. If there is good reporting and good editing, there should never be even the slightest question about malice. But where there is something other than good reporting and good editing, problems can arise. One of the things that helped to finish the Toronto *Sun* in the *Munro*[39] case was evidence that the younger investigative reporter had on occasion walked around the newsroom announcing to anyone who cared to listen, "I've got that fucking Munro." Statements like this did not help the *Sun* in its attempts to defend its story. The simple answer is that even if you happen to think things like this, keep them to yourself.

Courts have also held that where it is clear that the dominant motive in producing a particular story was the reporter's own personal ambition, that may amount to malice. Some of the case-law seems to suggest that reporters must appear to be noble creatures concerned only with truth and the public interest.[40]

Finally, neither a refusal by the defendant to apologize to the plaintiff, nor a determination to maintain the defence of justification — that is, continuing to assert that the story is true — will be taken as evidence of malice. Such would not, of course, be the case if it turned out that the defendant, in fact, knew the story to be false.

---

38   See *Botiuk, supra* note 26.
39   *Supra* note 14.
40   *Vogel, supra* note 13.

d) Consent

The fourth defence, one that seldom arises, is consent. In many different contexts the presence or absence of consent will determine the legal character of an act. To touch another person without that person's consent is unlawful. It is an assault that is civilly actionable and a criminal battery. To take a more concrete example, the practice of medicine is made legally possible because of consent on the part of patients. Just as an individual can consent to having someone else take a knife and cut him open, so too it is possible, in theory, to consent to being libelled. The problem is that it is difficult to imagine who, and under what circumstances, would be prepared to consent to this treatment. Do you mind if we call you a person of no morals, principles, or conscience?

One case that raises the issue is *Syms* v. *Warren*.[41] The plaintiff, who was the chair of the Manitoba Liquor Commission, went on an open-line radio show where a caller accused him of being an alcoholic. He sued the radio station, and its defence was consent. The station said that since Syms had consented to appear on the program, he must be taken to have consented to these remarks, or, presumably, any others being aired about him. The court agreed that a defence of consent existed, but said it did not arise in this case. The mere fact that this individual consented to appear on the open-line radio show could not be taken to mean that he consented to the publication of anything that anyone might conceivably say about him. It should be added that it is foolhardy for a radio station to air an open-line show without employing a delay mechanism.

As far as individual journalists are concerned, this question of consent can occasionally arise in relation to newspapers. Readers often write letters to the editor complaining about reporters or columnists. Some newspapers have a practice that before they print such a letter, they will show it to the staffer complained about. My view is that when an editor shows a reporter such a letter, by implication he is asking the reporter's consent to print it. And if the reporter is not enthusiastic about seeing the letter in print, he should say so, clearly and firmly.

3) Remedies

We turn now to remedies in civil libel actions. Concretely, we will investigate the question of what a successful plaintiff can receive.

We can begin to address this matter through an analogy with criminal prosecutions. In a criminal prosecution there are two separate and

---

41   (1976), 71 D.L.R. (3d) 558 (Man. Q.B.).

distinct stages. In the first, the court is concerned with the question of the guilt or innocence of the accused. If the accused is found not guilty, that is the end of the matter. If the accused is found guilty, however, the court moves to the second stage, which involves a determination of the appropriate punishment. Civil proceedings are not as clearly demarcated into two stages as are criminal proceedings, but there is at least a conceptual distinction. The first stage in all civil proceedings addresses the issue of liability. Who wins? Is the defendant liable to the plaintiff? If the defendant wins, if the court determines he is not liable to the plaintiff, that is the end of the matter. But if the plaintiff wins, the question that must be answered is: What does the defendant get?

People do not normally institute civil proceedings for the sole purpose of winning moral victories. They have some concrete goal in mind. In tort law the most common remedy is an award of money damages. It is also possible under certain circumstances that a plaintiff may seek an injunction to prevent the publication, or republication, of a libel. We will investigate issues relating to damages first and then turn to the matter of injunctions.

a) Damages

What standard is used to determine how much money should be awarded as damages? A recent English case has restated the traditional principle: "The general object underlying the rules for the assessment of damages is, so far as possible by means of a monetary award, to place the plaintiff in the position which he would have occupied if he had not suffered the wrong complained of."[42] So what a court is trying to do is give the plaintiff a sum of money which will, as far as possible, restore the status quo that existed prior to the defendant's unlawful act. The goal is to put the plaintiff back where the plaintiff would have been had it not been for the defendant's unlawful act.

Unfortunately, the matter gets more complicated in practice. In tort law there are two broad heads or categories of damages. The first is called "special damages." Special damages are easy and straightforward. Their purpose is to compensate plaintiffs for directly quantifiable pecuniary loss — out-of-pocket monetary loss. We can use the example of a tort claim arising out of a car accident, at least as it would have been dealt with prior to the creation of "no-fault" systems. The sorts of things a plaintiff could claim under the head of special damages as a result of a car accident would include loss of income, car repairs, medical bills, wheelchairs, drugs, and physiotherapy. These are all items for which a price can easily

---

42   *Dodd Properties (Kent) Ltd. v. Canterbury City Council*, [1980] 1 All E.R. 928 at 938 (C.A.).

be ascertained. The calculation of special damages is largely a matter of arithmetic. You write down all the things the plaintiff had to pay for and add them up. Did the plaintiff have to pay for this or did he not? Did he have to rent a wheelchair? If he did, for how long and what did it cost?

It should also be clear that there can be no limit or ceiling on "special damages." No one can say in advance that a particular sum is the maximum amount any plaintiff might claim by way of special damages. The only question is to determine the extent of the actual losses, which must, of course, be proved by the plaintiff. These are added up and the total is special damages.

Having said all this, special damages are not common in libel actions. The more obvious examples would be instances where the plaintiff loses a job or business as the result of the publication of a libel. Claims for special damages in libel actions will largely be confined to claims for lost income. Again, there are no particular problems with special damages in libel actions. The one obstacle confronting a plaintiff is that this is the only area of libel law where he must prove actual loss. The plaintiff has to prove that he suffered this out-of-pocket, monetary loss as a direct result of the publication of the libel. If he can, the loss is compensable by way of special damages. If he cannot, it isn't.

The real difficulties in libel actions arise in relation to general damages. General damages are awarded in respect of non-pecuniary, non-quantifiable losses. Once more, it is useful to look at analogies with personal injury claims. Someone who is injured in a car accident might, under the rubric of general damages, be able to claim for such things as pain and suffering, loss of the enjoyment of life, and reduced life expectancy. The difficulty with all these losses lies in assigning a monetary value to them. This has been a deeply vexed problem in personal injury litigation. How much is the loss of one leg worth? What about the pain and suffering and loss of enjoyment of life that result from such a loss? How many dollars are they worth? If the plaintiff lost both legs, should that be worth twice as many dollars as losing one leg?

In 1978 the Supreme Court of Canada decided three personal injury cases that have come to be called "The Trilogy."[43] These were very difficult cases. In one a little girl was playing around her house in the summer and heard an ice cream vendor. The ringing bells had the intended effect. The little girl went running after the ice cream vendor and was hit by a car. As a result, she was turned physically and mentally into a total vegetable. She would never do anything, never move, never think, never in any sense enjoy a human life, but would probably live another

---

43   *Andrews v. Grand & Toy Alberta Ltd.*, [1978] 2 S.C.R. 229; *Thornton v. School District No. 57 (Prince George)*, [1978] 2 S.C.R. 267; *Arnold v. Teno*, [1978] 2 S.C.R. 287.

fifty years. The award of special damages was enormous, but the Court had to address the question of how much should be given as general damages. The Court said that the maximum that could be awarded as general damages in respect of these non-quantifiable, non-monetary losses was $100,000. That remains the ceiling today in personal injury cases, except, of course, that it must be continually adjusted for inflation.

The point is that if it is difficult in personal injury litigation to assign a dollar value to things like pain and suffering and loss of the enjoyment of life, it is even more difficult with respect to the losses that general damages seek to compensate in libel actions. General damages in libel are said to be awarded to address two issues. First, there is to be compensation for injury to reputation and, second, solace for wounded feelings. How should a court go about determining a dollar amount to compensate for injury to reputation and to provide solace for wounded feelings? The difficulties are compounded by the principle that, apart from special damages, the plaintiff is not required to prove any actual loss.

These difficulties are further compounded because general damages in libel actions are said to be "at large." This means that where a libel case is tried before a jury, the jury is entitled to select any figure it wishes. Toronto lawyer Julian Porter put the matter this way:

> The magic of libel is that damages are at large and a jury can give whatever it sees fit. . . .
>
> Consequently counsel must adopt a baroque attitude with tears if possible. One must abandon and gush with vibrato. My view is that unlike other cases a plaintiff's counsel can ill afford to be cheery or chirp witty asides to a jury. A jury must be slowly and continually persuaded that the worst ailment on this earth is to be buried with a sullied name. All speeches should dwell on the illusory balm of money and the eternal pain of losing the quality of life that has been wrenched away by the monstrous libel. The great area to exploit is that damages are at large and that actual damages needn't be proved.[44]

To underline this point, we should refer again to *Hill* v. *Church of Scientology of Toronto.*[45] In this decision the Supreme Court affirmed the largest award of damages — $1,600,000 — ever reached in a Canadian defamation suit. After deliberating for four hours, the jury had asked the trial judge for some direction concerning the appropriate award. In particular, the jury asked about "realistic maximums" in recent cases. The

---

44   J. Porter, "Tangents" (1981) 5 Can. Law. 24.
45   *Supra* note 10.

judge's reply, which was endorsed by the Supreme Court, was: "I have discussed the question with counsel and we are all in agreement that the only answer that we can provide to you is that by law neither the parties nor the judge are entitled to advise the jury of maximums or minimums in these kinds of cases. So, I'm afraid you're on your own."

If there is a case for a ceiling on the amount that can be awarded as compensation for non-pecuniary loss in personal injury litigation, it would seem there would be an even stronger one for such a ceiling in libel litigation. In two recent decisions — *Snyder* v. *Montreal Gazette Ltd.*[46] in 1988 and *Hill* v. *Church of Scientology of Toronto* — the Supreme Court has rejected the idea, basing its rejection on the general ground that there is too much variation in the facts and circumstances of individual defamation cases to justify the establishment of an *a priori* ceiling. Despite this opinion, it is worth stressing that awards of general damages in Canadian libel cases are modest in comparison with awards in similar cases in the United States and the United Kingdom. To return to *Hill* v. *Church of Scientology of Toronto*, the Court noted that between 1987 and 1991 there were only twenty-seven reported — that is, reported in law reports — decisions in libel cases and that the average award of damages was $30,000. From 1992 to 1995 there were twenty-four judgments reported, with an average award of $20,000. And while *Hill* itself, as we have noted, saw the largest total award ever upheld by appellate courts, the award of general damages of $300,000 was consistent with existing Canadian standards. The Supreme Court made it clear that this was a figure either at or very near the upper end of the scale. In fact, it would not be unreasonable to view $300,000 as a *de facto* ceiling on general damages in libel actions.

The special role of the jury in determining the amount of a damage award must be emphasized. Where a libel action is tried with a jury, it is the jury's responsibility to determine exactly how much shall be awarded to the plaintiff. An appellate court will alter the figure awarded by a jury only if it is satisfied either that no reasonable jury could have awarded that amount or that the amount is so out of proportion to the libel as to shock the court's conscience and sense of justice.

General damages, and special damages, are two of the headings under which compensatory damages may be awarded. Since there is little more that can be said about special damages, we will continue our analysis of compensatory damages by looking in more detail at nominal, general, and aggravated damages.

---

46 [1988] 1 S.C.R. 494.

i) Compensatory Damages

a. Nominal Damages

A court may conclude that while the defendant has indeed libelled the plaintiff, the extent of the injury to the plaintiff's reputation has been so slight as to merit only a minimal or nominal award of damages. The main factor that would lead a court to such an award is the actual state of the plaintiff's reputation at the time of the publication of the libel. If it can be shown that the plaintiff had no reputation to speak of, a nominal award may follow. The defendant is permitted to introduce general evidence of the plaintiff's poor or non-existent reputation. "General," as used here, means evidence relating to matters other than what had been asserted in the original libellous statement about the plaintiff. This occurred in *Leonhard v. Sun Publishing Co.*[47] The Vancouver *Sun* had published an article in which it described the plaintiff as a "drug king." Although the *Sun* conceded that this assertion was libellous, it also introduced evidence showing that Jacob Leonhard was widely known as a gangster and had no reputation in the community. He was awarded $1.00 in damages. The risk in this tactic is that if the defendant's evidence as to the plaintiff's generally bad reputation fails to persuade the court, the defendant, as a result, may pay even more in damages.

b. General Damages

Here we will address the factors a court will look at in arriving at a final amount. We will look first at factors that relate to the plaintiff and then at factors that relate to the defendant.

It is unfortunate, but true, that in libel litigation some people are more equal than others. The more socially prominent a plaintiff is, the greater the amount he is likely to be awarded as general damages. The reasoning underlying this inequality is roughly as follows. It is assumed that the more significant someone is, the better his reputation must be. The better someone's reputation, it must follow, the more serious the injury to it will be. And the more serious the injury to reputation, the more substantial the award of damages needed to compensate for that injury. Thus, the Nova Scotia Court of Appeal could conclude in *Barltrop v. Canadian Broadcasting Corp.*[48]: "Here, a man of international reputation is vilified in the eyes of his professional confreres. He thus suffers greatly, though he may not lose a single dollar."

---

47   (1956), 4 D.L.R. (2d) 514 (B.C.S.C.).
48   (1978), 25 N.S.R. (2d) 637 at 665 (C.A.).

As we have seen, an incorporated organization can sue as a plaintiff in a libel action. But a successful corporate plaintiff can claim only special damages; it cannot seek general damages for injury to reputation.

Turning to the defendant newspaper or broadcaster, its exact nature and character are important. To begin with, other factors being equal, the extent of publication is important. The theory is that the more people who saw or read the libel, the more serious has been the injury to the plaintiff's reputation. This approach is not to be applied mechanically, however. In *Walker v. CFTO Ltd.*,[49] the jury awarded $1.00 in damages for each of the roughly 900,000 persons who had viewed the libellous broadcast. This amount was cut back drastically on appeal, the case being one of the few instances where an appellate court has interfered with a jury's award of damages.

The reputation of the defendant is also important. The better the reputation the defendant newspaper or broadcaster has, the more likely it is people will believe what it publishes and, therefore, the more serious the injury it can cause to the plaintiff's reputation. This issue was addressed in *Vogel v. Canadian Broadcasting Corp.*,[50] where the court said:

> In terms of prestige, power and influence . . . [the CBC] is at the opposite end of the spectrum from the sleazy scandal sheet. Created and maintained by Parliament to inform the Canadian public, its news services are accorded great respect throughout Canada. They have a well-merited reputation for reliability. For that very reason, C.B.C. has an enormous capacity to cause damage. The general run of right-thinking people tend to think that "it was on the C.B.C. news, so it must be so."

Awards of general damages made by Canadian courts, taking inflation into account, continue to be modest. Courts have generally recognized that they "must be careful not to award damages which may tend more to stifle the free expression of opinion than to rehabilitate the reputation of the defamed."[51] And it is worth noting that, with some exceptions, the awards at the higher end of the scale have not generally been against media defendants.

c. Aggravated Damages
The terminology used by the courts in discussing damages in libel actions is often confusing. Aggravated damages are awarded in addition to general damages, but are still regarded as compensatory. Aggravated damages rep-

---

49   (1987), 59 O.R. (2d) 104 (C.A.).
50   *Supra* note 13 at 178.
51   *Derrickson v. Tomat* (1992), 88 D.L.R. (4th) 401 at 411 (B.C.C.A.).

resent an additional amount of money awarded to the plaintiff to compensate him for a particularly serious injury to his reputation and, of course, to provide a more generous solace. The determining factor in leading a court to award aggravated damages is the conduct of the defendant.

In *Hill* v. *Church of Scientology of Toronto* the Supreme Court of Canada upheld an award of $500,000 as aggravated damages. The Court said such damages "take into account the additional harm caused to the plaintiff's feelings by the defendant's outrageous and malicious conduct." Other decisions have used words like "insulting," "high-handed," "spiteful," "malicious," or "oppressive" to describe the sorts of conduct that may result in aggravated damages.

A court will look at the entire course of conduct of the defendant from the time of the publication of the libel up until the conclusion of the trial. Among the factors to be considered, according to the Supreme Court, are whether the defendant sought widespread publicity for the libel; the presence or absence of a retraction or an apology by the defendant; repetition of the libel; and the conduct of the defendant and the defendant's counsel throughout the trial. This approach means, of course, that there can be a risk involved in mounting a vigorous, aggressive, and determined defence. If such a defence fails to persuade the court, the award may be higher than might otherwise have been the case.

ii) Punitive Damages

Punitive damages, or exemplary damages, are awarded in addition to compensatory damages. Their primary purpose is to punish the defendant, not compensate the plaintiff, since that, of course, has already been done. They are also awarded to deter others from engaging in conduct similar to that of the defendant.

The existence of punitive damages in tort actions is anomalous. First, they cause the distinctions between criminal law and tort law to become blurred. Second, they represent a windfall for a plaintiff who has already been fully compensated for any loss he may have suffered. Nonetheless, punitive damages are recognized in libel actions. In *Hill* v. *Church of Scientology of Toronto* the Supreme Court upheld an award of $800,000 as punitive damages. A court will only award punitive damages where it finds the defendant's behaviour to have been "truly outrageous," "so malicious, oppressive and high-handed that it offends the court's sense of decency."

It is inexcusable for aggravated damages or punitive damages to be awarded against a media defendant. Observing the rules of good reporting and good editing should ordinarily guarantee that this does not happen. Where these rules are not followed, aggravated damages or punitive damages may result. The cases in which this has happened exemplify egregious failures to observe basic standards of journalism. We have already looked at some of these cases, so for present purposes we will address only what the judges had to say in awarding larger than usual damages.

In *Vogel v. Canadian Broadcasting Corp.*,[52] the court spoke of the "reckless and deliberately damaging actions of the defendants" in reaching its conclusion to award aggravated damages. In *Thomas v. Canadian Broadcasting Corp.*,[53] aggravated damages were awarded because of the failure of the CBC to include in its broadcast information which it had in its possession and which tended both to be favourable to the plaintiff and to cast doubt on the CBC's interpretation of what had happened. In *Munro v. Toronto Sun Publishing Co.*,[54] punitive damages, although only in the amount of $25,000, were awarded, largely on the basis of the court's conclusion that the two investigative reporters "did deliberately intend harm to Mr. Munro." Among the evidence that led the court to this conclusion was the comment by the younger investigative reporter at the *Sun*, "I've got that fucking Munro," and, more generally, "the lack of care as to accuracy of the story and the falsity of the contents."

iii) Apology

The law gives a number of advantages to media defendants in libel actions. The most important of these have to do with an apology. A timely apology may permit a defendant to effectively avoid the consequences of libelling someone. In addition, the procedural rules governing apologies give an advantage to a media defendant.

The law places certain obligations on a potential plaintiff, obligations that are strictly enforced. Although there is some variation from province to province, a plaintiff must, as a precondition to being able to sue, serve a libel notice on a media defendant within a specified period of time.[55] A libel notice must be in writing and must indicate the material that the plaintiff claims is defamatory. Apart from these requirements, no particular form is specified for a libel notice. In Ontario a libel notice must be delivered to the newspaper or broadcaster within six weeks of the libellous material coming to the plaintiff's attention. This time limit is the shortest statutory period. In all cases, these limits are strictly interpreted.[56] Furthermore, it will likely be assumed that the

---

52   *Supra* note 13 at 184.
53   *Supra* note 3.
54   *Supra* note 14.
55   See Ontario, *LSA, supra* note 7, s. 5(1).
56   *Grossman v. CFTO-Television Ltd.* (1982), 39 O.R. (2d) 498 (C.A.).

alleged libel came to the plaintiff's attention on the same day it was published, unless there is some evidence to show why this could not have been the case. Even if a newspaper or broadcaster does libel someone, if that individual does not have a libel notice delivered within the statutory period specified by the law of the particular province, the newspaper or broadcaster is off the hook.

If a libel notice is received, the period immediately after its arrival is the most crucial of all. This period is when the decision to apologize, or not to apologize, must be made. The various Libel and Slander Acts or Defamation Acts give media defendants three days within which to decide to apologize. If the defendant apologizes — that is, publishes a "full and fair retraction" — within this period, the maximum amount that can be awarded against it is reduced to "actual damages." Actual damages means special damages and, since special damages are seldom awarded in libel actions, the practical result of an apology is that the matter is at an end. In the case of a defendant who operates a print publication other than a daily newspaper, an apology in the next regular issue after the receipt of the libel notice will suffice.

As soon as a libel notice is received, a lawyer should be called to review the material complained of carefully with the reporter and the editor who worked on it. Every aspect of this material should be checked. If, by the end of this review, it has become apparent that an error was made, an apology should be issued. If, however, it is clear that the facts complained of are accurate or that the opinions expressed are fair comment or that the assertions are a fair and accurate report of communications made on an occasion of privilege, there is no need to apologize. If a story is the result of good reporting and good editing, there is no reason to be intimidated by a libel notice. Far more libel notices are served than libel actions are instituted.

In fact, even if a defendant fails, for whatever reason, to publish an apology within the three days provided by the statute, an apology made at any time prior to judgment actually being given by a court will have the effect of reducing the amount of money that can be awarded as damages. The longer the defendant delays in issuing an apology, however, the less benefit there is to be gained from it.

To be effective, an apology must be real and it must be sincere. To quote from an old British Columbia case:

> That is surely not sufficient. It is not the offer nor even the publication of an apology at all, but an offer to offer an apology. And even in terms, it seems to reserve to the defendant a right of judging whether the plaintiff is reasonable in demanding any particular form *e.g.*, it offers

to make such an apology as the defendant thinks fit. Such an apology as merely "beg your pardon" or "sorry for it," is not sufficient in a case of libel. The defendant should admit that the charge was unfounded, that it was made without proper information, under an entire misapprehension of the real facts, etc., and that he regrets that it was published in his paper. . . . You should not offer to make, but actually make and publish at once, and unconditionally, such an apology, expressing sorrow, withdrawing the imputation, rehabilitating the plaintiff's character as well as you can; not stipulating that the plaintiff is to accept it; not making any terms but publishing it in the interests of truth, and because you are anxious to undo whatever harm which may have accrued from a wrong which you find you have been the unconscious instrument of inflicting.[57]

In other words, for an apology to be legally effective, it must contain an amount of grovelling.

Furthermore, if a purported apology is not a real apology, not only may the defendant not derive any benefit from it, it may actually have the effect of increasing the amount of money awarded as damages. In *Brannigan* v. *S.I.U.*,[58] the publication *Canadian Sailor* claimed to have apologized to Brannigan for calling him a communist. In a subsequent issue, under the heading "We Have Blundered," the magazine expressed its sorrow to Brannigan for having printed a photograph that did not, as the magazine had originally claimed, prove that he was a communist. But on the same page another story asserted "Picture That Should Have Appeared," and showed a fresh photograph, the photograph that, the magazine said, really established that Brannigan was a communist. As the trial judge noted, this sort of "apology" would aggravate, rather than mitigate, the damages.

A number of technical points about apologies should be borne in mind. First, it is common practice that the plaintiff's lawyer will send a suggested apology along with the libel notice. It is not necessary to publish this apology in order to gain the benefit of the statute. As long as the apology published is a real apology, it will have the intended effect. Second, a general rule of thumb is that the apology should be given the same prominence as the material complained of in the libel notice. If the offending story was on page 1 of a newspaper, the apology should go on page 1; if it was the lead item in a network newscast, the apology should, likewise, be the lead item. Third, it is essential in drafting an apology not to repeat the

57 *Hoste* v. *Victoria Times Publishing Co.* (1889), 1 B.C.R. (Pt. 2) 365 at 366 (S.C.).
58 *Supra* note 1.

defamatory statements. If this is done, not only will the benefit of apologizing have been lost, but a fresh libel will have been published.

A curious problem arose in the Ontario courts in the late 1980s. It was, for a time, feared that the practical value to media defendants of apologies might have been substantially eroded, but this appears not to have been the case.

The facts of *Teskey v. Canadian Newspapers Co.*[59] were decidedly unusual. A certain individual had been active in local politics in the Midland, Ontario, area. He was regarded as controversial and given to making sweeping and unsubstantiated statements about local issues and personalities. In order to get his views on a specific issue published in the weekly Midland *Free Press*, this individual sent them to the newspaper in the form of an advertisement. The difficulty with this course of action was that, while material to be published in the news or editorial pages of the newspaper was regularly vetted to determine if it was libellous, advertising copy was not.

The advertisement was published and Teskey, a local lawyer who was the object of the unfavourable comment in the advertisement, sued. The editorial staff at the paper received Teskey's libel notice, took one look at the advertisement, and issued an apology at once. The newspaper presumably thought that was the end of the matter, but it was not.

Teskey continued with his action, basing his argument on section 5(2) of the Ontario *Libel and Slander Act*. This section stipulates that in order for a media defendant to gain the benefit of an apology, the original libel must have been published in "good faith." Teskey argued that because no one at the newspaper had checked the advertisement to determine if it might be libellous, there had been a "complete disregard for whether it . . . [was] libel," which amounted to negligence. The court accepted this argument and held that the libel had not been published in good faith and that, as a result, the newspaper could not benefit from its apology.

Although facts like these are not likely to arise often, the *Teskey* decision should serve to reinforce the two principles set out at the beginning of our discussion of libel: that *anything* that appears in a newspaper or a broadcast can be the subject of a libel action; and that a newspaper or a broadcaster is responsible for everything it publishes.

The final point to note about apologies is that an apology will offer no assistance to a defendant if the libel complained of was an assertion that the plaintiff had committed a crime.

---

59   (1989), 68 O.R. (2d) 737 (C.A.).

b) Injunctions

A plaintiff may seek an injunction to prevent the publication, or republication, of a libel. The force of an injunction derives from the fact that to breach it is to disobey an order of a court — that is, to commit the offence of contempt of court.

As we have already noted in relation to non-statutory publication bans, an injunction is an order issued by a superior court which seeks to prevent the commission of an unlawful act. In the case of publication bans, an injunction may be issued to prevent the commission of a crime — namely, contempt of court. But injunctions may also be issued in the course of civil proceedings. The general principle is that an injunction should be made only in the clearest of cases, where the likelihood is that the plaintiff would succeed were the matter actually to go to trial and, further, where the plaintiff would suffer irreparable loss, loss that could not be compensated through an award of damages, if the defendant were allowed to proceed with his proposed unlawful conduct.

There are, however, problems with injunctions issued in the course of civil proceedings, particularly in the course of libel actions.

The first is that a plaintiff can apply for an interim, or temporary, injunction without having to give notice of such application to the other party. Concretely this means that an injunction could be made against a newspaper or a broadcaster without that newspaper or broadcaster having been given an opportunity to argue against it. The second problem is that an injunction issued during a libel action is as clear an example as one could ask of a prior restraint on publication — censorship in its most basic form.

The encouraging aspect is that few such injunctions are applied for and fewer are made. The reason few injunctions are applied for in libel actions is the obvious one that few plaintiffs know in advance that a libel is going to be published about them. This foreknowledge usually will happen only where there has been advance publicity concerning an upcoming television broadcast or an about-to-be-released novel or film. Most encouraging, however, are the established legal rules about the conditions that must be met before an injunction will be issued to restrain the publication of an alleged libel. These are:

a. the jurisdiction of the courts to make an interlocutory injunction is of a delicate nature and should only be exercised in the clearest of cases;

b. there must be no doubt that the material in issue is libellous of the plaintiff. Indeed the material before the court must be so evidently libellous that any jury would find it to be so, and that were a jury to find otherwise its verdict would be set aside as unreasonable;

c. an injunction will not be granted when the defendant indicates an intention to raise one of the recognised defences, unless such defence is, in the circumstances of the case, manifestly without foundation.[60] [Footnotes omitted.]

Although the Supreme Court of Canada refused in *Hill* v. *Church of Scientology* to "constitutionalize" defamation law, its decision in *Dagenais* v. *Canadian Broadcasting Corp.* is probably more relevant in this context. The clear direction of the *Dagenais* decision was that, as a matter of principle, courts should be very careful about issuing injunctions to prevent publication. There is no reason to imagine that this principle would not be followed in dealing with applications to prevent the publication of defamatory material. The result should be that the three rules set out above would be followed stringently. *Dagenais* also suggests that, because they involve limitations on freedom of expression, applications for publication bans should not be entertained by judges unless notice has been given to the party or parties against whom the ban is sought. I assume a similar approach would in future be followed in relation to applications for injunctions in libel actions.

The three rules set out above represent the position prior to the adoption of the *Charter*. Reading them together with the *Dagenais* decision, it is hard to imagine many circumstances in which a court would be prepared today to enjoin the publication of a libel. Indeed, the only conceivable circumstances would likely be as bizarre as those that arose in *Hill* v. *Church of Scientology of Toronto*. After a verdict was given against it at trial, Scientology repeated its original libel against the plaintiff. An injunction was issued to prevent further repetition.

4) Conclusion

There has been a great deal of talk over the last few years about something called "libel chill."[61] The theory of libel chill is that the fear of being sued for libel intimidates the mass media, that many good stories are not published because of this fear.

This seems unlikely. I personally have never heard a reporter or an editor point to an actual story that was not published because of the fear of a possible libel action if it were. As a matter of law, the Supreme Court

---

60 R. Martin, "Interlocutory Injunctions in Libel Actions" (1982) 20 U.W.O. L. Rev. 129 at 131–132.

61 See R. Martin, "Does Libel Have A 'Chilling Effect' in Canada?" (1990) 4 *Studies in Communications* 143.

of Canada appears to have decided in *Hill* v. *Church of Scientology of Toronto* that there is no such thing as libel chill. And such data as exist suggest that the extent of libel chill has been considerably exaggerated. In 1986, 1987, and 1988 the Canadian Daily Newspaper Publishers Association (now the Canadian Daily Newspaper Association) carried out *Libel Defence Costs Surveys*. Sixty-one daily newspapers responded in 1986, seventy in 1987, and eighty-five in 1988. In 1987 and 1988, 59 percent of these newspapers reported that they spent absolutely nothing defending libel actions, and in 1988, 73 percent of all daily newspapers spent less than $5000 defending libel actions. Forty-six percent of newspapers received no libel notices in 1988, and 71 percent did not have a libel action started against them. Most newspapers and broadcasters carry libel insurance. In 1988, 62 percent of the daily newspapers surveyed paid annual premiums under $5000.

It is useful also to remember the many advantages the law gives media defendants in libel actions. Libel is highly technical, and a plaintiff may conceivably engage a lawyer who is not particularly knowledgeable in the area. A libel notice must be issued quickly. An apology effectively concludes the matter. If the plaintiff decides to go ahead and sue, the formal action must be commenced quickly, within a far shorter period than that allowed for most other civil claims. Libel actions are very expensive, and legal aid is ordinarily not available. In many instances the defendant in a libel action can frustrate the plaintiff's litigation by asking for "security for costs," a procedure that can result in the plaintiff being required to post a bond with the court before being allowed to continue. Even if a media defendant should lose a libel action, awards of damages in Canada, as has been noted, are modest.

The really important thing about libel actions, as far as the mass media are concerned, is to avoid them. I have argued that the most effective means for achieving this goal are good reporting and good editing. But there is an additional practical point worth noting. What follows is based on the 1985 Iowa Libel Research Project,[62] but I suspect similar patterns and similar responses would be found in Canada. The first finding of this project was that people who believed they had been libelled in a newspaper tended to take the matter up with that newspaper before they went to a lawyer. The second, and crucial, point was that if such persons were treated by the newspaper with civility and respect, they would probably not contact a lawyer; if they weren't, they would. Once

---

62   See R.P. Bezanson, G. Cranberg & J. Soloski, "Libel Law and the Press: Setting the Record Straight" (1985) 71 Iowa L. Rev. 215.

again, both the law and good journalism suggest the same result. The people who read newspapers and the people they write about should both be treated in a professional and responsible manner.

A final point to note about libel actions relates to the individual journalist who did the story that led to the suit. It is overwhelmingly likely that the media corporation for whom that reporter works will be a defendant in the action and will, as a result, hire a lawyer to conduct the defence. This lawyer's professional duty is to represent his client, the employer, and not the reporter. Thus, this lawyer may well act in ways that are in his client's interests, but not necessarily in the interests of the reporter. There may well be situations, then, where it would be desirable for the reporter to retain his own lawyer to represent his own interests before the court.

B. PRIVACY

There is no general right to privacy in Canada. By that is meant that there is no general principle of Canadian law which prohibits the publication by the mass media of personal or private information about individuals. Put another way, assuming it can be proven to be true, there is nothing that the mass media may not say about someone.

The *Canadian Charter of Rights and Freedoms*[63] appears to enshrine a certain notion of privacy. Section 8 creates protection against unreasonable searches, which would include both unreasonable searches of residences and other premises and the unreasonable interception of postal and electronic communications.[64] Section 7 has also been interpreted as addressing certain privacy issues in that it has been seen as guaranteeing individuals against interference with either their bodily integrity or the making of personal and intimate decisions.[65] But this *Charter* right of privacy has so far been interpreted only as creating guarantees against the state, as protecting a certain personal sphere of action from interference by the state.[66] If this is the complete scope of any *Charter*-based right to privacy, it clearly says nothing about the ability of the mass media to publish private or personal information concerning individuals.

---

63   Part I of the *Constitution Act, 1982*, being Schedule B to the *Canada Act 1982* (U.K.), 1982, c. 11 [hereinafter *Charter*].

64   *R. v. Nicolucci*, [1985] C.S. 1245 (Que.).

65   *R. v. Morgentaler*, [1988] 1 S.C.R. 30.

66   *R. v. Dyment*, [1988] 2 S.C.R. 417.

There is a federal *Privacy Act*,[67] and a number of provinces have similar legislation. With certain exceptions to be noted below, however, these statutes address the use by the state of personal information about individuals which is in the possession of the state. As a broad principle, the federal statute provides that "Personal information under the control of a government institution shall not, without the consent of the individual to whom it relates, be disclosed by the institution." But the Act says nothing about the use of "personal information" by non-state organizations such as the mass media. A similar approach is found in provincial privacy legislation.

The common law has not so far recognized a tort of invasion of privacy. Although it might be relied upon in a variety of circumstances, such a tort, for present purposes, would give individuals some ability to protect themselves against the publication of certain kinds or categories of personal information. The recognition of such a tort would permit individuals to recover damages from persons or organizations who published protected information.

No Canadian superior court has expressly confirmed the existence of this precise tort, although a number of related claims have been upheld. In *Robbins* v. *Canadian Broadcasting Corp. (Que.)*,[68] the only one of the cases to be noted which involved the mass media, the plaintiff was awarded damages for what the court variously described as "humiliation," "invasion of privacy," "malicious mischief," and "nuisance." He had written a critical letter to the CBC television program *Tabloid*. After reading the letter on air, the host of the program invited viewers to write letters to Dr. Robbins to "cheer" him up. Robbins's mailing address appeared on screen. The result was that Robbins received an avalanche of harassing letters, telephone calls, and visits to his residence. In a similar vein, it was held in *Motherwell* v. *Motherwell*[69] that to subject someone to an uninterrupted flow of harassing telephone calls and letters over a period of two years was to commit a tort that the court described as "nuisance by invasion of privacy." There is also a related tort generally described as "appropriation of personality." This tort involves the unauthorized use of another person's name or likeness for a commercial purpose, as in, for example, an advertisement that falsely suggested that a well-known public figure had endorsed a particular product.[70] The closest a Canadian court has come to recognizing a tort of invasion of

67   R.S.C. 1985, c. P-21.
68   (1957), 12 D.L.R. (2d) 35 (Que. S.C.).
69   (1976), 1 A.R. 47 (C.A.).
70   *Krouse* v. *Chrysler Canada Ltd.* (1974), 1 O.R. (2d) 225 (C.A.).

privacy committed through the publication of private information was in a 1982 Ontario County Court decision, *Saccone* v. *Orr*.[71] A plaintiff was awarded damages against a defendant who tape-recorded a telephone conversation between the two without the plaintiff's permission or knowledge and subsequently played the tape at a public meeting.

The privacy legislation in British Columbia, Manitoba, Newfoundland, and Saskatchewan creates liability in tort for certain infringements of privacy interests.[72] Among the forms of conduct these statutes address are eavesdropping, surveillance, wire-tapping, and the use of personal documents. The legislation also creates broad defences against claims of invasion of privacy. These defences include publishing any of the following: a matter of public interest; a fair comment on a matter of public interest; and anything that would be privileged under the law of defamation. There has been little litigation under these statutes. An instructive case is *Silber* v. *British Columbia Broadcasting System Ltd.*,[73] a 1986 decision of the British Columbia Supreme Court. A strike was under way at a business owned by the plaintiff. On the day in question, the plaintiff discovered a camera crew from the defendant filming the strike from the parking lot of his business premises. He told the crew to leave the parking lot and, during the course of this exchange, he became involved in a physical struggle with some of its members. This struggle was videotaped, and tape that included the strike, the discussion, and the struggle was aired. The plaintiff sued for invasion of privacy. His claim was dismissed, the court holding, first, that while the parking lot was private property, everything happening there was clearly observable and, as a result, the plaintiff had no "reasonable expectation of privacy" with respect to it; and, second, that the altercation between the plaintiff and the camera crew was a matter of public interest. As a final point on these statutory torts of invasion of privacy, if they were to be interpreted in such a way as to constrain the ability of the mass media to gather or publish information, the relevant portions of the statutes which created them could then be open to a constitutional challenge on the basis of the *Charter*'s guarantee of freedom of expression.

Recent legislation in Quebec places restrictions on the ability of corporations and businesses to deal with personal information about individuals. As a general principle, personal information about an indi-

---

71   (1981), 34 O.R. (2d) 317 (Co. Ct.).

72   For B.C., see *Privacy Act*, R.S.B.C. 1979, c. 336; for Manitoba, *Privacy Act*, R.S.M. 1987, c. P125; Newfoundland, *Privacy Act*, R.S.N. 1990, c. P-22; and Saskatchewan, *The Privacy Act*, R.S.S. 1978, c. P-24.

73   (1986), 25 D.L.R. (4th) 345 (B.C.S.C.).

vidual may not be communicated to third parties without the consent of that individual.[74]

We will conclude the analysis of privacy issues with a discussion of the two situations that are of most practical concern to the mass media: the taking of photographs and the tape-recording of telephone conversations.

As a general matter, it is not necessary to seek or receive a person's permission before taking or publishing his photograph. Certain issues can, however, arise. First, the person photographed might be able to bring an action in trespass if the photographer physically invaded his land or premises in the course of taking the photograph. Despite this possibility, courts have held that there was no trespass in flying over a plaintiff's residence to take a photograph, or in taking photographs in front of the plaintiff's house while visiting the house to ask for an interview.[75] Second, it may amount to nuisance or harassment to subject a residence to constant surveillance in order to get a photograph. Third, the taking of a photograph may amount to the torts of assault or battery if it involves any physical restraint of or physical interference with the person being photographed. Fourth, the mass media may be restrained from publishing a photograph that has been obtained in breach of a confidence.[76] Finally, while this is not a privacy concern, any tampering with or alteration of a photograph may render it defamatory.

Once more, as a general matter, there is no need to seek someone's permission to tape-record a telephone conversation. However, two qualifications should be noted. First, the regulations made under the *Broadcasting Act*[77] specify that if a tape-recording of a telephone conversation is to be aired, the other person must, as a pre-condition, be informed and his permission granted. Second, the *Criminal Code*[78] makes it an offence to intercept telephone communications without lawful authority.

Closely related to privacy questions are issues of confidentiality. If I receive confidential information from my employer, or from my spouse or from a client or patient, I may be under a legally enforceable obligation not to disclose that information to anyone else. If I were to disclose such information to a third party — obviously, in the present context, a

74   *An Act Respecting the Protection of Personal Information in the Private Sector*, S.Q. 1993, c. 17.

75   *Bernstein of Leigh (Baron) v. Skyviews and General Ltd.*, [1978] 1 Q.B. 479; *Belzberg v. British Columbia Television Broadcasting System Ltd.*, [1981] 3 W.W.R. 85 (B.C.S.C.).

76   *Duchess of Argyll v. Duke of Argyll*, [1967] Ch. 302.

77   *Radio Regulations*, 1986, SOR/86-982, s. 3(e).

78   R.S.C. 1985, c. C-46, s. 184.

reporter — the individual or organization to whom I owe the obligation of confidentiality might be able to take legal action against me and I might be subject to either criminal or professional disciplinary proceedings. But none of this is directly relevant to the reporter to whom the information was given. What legal liability, if any, might the reporter face?

There is no recognized principle of Canadian law under which the reporter can be made liable for breach of confidence in such a circumstance. There is no legal relation, no legal nexus, between the reporter and the individual or organization from whom the reporter's source — the person disclosing the information — received the information.

Problems might arise if the reporter actively encouraged the source to give him information that both he and the source knew to be confidential. The reporter might be open, depending on the precise circumstances, to a tort action of inducing breach of contract or a charge of criminal conspiracy. But, to repeat, if the reporter, without offering inducement or persuasion, simply accepts the information that the source is proferring, no legal difficulties should result.[79]

FURTHER READINGS

As far as libel is concerned, good general introductions are A. Skarsgard, "Freedom of the Press: Availability of Defences to a Defamation Action" (1981) 45 Sask. L. Rev. 287, and G.A. Flaherty, *Defamation Law in Canada* (Ottawa: Canadian Bar Foundation, 1984). For a full and detailed statement of the law, R. E. Brown, *The Law of Defamation in Canada*, 2 vols., 2d ed. (Toronto: Carswell, 1994) should be consulted.

D. Gibson, ed., *Aspects of Privacy Law: Essays in Honour of John M. Sharp* (Toronto: Butterworths, 1980) provides an overview of privacy issues, but is very dated.

---

79   There is an exhaustive discussion in G.H. Fridman, *The Law of Torts in Canada*, vol. 2 (Toronto: Carswell, 1990) at 189–206. See also G.F. Proudfoot, *Privacy Law and the Media in Canada* (Ottawa: Canadian Bar Foundation, 1984) at 44–46.

CONCLUSION

This book was designed to achieve two goals. First, it aims to provide practical information, especially to working journalists. This information is necessary for a clear understanding of stories that raise political and legal issues. It is also essential if journalists are to avoid problems for themselves and their employers. Second, the book seeks to raise a number of important theoretical and social issues. Each of these issues has some connection with the way we understand freedom of expression and the devices employed in our legal system both to protect it and to limit it.

The most crucial of all these issues, and the starting point in any discussion of media law, must be: Why does freedom of expression matter? Our courts have not provided a coherent and consistent answer to this question. Recent decisions, especially those of the Supreme Court of Canada, are not only difficult to understand but manifest a variety of points of view. They often contradict each other. Indeed, it is not at all clear that the judges themselves are persuaded of the importance of free expression. In the *Keegstra*[1] decision, for example, then Chief Justice Brian Dickson appeared to suggest that free expression "values" should be accorded precedence over freedom of expression itself. In contrast, the judgment of Chief Justice Lyman Duff in the Alberta Press Bill decision sets out a justification for freedom of expression that is clearly stated and well rooted socially. He said: [The] right to free public discussion of pub-

---

1   *R. v. Keegstra*,[1990] 3 S.C.R. 697.

lic affairs . . . is the breath of life for parliamentary institutions."[2] Indeed, this assertion provides at the same time a definition of free expression and an argument in its favour. The essence of free expression is seen to be *political* expression. Its justification is a corollary to this definition. Freedom of expression is important because, without it, democratic institutions and, therefore, democratic politics would not be possible. Freedom of expression is an essential precondition to democracy.

The most unfortunate result of recent decisions by the Supreme Court of Canada has been a diminution in the clarity of thinking and in the significance imputed to free expression. It is a direct consequence of the Court's decision in *Irwin Toy*[3] to accord constitutional protection to virtually all forms of expression.

Despite this tendency, one Canadian tradition has continued: the notion that free expression is not absolute, that it can be limited in favour of other socially legitimate goals. In practice, litigation about free expression in Canada has been about balancing the imperatives of free expression against competing social claims. The bulk of the book has been devoted to explication and analysis of how that balancing has been carried out. Chapter 2 addressed the balance between certain claims of the state and free expression. Chapter 3 investigated the balance between the integrity of the judicial process and free expression. Chapter 4 looked at the balance between the protection of reputation and free expression.

It may be that the precise balance reached in each instance by our legal system is not ideal. There is always, in a democracy, room for disagreement on issues of this nature. And what is seen as an appropriate balance in one era may not be acceptable in another. But if debate on these matters is to flourish and if the mass media themselves are to play a role in that debate, it is essential that individual journalists maintain an active personal commitment to free expression. To achieve this commitment they need a theoretical understanding of free expression and a practical determination to make it a living reality in their day-to-day working life.

It is not always easy to maintain this knowledge and this determination. Many influences and pressures which work against it. Two seem specially important. The first is the most obvious and the most direct: the pressure, by no means always subtle, that employers can and do exert. A recent obituary in the *Economist* made the point with great force:

> He was the sort of character Humbert Wolfe had in mind when he wrote: 'You cannot hope / to bribe or twist, / thank God! the / British

2   *Reference Re Alberta Legislation*, [1938] S.C.R. 100.
3   *Irwin Toy v. Quebec (A.G.)*, [1989] 1 S.C.R. 927.

journalist./ But seeing what / the man will do / unbribed, there's / no occasion to.' George Malcolm Thomson was his master's pen, the obedient leader-writer who did the bidding of Lord Beaverbrook, press baron and politician manqué.[4]

The law does not address this matter. Owners and managers have substantial proprietary authority and the limits on this authority come down in practice to the integrity and courage of individual journalists.

The second pressure is orthodoxy and, in particular, pressure to make one's thoughts and one's writing conform to the demands of orthodox thought. The power of orthodoxy is obvious in Canada's mass media. Again, the extent of this power often comes down to a matter of the honesty and integrity of the journalist. Orwell expressed this point with his usual clarity:

> . . . [T]he controversy over freedom of speech and of the press is at the bottom a controversy over the desirability, or otherwise, of telling lies. What is really at issue is the right to report contemporary events truthfully, or as truthfully as is consistent with the ignorance, bias and self-deception from which every observer necessarily suffers.[5]

Canada's Constitution and laws create substantial protection for free expression. But no one, least of all working journalists, should imagine that this protection is the end of the matter. It is not enough to sit back confidently and assume that lawyers and judges can look after free expression, that it is not an issue of ongoing concern. At the end of the day, free expression demands from each journalist both nurturing and jealous protection.

---

4   *The Economist*, 1 June 1996, 86.
5   "The Prevention of Literature," *The Collected Essays, Journalism and Letters of George Orwell, Vol.4: In Front of Your Nose, 1945–1950* (Harmondsworth: Penguin 1970), 83.

TABLE OF CASES

INDEX

ABOUT THE AUTHOR

Robert Martin, B.A., LL.B., LL.M. is professor of law at the University of Western Ontario where he teaches constitutional law, and media law. He is also secretary-treasurer of the Commonwealth Association for Education in Journalism and Communication. Professor Martin has taught extensively in Africa where he has held appointments in law at the National University of Lesotho, the University of Mauritius, the University of Dar es Salaam (Tanzania), and the University of Nairobi (Kenya). He is the author of numerous books and articles including *A Sourcebook of Canadian Media Law*, 2d. ed., 1994 (with G. Stuart Adam).